**CHATTY AND SOCIABLE GEMINI?
DELIBERATE AND DETERMINED TAURUS?
TENDER HEARTED CANCER?
HOT-HEADED ARIES?
MAGNETIC AND A LITTLE SCARY SCORPIO?**

YOUR SIGN IS YOUR SUN SIGN

Every sign has tell-tale personality traits, good qualities, frailties, and special talents. Whatever your sign is, you have a unique approach to all the various aspects of life.

In this collection of Sun Sign articles originally published in *Dell Horoscope Magazine*, internationally acclaimed astrologer Nancy Frederick looks at all the signs from the perspectives of career and finance, love and romance, the trials and tribulations of life and how to handle them, and many more specifics.

Need a clue what to buy for that special someone? Check out *The Zen of Shopping.* In the doldrums and need a way to prod yourself out of that chair? Read *Motivate Yourself.* Want to find a meditation that will help you with some of your life issues? There are twelve from which to choose. Hoping for some vacation hints so you can have some fun? There are several articles to help you.

Your Sun Sign Book looks at you and your sign from many perspectives, giving you a fun way to learn more about yourself and your loved ones. For years readers have asked Nancy for reprints of her articles on Sun signs, and now, here they are all collected together. With her trademark humor and incisiveness, Nancy Frederick gives multi-faceted insight into the Sun signs from Aries through Pisces.

Also by Nancy Frederick

Love and Sex Under the Stars, 2014

The Astro Tutor

Dawn Any Minute

Hungry for Love

Touring the Afterlife

A Change of Heart

Starstruck

The Sportin' Life

Love and Sex Under the Stars, 1989

The Lover's Dream

Love Games: Psychic Paths to Love

Palmistry: All Lines Lead to Love

Tarot: Love is in the Cards

Want to learn astrology in depth? Check out Nancy's popular astrology book, **The Astro Tutor.** It's your guide to learning how to unravel the complexities of an astrological chart. With easy to understand lessons, each new detail builds on the previous one in clear language that demystifies horoscope interpretation.

Need in-depth information about your love life?

Want to know what really makes your lover happy?

Check out the newly updated and re-released version of Nancy's first, best-selling astrology book, *Love and Sex Under the Stars*, now available for kindle and print.

This is your chance to understand your own heart, and the needs and desires of those you love best. The planets Venus and Mars are the source of everything romantic and sexy about you. In this newly updated and expanded version of her first, best-selling astrology book, internationally acclaimed astrologer Nancy Frederick concentrates on Venus and Mars, the planets of love and sex, and gives detailed information about both planets in every sign. In addition, there are in-depth delineations of all the 144 Venus-Mars combinations. You need to have no prior knowledge of astrology to understand and benefit from the information in this book. Nancy Frederick shows you how to locate the exact position of Venus and Mars at your birth in the easy-to-navigate charts right here in this book. If you know your birthday, you can instantly look up your Venus and Mars—right here. Then she tells you what the planets reveal. To know the secrets of your lovestyle, all you need to know is your birthday! And the same goes for that special someone who's caught your eye. In this fascinating guide to the planets that rule the heart and the sensual passions, Nancy Frederick shows you how to discover your own romantic and sexual requirements: Find out if the lover who turns you on today is the one who will bring you happiness tomorrow and "forever after"; Look into the heart of a potential partner; Please your partner--and yourself; Liberate your sensual self. Love and Sex Under the Stars is an in-depth guide to your personal lovestyle and the key to the romantic needs and desires of everyone you meet.

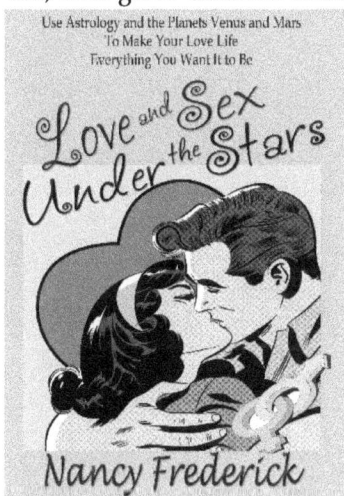

NANCY FREDERICK

Your Sun Sign Book

Nancy Frederick

Portions of this book previously published in *Dell Horoscope Magazine*; reprinted with permission by *Dell Horoscope Magazine*.

DEDICATION

For my beloved Tweetettes, the best sorority ever, and the most wonderful collection of besties any girl could have. Thank you for your friendship and affection. You bring light and joy into my life on a daily basis. Also for my dear astrology friends online and readers who contact me about enjoying my articles. It's heartwarming to hear that my articles give you pleasure as well as useful information. Thanks for supporting my work for so many years.

CONTENTS

Aries	Taurus	Gemini	Cancer
Leo	Virgo	Libra	Scorpio
Sagittarius	Capricorn	Aquarius	Pisces

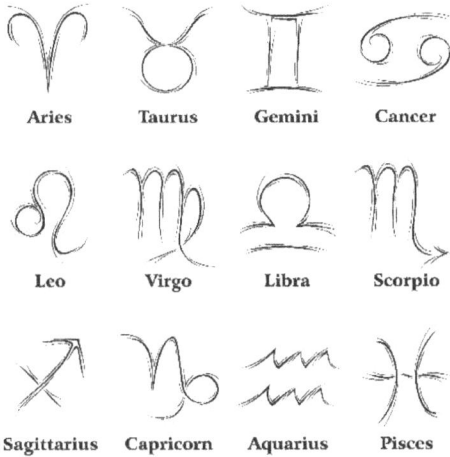

INTRODUCTION

YOUR SIGN IS YOUR SUN SIGN

"Hey, baby, what's your sign?"

Do you remember that as one of the most over-used come-ons in the singles' scene? You do know what someone means when asking you what's your sign. But this book is called Your Sun Sign. Isn't that something different?

Your sign is your Sun sign. We are concentrating completely on your Sun sign here, whether you're an Aries, a Pisces, or any of the ten signs in-between.

The sign of your Sun is very powerful, and many aspects of your personality are described by your zodiac sign. Learn all about that, and you'll gain insight into yourself and your basic purpose for living.

I've been an astrologer for more than thirty years. All that time I've been writing books and articles about the various aspects of astrology. My work has appeared constantly in all of the astrology magazines on your newsstand since the 1980's.

I've written a wide variety of articles on many topics within the broad scope of astrology. Probably the most beloved of all my articles are the ones about Sun signs. They are chatty and conversational, and they provide deep insights as well as some gentle ribbing about you and your sign.

Because I have a wonderful relationship with the editors of *Dell Horoscope Magazine*, they allowed me to reprint the Sun sign articles I've written over the years. And that has turned into this book.

I debated for a while about how best to present the information. Each article was published individually, and each has an introduction about the specific topic of the article (dealing with various specific problems, finding love, managing money, having fun, and so on). That introduction is followed by passages on each of the twelve signs, Aries through Pisces. I could have eliminated those introductions and divided this book up into twelve sections with all the bits and pieces on each sign gathered together. But somehow the idea of doing that made me sad. People love these articles because they're fun to read, and part of what makes them fun is the little introductions which have humorous anecdotes, personal details, and, okay let me be an egotist here, me, they have me. I didn't want to leave me out of the book. This is my work over many years. So here it is, articles presented according to topic, but preserved as they appeared originally.

The benefit of doing this is that chances are, unless you live alone in a cave, you know other people. Some of them you love. As you read the articles, certainly you'll want to read about yourself, but what about your mate, your kids, your lover, your mom and dad or siblings, or even your boss, whether nice or snarky. This way you learn some things about yourself and the other people in your life. Sometimes you get a chuckle at their expense. What's better than that?

The next time you find yourself in a position to be propositioned, when you hear the fateful, "What's your sign?" You can answer with some information about what makes you you, and you can know some things in advance about this new person you're encountering.

1
SUN SIGN BASICS

Without a doubt, you're an individual. There is nobody quite like you. In fact, even a single blade of grass is an individual, and each one is different from the other.

That said, you're also one of the twelve Sun signs. Each sign has certain things in common, such that if you're an Aries, you have more similarities to another Aries than you do to a Pisces. You thrust yourself into life in a certain manner, and that is an Aries way to be. Or a Taurus way to be. Or a Gemini way to be. One way to understand this is to read all the following passages, and you will most likely see that your sign is more like you than any other sign. Then you get the sense of the particular Sun sign energy blazing inside you.

Don't know your sign? Check below!

Aries ✸	March 21 - April 20
Taurus ✸	April 21 - May 21
Gemini ✸	May 22 - June 21
Cancer ✸	June 22 -July 22
Leo ✸	July 23 - August 22
Virgo ✸	August 23 - September 23
Libra ✸	September 24 - October 23
Scorpio ✸	October 24 – November 22
Sagittarius ✸	November 23 – December 21
Capricorn ✸	December 22 – January 20
Aquarius ✸	January 21 – February 19
Pisces ✸	February 20 – March 20

ARIES ✴
MARCH 21 - APRIL 20

Hello hot stuff! Fiery, impetuous, and passionate, you are the first sign in the zodiac, and you're all about action. You never stop to think about anything, because that could simply slow you down. Instead, like your symbol the Ram, you charge forward into life, and butt heads with anything that gets in your way.

You want to express yourself, and that's what you're here to do. Every action you take brings important experiences into your life, and it's those life experiences that help define you. Nobody more strongly learns through experience than you do. Other people can project themselves into the future and say, hmm, I might not like that so let's not do it. You rarely do that. Something sounds interesting, and you leap into the situation. Later you might learn, hmm I am afraid of heights, or hmm I don't like a job where I do the same thing all day, or hmm I don't mind getting my hands dirty. All these little nuances, the details of you, emerge through life experiences. That's how you come to a clear understanding of who you are as your life unfolds. Other people may know these things in advance, but you learn them moment by moment.

Excitement is very important to you. You enjoy expressing your passionate nature by living life on the edge. You're seldom afraid—at least at the beginning—and you're willing to go all or nothing toward pretty much everything. Being an action-oriented person can make you an inspiring leader, except that you're not terribly intent about having all those followers trailing after you. You tend to see life as a me-first sort of reality, and those you care about are welcome to tag along, as long as they don't get in your way.

Putting yourself first is quite natural to you, and you never get how some saps are so self-sacrificial. Why would they do that? It just seems obvious to you that each person should make himself the number one priority. Or herself, as the case may be. Even when you fall in love, you tend to incorporate your lover into your idea of yourself. *You* want to do something transitions into *we* want to do something, whether or not your mate actually wants to do that thing. It helps if you find a mate with similar interests, because then you won't be forced to compromise, which to you means that two people are miserable instead of one.

You take the same approach to your career. You want to be independent enough to make your own choices and free enough not to be shackled to anything. If you work at something you love, you don't mind it at all. If you work just for the money, every minute you're there, you think about leaving. You'd rather make less money doing something fun than grow rich selling your soul to daily tedium.

All of this taken together provides you with a youthful mentality that endures all your life. Even as you grow old, you still appreciate fun, and you might end up the only adult who understands your grandkids, because you see life from a similar perspective. If you can enjoy every moment while you live it, then you consider your life a success. You don't burden yourself with the rules and regulations that other people consider so necessary. If you try something and dislike it, then you stop. Why should you shoulder the burden of completion once you've discovered that a task is not for you? Life is filled with wondrous activities, and you're ready always to move on to the next one.

Your nature is cheerful and happy. You have a nice smile, which you know you can use to wiggle your way out of any situation involving other people. You're rarely self-critical, and are generally your own biggest fan.

TAURUS ✳
APRIL 21 - MAY 21

You have a practical nature, and are good at managing all the resources in your care. Making money is important to you, and starting as early as in childhood, you often save as much as possible. Life just has to make sense to you, and that's why you take your time considering the pros and cons of every decision. Some say you lose opportunities that way, but you feel that you'd rather be reasonably assured of the outcome before taking definitive steps in any direction.

Your nature is slow and steady, which is why you like to think things through. Once you begin something, you rarely abandon it, so should you make a hasty choice, you could find yourself mired in an unwelcome situation that lasts for decades. Other people suggest that this is a needless approach, for anything once begun can just as easily be ended, but you don't see it that way. Change disturbs you. It feels far more comforting to endure, to choose a situation, a mate, a home, a job, or whatever, and just to remain with it all your life. The sense of continuity is just too comforting to abandon.

You have a reputation for being stubborn, and perhaps that is true, for once you choose an idea as your own, you seldom change your mind without a very good reason. You tend to make similar choices, approach problems from a similar perspective, and primarily to resist change on all fronts. So, yes, you are rather stubborn, but really it's more of a lack of flexibility. This can cause problems if a better solution to a problem is available, and you reject it only because it's new. For the most part, though, you're content with the tried and true, and this approach works for you.

Security on a financial level is important to you, but there is more to security than money. Security is another aspect of continuity. If you own your home, you'll always have a place to live, one that you find attractive and comforting. If you choose the right mate, there will always be someone by your side, in good days and bad. This is how you look at life—as chances to make decisions that will stand you in good stead for the rest of your life.

You enjoy life and all its pleasures. Nobody adores fine dining more than you do, and you might be a superlative cook. Food is just so wonderful, and you don't mind admitting that you have a bit of an oral fixation. Your lovers don't complain, so why should you? In addition to the pleasures of food, you like nice clothes of good quality. You're not so fashion oriented that your clothing goes out of style. Instead, you like your collection of cuddly cashmere sweaters in classic styles. Well-made things that will always be in fashion appeal to you for their quality and staying power. They remind you of yourself.

Known for your sensuality, you love to touch and be touched. Yes, you're a hard worker, but you're also a physical person who appreciates the beauty in life, and who rarely resists stopping to smell the flowers.

GEMINI ✸
MAY 22 - JUNE 21

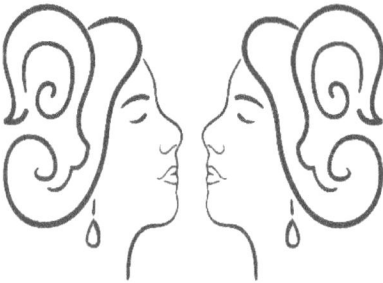

You're an outgoing, conversational person who lives to connect with other people. You require almost constant stimulation, so if you're not on the phone, you're reading or watching television, riding your bike, or doing all these things at once. Your mind races along on many channels simultaneously, so you feel capable of handling many forms of stimulus without feeling overburdened.

You have an active mind, and that's why you're always immersed in new ideas. It's not that you're an intellectual, for that sounds a bit boring. Yes, you like intellectual stimulation, but it can be of the less than scholarly type. You don't spend all your time wrestling with life's biggest issues. Sometimes you're content to mumble limericks or read the funny paper. You just like mental playtime, and for you that's almost all the time. Even if you read constantly, you might just be reading pulpy novels or cereal boxes. You don't care. It's all interesting enough to fill the moment.

The humdrum of life is not for you. You need change and excitement, and you seldom worry about meeting a schedule or punching a clock. You make a date, and then when something better comes along, you have no problem switching plans. Likewise in your daily life, you need the possibility of the unknown. You don't want to spend your life attaching the same widget to the same doodad. You want each day to be different. That might mean that you're a serial careerist, that you do a job that allows for travel, or one which brings different people into your life daily.

Fun is what it's really all about. You need fun. You like talking and laughing, and everywhere you go, you bring a sort of magical sparkle. You take the same approach to your human interactions. Other people crave commitment and continuity. You often seek to avoid them. Nothing is worse than being trapped with someone with whom you've run out of conversation. You don't worry about being old and alone. You worry about being bored, so you'd rather break free of current entanglements and skip along to what's next. Many people are better than a few, for one friend could be your Scrabble partner while another likes to jog by your side. As long as you have enough people to share your varied interests, you feel intellectually stimulated and emotionally content.

One of the great things about you is your flexibility. You try new things without a qualm, and if a tried and true solution fails, you're more than content to attempt a new approach. You don't feel obliged to remain in your childhood hometown, and you happily add new friends to your collection of old ones. Because of this, you can find satisfaction and success in many different approaches to life. You're happy to try a job for a while, and then if it becomes dull, you move on to a completely new career. Life is too short to be lived stuck in quicksand. You'd rather get up and move on to the next cool thing.

CANCER ✳
JUNE 22 -JULY 22

You're a sensitive person who requires security in many forms. You need to be surrounded by loved ones, and even if you don't like your family, you still love them and want to spend time in their company. You need to feel that sense that you're being cared for and nurtured, as a child by your mother, and as an adult by the various significant others in your life. As much as you need to receive, you also want to give back, and you enjoy taking care of those you love, whether a mate, a child, or a pet. These connections that bind are life's most important, and in your mind there's no question that life should add up to a scrapbook of tender attachments and sweet memories.

You're about as far from the bachelor type as can be. Even as a child, you loved to play house, and you could always envision yourself married and surrounded by a happy family of your own. People are the basis for your security, that loving connection that builds in your life a hammock of tenderness in which you can always languish. Once you connect, you want that relationship to endure. You like continuity, and may even still be close with those grammar school chums you enjoyed in your childhood.

You're a collector, whether of people or things. You don't like tossing anything or anyone aside, because to you it feels as though you're losing something of deep and permanent value. If a relationship isn't working, you do what you can to repair it. If it must end, that takes a great deal out of you, even if you know it was the right choice to make. Your feelings are usually uppermost in your mind, and although you're invested in all of your relationships, understanding the emotions of other people isn't always your strong suit, because you're so immersed in your own feelings.

Another aspect of security is financial resources, a home of your own, and a solid foundation on which to rest your life. Despite all your sensitivity—or because of it—you are success oriented, and you work hard all your life to create this foundation. At work you can be quite a dynamo, and other people realize that you're sensitive, but they don't always know that it's an emotional tsunami inside you which motivates you to keep going.

If someone hurts your feelings, you can lash out, but certainly you'll become wary of that person ever after. You remember everything long after everyone else has forgotten, and you don't forgive easily. Any thorn in your side remains there, festers, and reminds you always of whatever betrayal caused that pain.

Often you take solace in food, for what is more comforting than a treat that brings you back to the happy memories of childhood. Being around the table with family members provides much happiness as does an ice cream cone gobbled on a solitary walk.

The truth is, you are a complex person, one who needs a great deal of attention and TLC to go through life in a happy, contented manner, but your heart is always in the right place, and you know that nurturing and being nurtured are the essence of life.

LEO ✳
JULY 23 - AUGUST 22

Even if other people think your ego is too large, you say nonsense, for what's more important than looking and being your best? You try hard to live up to your own highest standards, and you always have an eye toward whatever impression you're making. You care very much that other people see you in a positive light, and you work hard to deserve the praise you wish to receive.

Yes, you enjoy being the center of attention, and in your mind, who doesn't? Those shy, modest people are just pretending they don't like the applause and the attention, because it feels so good to you, it must therefore feel good to them as well. Expressing yourself is one of your most important tasks in this lifetime, and it feels wonderful to do something well enough such that other people admire you. If every day has some of that admiration and applause, you feel it's a good day. Perhaps that's why so many Leos want to be actors. Certainly you are star-struck, even if it's just about the celebrities with whom you connect on a profound level—without ever having to know them personally.

You have a strong sense of quality, and you always want the best. You like a nice life, filled with nice things. Even male Leos like good jewelry, and you don't feel out of place at all wearing jewelry and being dressed up. Lady Leos are the same way, and sometimes you're a little over the top, but you don't mind because being glam suits you. Why should you go through life seeming dowdy when you're so spectacular, inside and out.

Outgoing, friendly, and usually happy, you have a sunny personality to which other people gravitate. Having good friends in your life is very important because you crave social interaction. You like all manner of social events because it's fun to be around people and show your sparkle, and also because it's a chance to wear whatever new garments you just acquired.

Money and material possessions are important to you, because nobody can achieve a suitable state of glamour without them. You need a nice home because you can't throw a memorable party in a slum, now can you. You'd never want a Bette Davis type entering your home and sneering, "What a dump." It's all about pride, like the lion which is your symbol. You have a never-ending supply of pride, and it functions in all areas of your life. You want people to admire you for your appearance, your mate, your children, your job, your home, your bank account, and even your charitable contributions. Being envied is the best thing in the world.

As much as you like money, you don't always like working to get it. A job can excise such a big chunk out of your day that it's hard to want one unless you're doing something thrilling. That's why movie stars are so lucky. Everyone wants to be them and their work is so exciting. And they're rich. It's win-win-win. Thus it's important for you to be in a career that is as much fun as it is financially rewarding.

Loyalty is another of your strong suits. You like to keep all your friends forever, and in general you hold onto things. You're just not a cut and run sort of person. You like the sense of continuity far more than the idea of change. You want to find the most perfectly glamorous life possible and to keep on living it—forever and ever.

VIRGO ✸
AUGUST 23 - SEPTEMBER 23

You like things just so. Your eye is discerning, and you have standards for just about everything. If you find a certain person vulgar, you won't want him or her in your life. Tacky environments, well, no. Ugly clothes, even if they're the height of fashion, forget it. You don't care what anyone else thinks, because you believe in your own standards and intend always to stick to them.

Your nature is practical. Things must make sense to you for you to endorse them. You like taking care of your possessions, and you don't buy things on whim. You have to really love something to buy it, and then you keep it for a long time. That doesn't mean you're a collector, for to you that's just something else you'd have to maintain. Thus you care about financial security, but greed and excess are no part of your make up at all. You want no more than just what you need, with a little extra for a rainy day.

You are kindly and helpful, and because of that discerning eye, you can easily see where there's a problem, and you're content to glide into the situation and untangle the mess with ease, no thanks needed. It's some sort of Girl Scout or Boy Scout inside you that prevents you from ignoring those in need. If an old lady dropped something, you just have to stop to help search. If someone is trying to choose a baking dish, well of course they need to know what you think. Otherwise they could choose the wrong model.

Because of this natural kindness, it's easy for you to put the needs of others first. When it comes to family members, this is fine, because they love you and will sometimes put you first. But if you're surrounded by people in need, and you do tend to attract them, it can become exhausting, and then you just want to lock yourself away from the chaos for a while so you can restore your depleted energies.

You are quite content to spend time alone, and yours is one of the bachelor signs. You spend so much time helping others that you feel at peace when alone. You don't go crazy in silence, for you have your interesting thoughts to keep you company. Of course you want a partner, but if you end up single, that's okay too. More than anything else, you crave peace of mind, where nothing too much is nagging at you.

You have a good level of flexibility. You don't mind changing plans and doing things at a moment's notice, although you do enjoy planning special outings and events. You also find solutions easily, for you know that if one approach fails, another will present itself to you which will then succeed.

Other people see you as kind and competent, and you like that about yourself very much.

LIBRA ✸
SEPTEMBER 24 - OCTOBER 23

You're a people person, not just because you require social and intellectual interaction to be happy (you do), but because it's through other people and your relationships with them that you learn about yourself. You see yourself most clearly and profoundly through the eyes of other people, and your idea of yourself is usually in relation to the significant others in your life. You're not the sort to do well shipwrecked alone on a deserted island. You need other people to provide joy and meaning in your life.

You're a charming person with an excellent set of social skills. People enjoy your company, and you're often the first person added to your friends' guest lists. You just naturally function well in social situations, and you have the ability to put other people at ease while doing so. Your manners are excellent, not because you read an etiquette book (although you may well have done so), but because you have an innate grace that allows you to express yourself in a way that never infringes on anyone else's individuality. Good taste is very important to you. You dislike vulgar people, and avoid their company. You like people who are congenial and who can display the right degree of charm, as you do yourself. Not only do you expect those around you to behave properly, you like them to look good too. It's all part of the genteel package that you want your life to embody.

Relationships are essential to you. You need that significant other to mirror yourself back to you, but it's more than just a need, deep in your soul, for romance. You like socializing. You even like dating. Being able to dress up and go out with someone special just feels wonderful. It's a sort of fairy tale magic that you enjoy having in your own life. As early as grade school, you enjoyed dances that all the other kids wanted to avoid, and you enthusiastically became involved in those sweet little-kid romances, even if your crush shoved you into the sandbox. As an adult, you're unfulfilled without a mate, and you want to be married. If you're not content with a partner, you'll weep, but you will break up, because you have the image in your mind of what a happy relationship should be, and you're unwilling to suffer along in misery just to be connected.

You have many friends, and they can tide you over in dry romantic periods. You need a good deal of social interaction, so it's important for you to have a group of best pals with whom you can do fun things, like attend luncheons or fancy teas, shop, and share fun gossip. It's not that you'd be unkind, but it is fun to discuss what's going on with other people.

You need a sense of balance in your life, but unfortunately, seeking balance sometimes means that there's a seesaw effect where everything swings back and forth, perpetually out of balance. You relate to this idea, but you know there's little you can do about it. You just have to keep trying to make things the way you want them.

Although money is essential to fund the sort of elegant life you desire, it's not the number one thing on your mind. Often your job is secondary to your social life, and if you don't need the money, then it doesn't matter. You can be quite successful in a field where you feel comfortable, such as fashion, design, or even party planning. Once you achieve that success, the job becomes part of your life and your colleagues part of your social life. That's the best of all possible worlds.

SCORPIO ✹
OCTOBER 24 – NOVEMBER 22

Okay, so it *is* true. You really are that intense. People can feel your presence as you enter a room. You make a substantial impression. Maybe you're shrugging right about now, because you don't see the big deal of it all. It's not like you're one of those fools dancing on a table with a lampshade on your head. It's not like you go out of your way to force people to notice you. In fact, it's quite the opposite. You're subtle, often shy. In social gatherings you might be the seemingly subdued person sitting innocently in a darkened corner, all alone, just watching. But all you need to do is set your sights on the most interesting person in the room, and strangely, magnetically, inexplicably, that person meanders your way. That's personal magnetism, and you have it in spades.

Scorpio is known as the sexy sign, and you don't dispute that at all. Sometimes you're a wanton libertine, out there romancing and bedding everyone in sight. But even if that's true, it won't always be true, because your nature is exclusionary, and in your heart you know you want to be with only that one soulmate who completes your destiny. You believe in true love and love at first sight. You just know. But until that sense of destiny comes calling, you're often willing to dally.

Because you're so intense, you're good at getting what you want. Once you have an idea, a desire, a plan, or even an inkling, you stick to it unwaveringly. You're steady, determined, and fixed, and you like it that way. If other people disagree with you, that's their problem, although you don't find it that hard to change their minds.

Part of being intense is being emotional, and you're a very sensitive person. Your feelings easily get hurt, and you definitely hold a grudge. Elephants forget sooner than you do. Sometimes you can be downright mean, using someone's frailties against him or her, and in your mind it's all right to do so.

You care very much about security, and that's just part of you building a life that becomes like your fort of power, your secure stronghold, where you can feel safe and happy. You work hard and you play hard. Any goal you set for yourself, you can easily achieve, by the sheer power of your will. If you want to be a millionaire, you will achieve that goal. What you seek in a job is not only money, but the sense that you are captaining your own ship. You can work for someone else, but there must be a sense of independence, that things are being done the way you choose.

You have a great deal of healing energy, which can help other people. You make an excellent therapist because it's so easy for you to unearth everyone's secrets and to see what's deep inside those around you. That might make you seem a little scary to other people, but that's okay with you.

SAGITTARIUS ✴
NOVEMBER 23 – DECEMBER 21

You're playful but never a player. You're probably the most direct, honest, and forthright person in the world. You don't see the point of lying, even if just those silly white lies designed to assure a friend that no, that outfit doesn't make your butt look too big. Who cares about silly stuff like that anyway? Your mind is often on much bigger issues.

You're a natural philosopher, and you enjoy pondering the deep truths of life. It's interesting to hear the points of view of other people, even if you don't agree with that perspective, because there's a whole panorama of ideas in the world, and you find them all endlessly fascinating. You're also interested in various forms of spirituality. Sometimes you're religious, and if so, that provides you with a sense of connection. If not, you take a more intellectual approach to spirituality, finding it interesting to learn about the different ways people find God within themselves.

You're quite physical, although some people regard you as lazy. You like being outdoors so that you can breathe fresh air and be inspired by the beauty in nature. You could take a twenty mile hike and emerge exhilarated, so is that lazy? Only if it means you call in sick at work to do it. But you have your priorities straight, and it's rarely a job that is tops on your list. You know that everyone has to make a living, but the idea of selling your soul for a buck seems so painful to you. It's important that you find a career that allows you to become involved in what you're doing so that when that alarm clock buzzes, you're up and at'em with a sense of joy rather than dread.

You're a mellow sort for the most part, and that means you rarely buy into the annoyances of life that cause other people to live with so much stress. *Don't worry, be happy* is your motto, and that makes you a very engaging companion. Other people enjoy your company and your fresh, fun-loving attitude to life. You'll laugh at any joke, will embark on any adventure at a moment's notice, and are willing to change your plans on whim. You're easy.

You like people and they like you, so perhaps that's why you're one of the bachelor signs. If you don't find a spouse, you don't mind at all, because there are so many ways to enjoy life and all the people in it. Good friends fill your days and your nights, and if there's no one and only, you shrug and enjoy what you do have.

Travel is one of the many pleasures on your to-do list, not just because you like adventure, but because you feel yourself a citizen of the world, and you like to be out in it, seeing all the many avenues for life here and now on this planet.

CAPRICORN ✳
DECEMBER 22 – JANUARY 20

You're an eye on the prize sort of person. Your goals are always first and foremost on your mind. Even as a child, you probably had a five year plan, a ten year plan, and maybe even a whole life plan. Work is number one in your book, not just because you love working, but because it's the means to an end—to achieving the goals you set for yourself. You take life seriously, and even though you often have a killer sense of humor, you know what matters. Anyone important to you needs to understand that you have certain priorities, and success is at the top of your list.

There are many career areas in which you can succeed, mainly because you're so good at immersing yourself in any professional milieu, learning what you need to do to climb to the top of the ladder, and then doing it. People who languish along, focusing only on fun, or who bale on responsibilities in favor of fun, well, they're not your sort at all. Does that mean you don't enjoy fun? Of course not. You like your hobbies, your entertainment, and your family activities as much as anyone. You just don't allow them to thwart your goals or derail your objectives.

Your outlook on life is rather traditional. You believe in marriage, in having a home and a family, and you want all those things. You value those things. Early in your adult life, you might not have time to make those things happen, however, even if you want to. You might be someone who thinks hiring a matchmaker is an excellent idea. That way someone other than you pre-screens mates so you don't have to waste time and money on dates with people who won't work out. This is your practical nature, and it works for you.

You take a similarly practical approach to everything. Yes, you must look like a success, so you own nice clothes, but you find ways to get them on sale or at a discount, and you choose the classic styles that won't be in a donation bag next season. Being a fashion plate rarely appeals to you anyway, because it seems so shallow. You work out because it's just another responsibility—your body needs to be maintained as much as your car. Your life has many check lists, and you feel comforted when you can go to bed at night knowing that everything you should have done you did do.

They do say that Capricorn is old when young and young when old, and by that it's meant that as you age, you relax a little, so that you can enjoy the casual moments that passed you by while you were so busy building the secure foundation of your life. Once you've achieved all your goals, you're willing to spend some of that money you struggled so hard to amass. Then you can spend time playing with your grandchildren, and showing them how they can climb up that ladder of success in your footsteps.

AQUARIUS ✸
JANUARY 21 – FEBRUARY 19

Of course everyone is unique, even if they're boring, but you are a true individual. Life has to make sense to you on your own terms, and then you express yourself in ways that are as unique as you are, whether anyone else approves or not. You're not here to get thumbs up from other people—how silly that would be—when it's far more important to know that you're following your own rules and acting according to your own solid and sane principles.

Yes, you like to be quirky, and the more staid the people around you, the more outrageous you can become. It's sort of fun to tweak other people's noses, isn't it? Most of your life isn't about that at all, however. It's about seeing reality in a unique way and making your own world fit into that vision.

You appreciate the new and interesting. You're often a techy, or at least someone who sees technology as an essential aspect of the future. Maybe as a kid you were a big fan of science fiction, and now you love movies and television shows that use imaginary technology that has yet to be invented. It's a brave new world, and you want to be part of it.

Despite your quirky individuality, you're a people person, and you'd never be very happy living as a hermit all alone. You need to connect. You like to talk and to share ideas, and you always want to be surrounded by a group of friends who are like a second family to you, like-minded people whose ideas and visions are compatible with your own. You can be quite a visionary, and you love the idea of sharing your brave ideas with the people who can use them. It can be irksome when dealing with those you see as too fixed to be ready to embrace new ideas, and in that case you will repeat yourself over and over until they finally see that your idea is the answer. Of course, that too is being fixed, but you don't see it that way. You don't see yourself as stubborn either, although you are. Once you know something is right, you hold fast to that idea.

Nothing about you is terribly traditional. You're okay with far-out ideas like living in a commune and sharing everything—including mates. You're usually not the jealous sort, and you can keep an ex lover as a friend forever, because you feel that the mental bond you share is the most important part. The physical is fun, but there's no reason to be domineering about it. Life is varied and romances come and go. Friendship is forever.

Whatever path in life you choose, it must make sense to you. A job that bores you or seems pointless is rarely what you'll do, and even if you need to make money, you'd rather earn less doing something interesting and challenging than to grow rich by selling your soul and numbing your brain. You're a serious person, and whether having fun or doing something practical, you approach life in an intellectual manner.

PISCES ✸
FEBRUARY 20 – MARCH 20

You're sweet and sensitive, and everyone's favorite friend. You just care about other people so much, and they appreciate this about you. People naturally gravitate toward you because your sense of empathy is so strong, and they can feel in you a sympathetic listener, which you are. You too easily feel another's pain, and this can be wearying, particularly if you know many people with problems who need you as an amateur therapist. It's better for you to spend time with cheerful, happy people, just enjoying each other's company and laughing, so that you don't absorb too much of the negativity of those who need you to be their permanent sounding board.

Your nature is quite social, and when in the company of happy friends, you're in your element. You feel lonely when you have too few social opportunities, so make the effort to join clubs or groups whose purpose appeals to you so that you can find compatible people with whom to spend time.

You're also quite romantic, and you feel sad if you don't have someone you consider a soulmate. There are so many little nuances in life, that having that special someone with whom to share them makes life even sweeter. You want to have a home and family, so that you can have people in your life you can love and trust.

You're creative and artistic, and you have an excellent imagination. You can spin tall tales for the amusement of the children in your life, and you enjoy playing all sorts of games as much as your kids do. Even if you don't work as an artist, you will likely have some sort of creative outlet as a hobby which you do often. It helps you to focus and feel centered, and you like the idea that you have created something.

Focus is definitely an issue for you, and it's easy for you to become distracted. You start one thing, grow fuzzy, and move on to another. This can be a source of frustration at the end of the day if nothing has been completed, even if you did do a lot. If you have certain goals to accomplish, the first step is to engage your mind, invoke some sense of focus, and make a list of all the steps you must take to meet that goal. That way you don't get lost along the way.

You have some natural psychic ability, and that can translate into an appreciation for the spiritual side of life. Meditation restores your energies, or even just a walk in nature can bring back your sense of balance. In a way, you're like a kite, soaring into the heavens and then being brought back to earth. As long as you can do both, you'll have a happy life that fulfills you and is a pleasure to share with loved ones.

2
CAREER AND FINANCES

We live in some pretty scary times. Many of us are in a job market we never expected to encounter. Most of us have had to deal with financial loss and too-slow recovery. Some signs find this easier to manage than others, but all of us can use some pertinent tips about how to make the best impression at a job interview, how to turn that interview into a successful process, and how to land that job. In *Job Seeking Strategies*, I discuss ways everyone can be more successful at the process, and how your specific sign can use certain pointers to succeed at a job interview and bag the job. In *The $ign of the Times,* I consider the economy from the perspective of the first decade of the current century and look at ways each sign approaches the need to conserve on finances. We're all different, and sometimes a tip or two about your own sign—or even one borrowed from another sign—can be all you need to look at a difficult situation from a more hopeful perspective.

JOB SEEKING STRATEGIES

An aspiring screenwriter friend told me a story some years back. She had just taken a tumble on some stairs, spraining her ankle and tearing some ligaments. Then a source of income on which she depended dried up. It was a matter of finding a survival job or packing it in and giving up her dream of making it in Hollywood. So off she hobbled to an interview for a customer service telephone job. The hours were great, she knew she could do the job, and she dressed professionally. After explaining the ankle situation to the interviewer, he was sympathetic and even shared some information from a friend's similar sprain. He showed her around the office, and she stumbled behind him on the side of her foot, the only way she could walk. Despite all that, it seemed like a pretty good interview and when she learned the job had been offered to someone else, my friend was sad but not surprised. Most people don't want to hire someone in the middle of a health crisis. Just as in the movies, though, the tide turned. The person offered the job didn't take it, and she was hired. Maybe it wasn't a Hollywood ending, but it was a happy one.

I don't know of anyone who likes interviewing for a job. Most people hate dating—and they liken it to a job interview, so imagine how much worse an actual interview is. Nobody likes the idea of being merchandise, up for inspection and approval, and many would agree a check up at the doctor or dentist is less stressful.

Nowadays it's even more worrisome, because of the economy. There are fewer opportunities to attend a job interview because there are fewer jobs available. And everyone being interviewed knows that the odds are not exactly positive when it comes to getting hired. That doesn't mean you shouldn't give it your all though, because that job is going to someone and it might as well be to you.

Social skills are important during an interview, just as they are during a first date. Being able to relax and present yourself as a nice person who has necessary skills is key. The emphasis here is on the nice person part. It's an interview. You have to connect with the other person, just as in a date. Even if you are as brilliant as a savant, if you can't connect, chances are the position will go to someone a little less brilliant and a little more conversational. I've read many stories online about crazy job interviews, one of which involved going out to lunch with potential colleagues and being able to eat crawfish—and dance. That seems way above and beyond the call of duty, but that's the thing—you never know. Going for a job interview might be similar to pledging a fraternity or sorority. You have to make yourself a desirable commodity, someone who would fit in with the group. And sometimes displaying the right chemistry is enough.

I'm a big fan of the TV show *Friends*, and can still happily sit and entertain myself with the reruns. Remember the one where Rachel interviewed for the job at Ralph Lauren? She inadvertently kissed her interviewer, then went back to explain, then seemed to be touching him inappropriately. It was a comedy of errors—but she got the job because despite the craziness, because she was right for it, and she communicated her genuine interest coherently and enthusiastically.

Being able to edit yourself is probably the best skill any job seeker can have. Hear your words in your mind before they exit your mouth. That way if what you're about to say sounds stupid, don't say it. Listen to how you could sound from the perspective of the other person—that helps immensely in choosing what and how to communicate. The point is to say things that do truly express yourself but which don't make you sound like a bad risk as did a guy I read about online who when asked would he be willing to submit to random drugs tests, said not on a Monday. Likewise even if you're seeking a part-time or flexible schedule, it's best not to say you want Mondays off in case you're hung over. Not only does this represent bad judgment in lifestyle, it's what the kids call TMI—too much information.

An interviewer wants to hear positive things. So if he asks what you liked best about your last job and you say "nothing," that isn't the best route to take. It reminds me of my daughter, when in grammar school, and I asked her what her favorite subject was. "Free time!" she crowed. She wasn't interviewing for a job, but you can bet showing the me-me-me side of your personality isn't the best approach to get one.

The same is true if someone asks how you handle down time. If you used it to write the great American novel at your last job, fine, just don't say that at an interview. Say you'll work on future deadlines, organize something, or offer to help a colleague who's buried with work. Show some team spirit! And make an effort to say things that sound good to the person on the other side of the desk. That's the best way to sell yourself. And although nobody wants to think of him or herself as a used car, basically that's just what you are in an interview, a vehicle to get the job done, one with some useful mileage so you don't need too much breaking in, and a reliable asset for the future.

Unless you're going for a job that is precisely the same as a position you've already held, there will be things you won't know. I always feel that any job can be learned in two weeks, but I'd never say that. Nobody wants to know that you feel their job is simple—and thus stupid. One interviewer laughingly told a tale about a woman who was applying for a computer job but had no computer skills whatsoever, nor did she own a computer. She insisted she was a quick enough study to pick it up. The interviewer felt sorry for her because she seemed childish—and was wearing one of those kids' giveaway watches from a fast food chain. I'm guessing she was a mom who decided either out of financial desperation or on whim to change her life and off she went to an interview. At least it did provide her with one thing—practice interviewing. Of course it didn't get her a job.

You can get a job that requires more skill than you possess—if you do have some of the skills necessary and can present yourself as a professional person who routinely learns new tasks as well as excelling at the old ones. You just can't get a job where you possess none of the skills involved. Nobody will hire me to be an accountant. I don't know that stuff. But if there were a job involving stuff I do know and some bookkeeping, maybe they would, heaven help me!

A job should seem like a wonderful thing, a source of more than just money. Saying you want a job just for the paycheck might be honest but it's a sad assessment. If you are doing something interesting, enthralling, and rewarding, and getting paid, then you are living a much better life and can discuss that possibility in a far more enthusiastic manner, making yourself someone an interviewer would put to the top of the list. Being psyched about doing the job, giving it your all, and producing quality work is the best possible attitude—and the best way to live.

Asking good questions is another positive job seeking skill. Of course the interviewer will ask you things, but there must be some things about the company or the position you don't already know. Go ahead and ask. Show your interest. Don't ask things that put you in a bad light, though, such as what happens if you use up all your sick and personal days and need more time off to visit a family member in prison.

Like many things in life, job hunting requires some strategy. If you haven't been on an interview in a while and you suddenly must look for work, it might not be a bad idea to seek out some temp agencies. Even if they have no positions available, they usually keep interviewing, and yes you will waste several hours of your time filling out paperwork and taking tests, but out of it you'll get something useful—practice interviewing. This can be very worthwhile even if you have immediate plans to interview for a non-temp job because you can iron out the kinks in your interviewing techniques in a situation that isn't as threatening. Then when a real interview comes along, you'll remember not to make this mistake I read about online: when he realized he didn't have dark socks to wear with his suit, a candidate colored his ankles with a magic marker. Obviously don't wait until the last minute to choose your wardrobe, do be creative, but don't be an idiot!

Now let's see what particular strengths and pitfalls we can identify based on your own Sun sign. And don't forget—there could be tips that would serve you well listed under a sign which isn't your own, so read each one and take what you need to create your own success in the job market.

ARIES: Your greatest strength and greatest weakness ironically are the same thing—the ability to talk endlessly about yourself. Many people feel awkward sounding off about themselves, but not you. It feels natural, happy, and even pleasant to ramble on about that fabulous person—yourself. This comes in handy because a job interview is your chance to share the pertinent details about yourself with someone who is there to determine if you're the round peg that will perfectly fit in the round hole. But remember that although a job interview is about you sharing your qualifications, it also is a conversation and that means the other person should be allowed to speak as well—the same code of manners you resist implementing in dates. There has to be a sense of connection in an interview and if you're doing nothing but talking, then it becomes tiring for the other person. Even a person as interesting as you obviously are can be tiresome when someone has talk lobbed at him endlessly. So know when to stop and to listen. Know when to share information, to ask about what you've just heard, or to let the other person make a joke. It's also good to remember that an interview is basically a formal situation. No matter how much fun you're having if a good connection has been made, don't slip and pretend you're having cocktails with a school buddy and it's all right to share some information that is best classified as personal, sensitive, or risqué. It's your job not just to show how fabulous you are via tales of yourself, but to pigeonhole your best—and most appropriate—skills. That way if the interviewer says the job is about this, this, and this, you can say, I did such and such at my last job and it worked out this way—showing that you have a direct connection with the company's needs. Thus you're making them see that yes, you are great, but also that you're precisely the person they've been seeking.

TAURUS: If there's one sign in whom I have faith that

you'll be employed from birth virtually to death, it's you. Your tendency to stick to a job could mean you go on one and only one interview your whole life long. If not, you can certainly point out that you have a long and steady work history and that will speak well for you in this era of downsizing. Stability is an admirable quality, one which all employers appreciate. You are wise enough to realize that discussing money is relevant in a job interview. It's only novices who go to discuss employment and return home and say gee I never thought to ask about the salary. Anyone desperate enough to want a job which pays a completely undisclosed amount looks immature. It's also all right to discuss the various benefits attached to the job such as insurance and retirement perks, but it's not all right to bring them up immediately as the interview commences. It's better to talk about the thrills of the job, the exciting work you'll be doing, the ways in which you can contribute to the company, and how you can be an invaluable asset not only to your boss but to the team. Remember also, that if you've been at one job for a long time and now must be flexible enough to pick up new skills, it's good to display something that isn't always your strong suit—a flexible mindset. You're there to be the cog that fits into their machine and that means you can't look for ways to bend the job to your current skill set and customary tasks. Instead you are a highly skilled individual who is a brave pioneer, ready to blaze new paths of achievement and not only willing but enthusiastic about learning new tasks.

GEMINI: When it comes to being flexible, there in the dictionary is your picture as a shining beacon of, you know it—flexibility. You can learn quickly, adapt to circumstances, and fit in well in so many different milieus that you're the Zodiac's true chameleon. There's no question that these are great qualities to emphasize in any interview because it gives the interviewer hope that you can in fact do the job. What you have to watch out for is the same tendency that helps sell you—your chameleon nature. It's possible you've had so many different jobs that your resume needs to be printed on a long, long scroll. This is not a good thing. No employer wants to think that you're just there biding your time, waiting to become bored, something that in your case could occur way too quickly. So if you do have such a resume, you may need to edit it carefully. Or you might need to devise a reasonable, believable, and positive excuse why you've had so many jobs. If you worked your way up the ladder, that is one potential reason that speaks well for your talents but again could strike fear into the heart of a future boss because if you fled previous jobs you could depart this one too soon— after he spent the time and money to train you. So the best approach you can take in any interview is to put yourself in the boss' place. What does he want to see and hear and find a way to pigeonhole yourself into that mindset. Your charm, wit, and good personality can go a long way here because it gives the interviewer a reason really to make a connection with you and to like you. That helps immensely to short circuit any doubts that may arise as to your potential longevity in the job.

CANCER: Even though you're a soft and cuddly family-oriented person, there's another side to your Cancer nature and that's the driven, achievement-focused person who's fixed on success. These traits come through clearly in any interview and that's very good because it communicates to the interviewer that you're someone who feels like a friend but who will go the distance. Being able to relate to an interviewer as an equal who is competent, successful, and determined is a very good thing because it balances the power but in a non-threatening way. The goal is to make the meeting feel as though you both have the same objective— filling the position in the best possible way and that in the future you could become not only colleagues, but colleagues who feel like friends. This is something you can really carry off and it can benefit you enormously, even if you don't consciously manufacture the energy but rather just let nature take its course. It's probably wisest to keep things formal, however, and even if there are darling pictures of the interviewer's family in the room, you can't spend too much time discussing how cute those kids are or pulling out a brag book of your own splendid progeny. Well, probably you shouldn't. If the tide turns and you end up talking about families, gauge what's appropriate. What you don't want to do is talk about junior's therapy, many sports teams or anything else that sounds like it could provide competition to doing the job. Obviously a person should have a wealth of involvements in his or her life, including family pleasures and obligations, but it's always smartest to limit mention of any competing obligations. It's also wise to discuss the future with the interviewer, ways in which you can envision being of service to the company. This way you keep the talk focused around the subject that has brought you together—the job you very much want to secure.

LEO: Ryan Seacrest recently tweeted about a beautiful girl who was fired from her job at a bank because (she claimed) she was too "hot." There was a link with pictures of this, yes very beautiful, girl in her work attire, which was too shimmery, too fitted, too glam. Apparently she was confused about what bankers wear because she must have been copying styling mores from fashionable pseudo-execs on soap operas. Looking the part is important in any job, and you can't really look better than the job. She looked like a cosmetics assistant going for cocktails after hours, not like someone who's meant to handle anyone else's finances. Your appearance is very important to you, and chances are you are the snazziest dresser on not only your block but any block, but remember to look the part not only at a job but in an interview. You don't want to look out of place, even if you look gorgeous. You don't want the interviewer to be struck dumb with lust—or fashion envy—unless you're interviewing for a fashion position. Showing up properly dressed shows you have respect for the job, and more than that it shows that you see yourself in that position, and even more than that, it shows that you consider the job a good thing, not something that is beneath you. The irony here is that dressing too badly is no worse than dressing too well. A job interview is almost like Halloween and you must go in costume, as one of 'them.' Once you're properly attired, even if you feel you look a bit dull, it's up to you to wow them with your talents, skills, and personal qualities that make you the perfect candidate for the job. If you're entering a new field, you might have to take an entry level position, one far below where you feel your talents lie. If you convey to the interviewer that you hope that position won't last too long before you're elevated to a better one, you might not get that foot in the door. Focus on immediate goals as well as on long-term ones and remember job one is getting the job.

VIRGO: Interestingly, although you have little in common with the sign Aries, like them your best skill is also your worst liability. You can see the slightest little problem, the teensiest issue that must be corrected, and nobody is better than you are at charging in and fixing this no-no. No matter in what area of life, you see the details. That makes you an invaluable shopping partner, because nobody else will see all the flaws in a car, an apartment, or even an ice cream soda, that you as second nature spot in one glance. That could mean that you were the toughest trouble shooter at your previous job, and if that is the sort of position for which you're interviewing, then it's all right to share the various problems you vanquished. On the other hand if you're going for less of a sheriff-who-will-get-those-baddies-out-of-Dodge sort of job, you can't go on and on about the problems in your previous job. It makes you sound cranky. And it could confuse the interviewer into thinking that you complain too much and will always be bending someone's ear about things that you see as wrong but which disturb nobody else. This is one of those situations where you must put yourself into the place of the interviewer, and gauge what this person really wants to hear. Sharing a positive perspective is always a good choice, because it shows you as a happy person who will be delighted to join their team and be a colleague they all will enjoy collaborating with. And you can certainly share ways in which you were an asset to your last firm, thus putting a positive spin on the problem solving issue. Then once you have the job, you can sneak in and fix all the problems that desperately need your deft touch.

LIBRA: Having your particular skill set comes in super handy at job interviews. You're a people person, and pretty much everyone adores you on first meeting. You just know how to connect with people, put them at ease, and make any conversation fun. Obviously this provides a huge leg up in any job interview. Not only do you make a conversation worthwhile, you make it fun, and people just don't want to stop interacting with you. So many people in your sign work in personnel jobs so you might usually be the person on the other side of the desk. If so, you know all the tricks, but chances are what you realize is that it's not about tricks, it's about being yourself—in the best possible way—and nobody is better than that than you are. Because you're so socially adept and socially oriented, you might not even be nervous about interviewing. You wisely conclude that it's just two people who are there hoping to make a positive connection that will benefit both of them. Remember though, that although it's easy to enjoy the social aspects of the interview, you also must cover the brass tacks, so be sure to ask the right questions, allowing the interviewer to share completely with you the details of the job. That also gives you the opportunity to share ways in which you've done similar things in other jobs and would be able to plug right into this new job. And also remember it's not tacky to discuss money. It's a job interview, not a date, and you should know the numbers in advance of considering the job seriously. By being willing to bring up these less than delicate subjects you show yourself to be not just a pleasant, socially-adept person, but a professional within the field and someone who is capable of dealing with issues of all sorts.

SCORPIO: It's not for nothing that you come across as rather mysterious. You like being mysterious and your naturally private nature can cause you to keep secret some details about yourself that other people would regard as relatively mundane. In a job interview, being mysterious isn't really a good thing, unless it's an audition to be the new Garbo. You want to seem friendly, professional, and yes, accessible. It's really not so much about what you reveal, and I'm certainly not saying this is the time to provide full disclosure including the harrowing details of your gallbladder surgery. Instead it's about a vibe you project of being open and available. The question is, how easy/difficult is it to adjust the vibe that emanates from you. You might want to do a little exercise before entering the interview room. See yourself smiling, your heart broad and open, beaming a nice, friendly ray, perhaps yellow, of happy energy, and even consider seeing yourself for a few seconds as a dog, with your tail wagging. Obviously you don't have to walk up to the desk and wag your hips, but doing those exercises can help you project an amiable countenance. Don't forget to smile, not a giant, huge, you-just-found-a-long-lost-relative smile, but a casual, cheerful grin. You're a happy person who's glad to be there and who's looking forward to discussing this new job because it's perfect for you and you're perfect for it. Nobody is better at seduction than you are, and although it's not romantic seduction you're performing at a job interview, it is still a kind of seduction—you're winning over the interviewer. So use your abilities to do this. Then you can relax and seriously discuss the details of the job and your various qualifications to do it. You can see yourself there to make a friend, and just like in the bestseller, you can win friends, influence people, *and* get a new job.

SAGITTARIUS: Although technically my sign, Virgo, isn't supposed to get along all that well with your sign, I must admit that Sag people are among my favorites in the Zodiac. This is because of your affable nature. You know how to be mellow, how to get along with people, and how to enjoy life. Maybe it's part of being ruled by Jupiter, planet of expansion, and some say luck, but whatever it is, you just seem like good people to me. And if I, a cranky Virgo, can sing your praises, imagine how well you can do with every other sign. That aside, your casual nature could do you in at a job interview. Like the guy who ran out of socks, five minutes before you're due to exit the house isn't the time to discover you're not prepared with proper attire. Being prepared is more a Virgo motto than a Saggie one, but it's one you nevertheless must adopt when job hunting. This means looking through your wardrobe days before you start pounding the pavement and making sure you have what you need to dress the part. Admittedly, being gussied up isn't usually your favorite thing to do, but as I said before, a job interview is a costume party, and you must look the part. Even if it's a mostly casual position, you don't want to arrive all rumply (or with magic markered ankles). That's not to say if you're a software engineer, you don't want to be made fun of for arriving at an interview looking like a banker. Look the part, be unrumpled, and play the game. That's the hardest thing for you, because you're a deep person and you see beyond the silly stuff of life, but this is not one of those times to get preposterously philosophical. Although it's possible once you get the job the rules will relax and it will all be more casual, in the interview, it's as formal as it's ever going to be, so crank up your game and win the job.

CAPRICORN: You have the opposite mentality of Sagittarius. You take everything very seriously and recognize how truly important a job interview is. You're right of course, but that could mean that you feel and project a sort of tension, a clenched energy, that can make the interviewer feel ill at ease without even knowing why. Other than getting the job of course, which is the ultimate goal, an interview really is about meeting two short-term goals—making the person like you, and sharing how you're right for the job. You know that speed dating that is popular now with singles? Imagine it's like that. In ten minutes you have to share interesting and pertinent facts about yourself, but in a way that makes you appealing and likable enough for the other person to want more. Some people might say—hey learn a joke and tell it, but to me that seems pretty silly. Instead, be warm, be friendly, shake hands with firm but congenial pressure, and send out the vibe that you are someone the interviewer would love to have as a neighbor—or a colleague. The way to do this is to seem both affable and competent. What are the qualities you'd most like in a neighbor? You want someone you'd enjoy greeting over a fence, perhaps having a meal with and who isn't stupid enough to burn down the place. The same is true of a job interview. As you start thinking of it in these sorts of other terms, it becomes easier to get a handle on the persona you want to project because you can view it from many different angles, thus giving yourself a needed boost in confidence. What's hard for other people will be easiest for you—discussing your abilities and ways in which you can do a great job. You know the examples from the jobs you've done so far and can communicate them clearly and in reasonable detail, so after you win them over with your charm, be your serious self.

AQUARIUS: Take a page from the book of another stubborn sign, Taurus. Despite being determined that everything in life should be done a particular way—theirs—Taurus knows how to get a job, because pretty much nothing is as important to this practical sign. With Taurus, you have in common the stubbornness and the tendency to want things just as you want them, but you don't always know that you can't present this side of yourself to a job interviewer or else it may seem that instead of being the interviewee, you're the interviewer. A certain degree of flexibility is a necessity when working for anyone else, and even if you don't plan to be as flexible as they might want, you certainly can't let them know this. Maybe you're management and other people will have to kow-tow to you. This feels comfortable. In such a case, your management style might actually be discussed, and if so, it's all right to share your approach to this task, as long as you don't sound like a general about to storm Normandy. Balance is the key in a job interview. Obviously they are looking for the best person for the job, and certainly that person might be you, but they're also looking for someone who can fit in well and be an asset—also probably you, and it's up to you to communicate that, in a congenial and relatively direct manner, all the while generating some good will and positive vibes. As the sign of friendship, that should be something you easily can do, once you relax a little, slip into a flexibility mode, and allow yourself to come across as a reasonable person who isn't driven by fixed ideas.

PISCES: The greatest thing about your sign is how nice you are. People naturally love you and want to be your friend because you have a nurturing, friendly quality that feels as though you'd be the perfect person to have in someone's corner at any given moment. Being likable goes a very long way toward getting you a job. You are able to make a congenial impression during the interview and come across as an asset to the company. That is a very up version of the up side. The down side? You're not always organized, timely, or prepared. Time does get away from you now and then and you don't always estimate correctly how long anything will take. Arriving late for a job interview is not the best way to make a good first impression. Arriving way too early is (in my opinion) also bad, tho being early for an interview isn't as bad as being early to a dinner party. Arrive early, wait to go in, and thus be there right on time is my advice on that score. Carefully checking your resume is another essential task, and if you find it hard to discover typos or any writing errors, beg or hire someone to proof it for you. A resume with mistakes makes the worst sort of bad impression, and it's easy enough to avoid. The other issue may be that you, a likely Renaissance person, have experience in many different areas. While this could imply that you're well-rounded and capable to do many things, it also might say that you can't focus. Find a way to share your experience that gives it focus, makes it seem a natural progression, and which also connects it to the new job you're seeking. That way the interviewer won't assume you'll soon be bored and off to the next challenge.

Job hunting can be stressful, as anyone will agree, but armed with a few techniques, you'll soon be off the market and back among the ranks of the employed.

THE $IGN OF THE TIMES

Reading the paper lately is a daunting task, one which can lead to much fingernail biting and angst. The news seems to run the gamut from worse to horrific, and recently I read that economists predicted that the global slowdown could be just as bad four years hence as it is right now (January, 2009, as I'm writing this). Their theory was that America's now-constrained consumerism is responsible for economic woes all across the globe.

A friend's broke but travel-loving Sag sister asked him along on a vacation—and asked that he foot the bill for their broke brother. I said well gee how can you justify spending money on travel when you're broke, but my friend said that her kids gave her the trip for a birthday present. Nevertheless, it seems to me that if you're financially under the weather, it makes sense to use whatever resources you have in a more practical manner. But see—that's the difference between Virgo (me) and Sagittarius. They feel life is difficult and a break will be a necessary restorative. I feel well gee you could eat for several months on what a good vacation costs. And several months of less stress trumps a couple weeks of vacationing.

Cancer Harrison Ford took much chiding because when he and girlfriend Calista went to the movies, he purchased a senior citizen ticket for himself. This mega star who earns over twenty-five million a movie joked on a talk show that after all the savings is not insignificant. That's Midwest flintiness in action. But doesn't it make you wonder if his affinity for frighteningly undersize women could be because when they dine out nobody will raise an eyebrow if she orders from the children's menu—and still needs a doggy bag.

Leo Dustin Hoffman recently confided to Taurus Jay

Leno that he is a kleptomaniac. Apparently whenever he's in a city—and foreign ones are his preference—he will pinch note paper, scratch pads, or robes from the hotel. The voice of reason, Leno said that well yes but hotels put that sort of thing right on your tab. Hoffman shrugged and admitted that well the studio pays for the tab, didn't they do the same for Leno? Leos like their luxury and some like it as perks.

Some megastar, whose name inexplicably escapes me, was commenting on Taurus Al Pacino, who apparently has gobs of money, not so much because he's been working forever at a very nice rate, but because he never picks up a tab for anything. He's always comped wherever he goes and he's been dining out on his celebrity for decades. Nobody is better than Taurus about conserving and just plain being cheap.

The actor Jeffrey Donovan, from TV's Burn Notice recently confided in an interview that he was extremely poor as a child and that growing up on welfare has given him a very conservative outlook about his finances. Taurus Donovan recounted seeing a very "pretty young man," arriving at a hotel in a $60,000 car, which he'd bought because he'd been cast in a new TV show—one which ultimately never aired. A few months down the road, that fine fellow will be selling that vehicle, predicted the steadily-employed Donovan, who nevertheless drives a much lower-rent Camry. Like most people with money to invest, his resources have diminished recently, but he says he owns his home and buys land, something that can't just vanish.

Many people are feeling that sort of pinch, and are focused more on what they lost than on what they have. In the supermarket recently I saw a guy morosely walking around, without even a cart, talking on his cell phone about devastation to his investment funds. "Now I'll never be able to retire," he moaned. The rub? He looked to be barely forty! Was retirement so imminent for him that it was rendered impossible by the current economic downturn? Did he have no faith in a future recovery? It seems that that is indeed the climate of the times.

Every time I watched Martha as last year was ending, she

managed to mention how depressed everyone is over finances. Her friends are certainly in the upper echelon of income in this country, and apparently they lost more than most of us, and it has depressed them. Losing money is no fun. But you'd think people with that much money would be a little less depressed when they look out at the world and so many other people in genuinely dire straits. I watched Martha make—out of season—a recipe calling for at least a quart of berries—maybe two. Not strawberries—the expensive ones—and they cost at least four bucks for a handful at the time. She uncharacteristically mentioned that this would not be a financially prudent recipe unless you'd frozen some berries at the height of the summer season. Sometimes I suspect that she doesn't know what she will be doing on her show until she does it because Martha is very anti-waste and despite being a luxury-loving Leo, she can be frugal where it matters. Recently I've read that some heads have rolled at Martha's company in an apparent effort at conservation. This to me is amazing. At pretty much every level of the economy, business and the people involved are dealing with the need to tighten their belts. Just yesterday Martha suggested that we all conserve by growing our own veggies. Then she cut to a resplendent photo of her estate in New York with its acres of majestic gardens.

Movie star Kevin Bacon, a Cancer, was one of the celebrities bilked in that Madoff Ponzi scheme scandal. In an interview, rather than focusing on his losses, he said yes it's terrible but that he had just so much to be thankful for—his family, his health, his family's health. He would simply keep working, more important now than ever. That's the sort of attitude that can get us all through tough times, whatever they are. We would of course expect a Cancer to count his blessings and put family at the top of the list but still he expressed a really good attitude, one we should all try to emulate.

There's no question that we've become a much more frugal country. Even if we still have the resources, pretty much everyone has resorted to belt-tightening. Fostering a sense of economy in these times gives many people a positive feeling of control. Buy what you need and conserve the rest. Don't splurge. Be rational. Of course that attitude has caused many retailers to shutter their doors across the globe, and it's probably just temporary. But what does your Sun sign tell you about your approach to enforced economy? Just how willing are you to be frugal?

The sign least likely to enjoy belt-tightening (except during a diet) is probably **Aries**. To your credit, you have this whole Alfred E. Newman thing going and you know what his motto is—*what—me worry?* You do not sit and ponder dire consequences to anything and maybe that's why you can so easily be persuaded to leap out of a plane or bungee jump. You're not the sort to keep a ledger of expenses, and you might not even bother with a checkbook. You go to an ATM machine, yank some cash from it, and spend it as you please. When the bills come, if you're inclined to atypical neatness, you toss them in a drawer. Your intention is to pay them, certainly, but if the money isn't there, you don't sit and wring your hands about when it will come. And when the money does come, you'll think well gee I worked hard for that money and I deserve to treat myself to something nice. So that could mean a night on the town, a flight to Paris for lunch (as did Aries director Francis Ford Coppola during his bankruptcy ordeal some years back), or a purchase of something you really desire. Two plus two is not usually in your lexicon, so you would not normally say to yourself well gee, if I keep buying stuff and dining out with all my pals on my own dime, there won't be money for the electric bill. As long as the power is still on, you don't worry about it being shut off. If it is discontinued, then you will do what's necessary to restore it, even if you have to cry on the shoulder of a friend who is only just a little better off than you are. Although you're much in favor of the idea of retirement, which usually in your own mind just means living pretty much as you're already doing but with more money and less work, you're seldom the practical little squirrel who will bury some assets for the future. The future always seems so far away to you, the person who more than any other lives in the here and now, focused only on today and today's whims. Although you might not like it, you could benefit from a little Virgo-inspired organization. Even a simple sheet of paper will do. List all your bills for the month and the amounts you will owe. Keep it on a desk where you will see it so you have it in your mind. And when each one is paid, scribble a check mark. At least then when you do have money, you'll be more in tune with the idea that as money comes, at least a good chunk of it should go for life's necessities. And if that means you have to cut back on some of the fun, well it stinks but that's what grownups sometimes have to do.

As we said, nobody is a better skinflint than a **Taurus.** My Taurus aunt once said when we were at a buffet restaurant, that she chose a blueberry muffin because it could be both her bread and her dessert. Like the other earth signs Virgo and Capricorn, Taurus really understands the thrill of being practical, but as a Virgo all I can say is bah-humbug, I want a French roll, *and* a really nice dessert. Some people say I'm not true to my sign and they could be right. Taurus loves to save and to conserve, and you might have such a perfect system in place for squeezing the last bit of oomph out of every nickel that the current economic climate doesn't worry you a bit. You're already buying only what you need, and are careful to use what you buy. Waste is a four-letter word to Taurus. You shop carefully and you make sure you have received the absolute best bargain out there, but you're never penny wise and pound foolish. You don't buy crap, in other words; you buy the good stuff and make sure it will both last and not set you back unreasonably. You're one of those types who is always careful to save money and you probably make only the most conservative of investments. Even if you have been hit by the various financial crises plaguing our country, you probably have taken the long-sighted approach and you realize that as long as investments don't reach zero, they can balloon back up again. Like Jeffrey Donovan, you believe in land as a good investment, not flashy cars or anything that depreciates. You always look toward the future and consider the best approach for tomorrow. Even though you do tend to enjoy working and hate the thought of giving up a paycheck, you might one day want to retire or at least slow down your schedule a little and you will always take financial steps so that can happen. But you know yourself pretty well and may even joke that you're the type to die with your boots on. That footwear might have a Prada logo, but you can bet it wasn't bought retail unless a spectacular sale was in progress.

Without planets in neighboring Taurus, most **Gemini** types aren't big on conservation. You buy what you like, but usually shopping isn't your favorite pastime. You like to be involved intellectually and will acquire books, magazines, and maybe a huge TV, so that you can be plugged in. If it's necessary for you to cut corners, you don't mind getting that reading material at the library or even at a thrift store. You're also not averse to having several part-time jobs, which is a good idea in these times. Some people went to the mall over the holidays to join the workforce even if retail was far from their true calling. You would enjoy this prospect because it would be fun for you and you'd meet new people with whom you could converse. You also would love to be a tutor and there are companies which employ tutors on a part-time basis. When the cash isn't flowing, such options can be good choices for gadfly Gemini. You also don't mind cleaning out closets, although you seldom tend to be a packrat and thus might not have storage areas bursting with items that can be turned into cash. On the plus side, you also might not have the heavy credit card debt that so many Americans carry now because you don't over-consume. A casual life really appeals to you, and there's no question that casual can be easier to bankroll than opulent. A bike ride and a picnic is the perfect Gemini outing, and that's a lot cheaper to manage than a lunch in Paris. If you have a history of poverty or enforced conservation, well you will turn that into a number of amusing anecdotes which your children and grandchildren will love hearing. "We were so poor my sister and I had to go to school on different days so we could share the same pair of shoes." That's the sort of tale children love hearing, even when they know it might not be true, because then they're willing to pitch in and make a homemade pizza for their sleepover party instead of splurging on fifty bucks worth of delivered food. Anything that can be made into fun, you will do so, and that's the happiest way to tighten a belt.

Cancer people have a strong need for security, and even though you're dynamic, achievement-oriented, self-starters, the idea that something could threaten your security can send you into hysterics. Right now, with the current economic downturn, you're probably freaking out daily, even if you're still employed and are making plenty of money. You're generous by nature, and you may be supporting more people than in your immediate family. If someone close to you is in trouble, you are ready and willing to lend a hand, even in hard times. Although this isn't the path to wealth, it is in a way a comfort, because the more people you have in your corner, the safer you feel. Perhaps in the future, if you needed a helping hand, the ones you're supporting now will reach out to you then. This is the Golden Rule and it has a very important place in today's economy. Unlike neighboring sign Gemini, you do tend to be a pack rat, and chances are you could clean out closets and have a garage sale and raise some cash in a pinch. In fact, you might even tell yourself that as a means of comforting a faint heart on a bad day. You can be frugal, although it's not in your nature. You can shop at cheaper markets, and sometimes it feels like quite a triumph, as my Cancer daughter tells me when insisting on taking me to tour the new discount food market from England, Fresh 'N' Easy, right in her neighborhood. Of course she did fill a basket with stuff, even though we'd just come from dinner on my dime, and you know who paid for it at the checkout stand. That's another way Cancers conserve—by having a mom who dotes on you, but that's the Cancer thing—family—and as long as you're rich in family, everything else comes second.

Leo, the second fire sign, along with Aries and Sagittarius, is probably just as apt as Aries not to want to conserve. You don't tend to stash and ignore your bills, but you do like to live a nice life and you'd never opt to have a picnic instead of a resplendent birthday dinner at a luxe establishment. Even if you're springing for the tab, you still want the event to be up to your standards, and the thrill of enjoying good times makes it all worthwhile to you. A Leo friend who's been involved in some home improvements told me today that with this economy he should stop spending, but I say no, in this economy if you have the money, you should spend it. You're helping the country, providing other people with employment, and your home will rise in value eventually when the economy turns around. No, I am no expert on finance, as my bank balance would attest, but it does make sense, doesn't it? That doesn't mean you should go into deep debt now, but if you have some expendable income and a project that calls out to you, do it. The problem with asking a Leo to conserve is that by cutting corners you feel as though you're somehow denying some essential part of your being. Standing on a corner, singing "Brother can you spare a dime," is so far from the Leo ethos that the very idea chills you to the core. You can conserve if you really want to. You can eat those leftovers, even if they bore you. You can shop more carefully, even for presents, and get a better deal. You can take any extra money you have and pay down your own debt. That's sort of a Green approach to finance, and green is the color of money.

The thing about being a **Virgo,** is that it's not so much about being cheap but being orderly. I clip coupons from the paper but sometimes forget to use them and it galls me. If I pay more for an item and find it cheaper somewhere else, ohh the indignity. It's not so much about the dollars I might have overspent, usually just two or three, but the idea that somehow I'm being lazy, doing a poor job, and simply not paying attention. That is something a Virgo can't tolerate. Everything in the Virgo world should be just so. Checks should not bounce, and the checkbook should be nicely kept in order. While it's all right to dine out when the urge hits, you don't want to overpay for a dish that isn't up to par. An expensive entrée should taste better than what you could make at home in fifteen minutes or you feel robbed. Even the Virgos who like to shop, such as me, won't buy unless the item makes sense. Knick knacks—forget it. You make shopping a challenge and wait until the sale is just right. This way you don't overspend, don't buy too often, and get some exercise. Your drive for order comes in very handy when some conservation is necessary. You can buy food on a credit card that gives you points and pay off the balance before interest is levied. You despise waste and try to need what you buy and use it at peak. An overly full fridge makes you feel pressured and guilty. Single Virgos—and this is one of the bachelor signs—might not buy a take-out chicken on a Wednesday because if you're going out on the weekend, you know it won't be fully consumed. Do as I do—make large batches of food and freeze them in individual containers for lazy nights. It's certainly a better alternative to those icky frozen dinners. You're always the type to expend energy rather than wasting assets. You probably clean your own home, not just because of the expense but because you don't want to waste time entertaining a maid, and no doubt making her lunch. Your world must be orderly and everything must make sense to you at all times, which is the perfect attitude for managing money.

Libra is a very social sign, and one which likes everything to be pretty. For you, that could mean that the tendency to replace your wardrobe yearly is more of a necessity than a whim. Looking good is what you're all about, and you might toss perfectly good items just because they're no longer in style. You could be like me—wearing the same boring classics for twenty years, and then they'd never be in—or out—of style, but then you wouldn't be a Libra. You can be dynamic and assertive, Libra clichés to the contrary, but somehow the idea of money just sort of makes you cringe. You don't want to talk about your finances and you certainly don't want to hear about anyone else's. It's tasteless. That could mean you don't make a very soft touch when someone needs your help because you tactfully change the subject. One thing you're very good at is organizing social events, and you might be persuaded to do this for charity. It could be a good way to raise some cash for the homeless shelter—or severely under funded animal charity—in your area. You could decide to donate those castoff fashions to a shelter or to one of the organizations which help the unemployed get back into the work force via donated wardrobes. Like Martha, you might realize that conserving assets is now in style and you could tone down some of your social events and make them simpler. And if you're a Libra with a partner who's the major breadwinner, you might opt to look for work, a daunting task today. That would keep you busy, and you could contribute more to the family coffers.

Like other water signs Cancer (and Pisces to a certain degree), **Scorpio** requires security. You worry about the future and want to make sure you will be safe. You know you're not exactly one of the world's most flexible types, and thus are less likely suddenly to change your career when it seems to be floundering. This could be bad or good, depending on what your actual situation is. Going down with a sinking ship hurts, but then maybe determined paddling can put that boat back on track. Your tendency is to save for the future and as long as you have done what makes sense to you, you don't worry too very much. Because you have such excellent will power, you can easily cut back and it won't be too terrible a prospect. If your habit is to dine out too often, you can force yourself to cut back by a certain percentage and it will work to your advantage. You can institute a family meatless spaghetti night once a week and nobody will complain, not even you. You also have the tendency to hold onto what you have and that can work where your wardrobe is concerned. You like unusual and sometimes flamboyant attire, and a conversation piece remains such years after it's acquired. If there's something you must buy, you don't mind delayed gratification a bit. You'll happily save up the money and then go pay for that item with cash. Likewise, you're savvy about credit, which is still available, despite what they say on television. You may already have refinanced credit cards at zero interest—and you may be watching with a little trepidation as that lender is taken over by a different one because you're not sure if the deal you made will be honored. But still, it's usually worth it to save some money on interest while focusing on reducing debt.

As you already surmised, **Sagittarius,** the last of the fire signs, is not particularly frugal. In your defense, you're also seldom a spendthrift. In fact, you may hate to shop and as you don't mind wearing clothes you found on a corner ten years ago, it's not too much of a problem for you. You like to travel and never begrudge what you spend on going to exotic places because that money enriches your soul as it depletes your wallet, a trade you happily make. Unlike neighboring sign Scorpio, you do resent delayed gratification and if you can travel on plastic and pay it back later, you'll be out the door in a wink. Also to your credit, you seldom mind roughing it. You will happily go camping, backpacking, or on a bike tour cross-country. Bugs in your teeth? So what. You also seldom spend big money on luxuries like dining out or fancy cars, unless you have a mate who really demands it. That way your basic expenses are relatively low and you're content with that life. The thrift store couch you got in college is still comfy enough years later. There's nobody you need to impress. Thus if you need to cut back, you will happily grab a slice of pizza or a burger and consider it a bargain. You'll even camp out on a friend's couch and crash a dinner if need be. That's what friends are for. Although we joke a lot about your very casual set of standards, in a way you have the right idea. Focus on the ethereal and keep the practical to a minimum.

Capricorn is the third earth sign, and you really love being a skinflint. Even if your family is ordering an expensive meal, you'll be willing to order something cheaper and "take one for the team," as my Cap son-in-law once said. What team was that I wondered, since I was paying for the meal and wouldn't allow him to do it. Of course, the flip side is often this skinny boy, who can eat like Dumbo and never gain an ounce, orders more than the rest of us put together, and sometimes that irks me because I know he's enjoying my largesse a little too much. This is the sort of typical Cap-Virgo debate. Cap can be selfish and Virgo wants things to be balanced. I'll happily give but don't like to be taken! Capricorn is very skilled at managing the resources of the earth—it's your Karmic task, so of course you can belt-tighten better than an anorexic. You love finding a good bargain, will combine your phone, cable TV, and internet bills to save a few bucks and generally enjoy working the system to your advantage. To you this is only good sense, and it's not just about the money you're saving but also about managing your life in a capable manner—something you do have in common with Virgo—and sometimes Taurus. You're always working toward a goal, and saving for the future is important to you, but not the most important thing. Your goal is to achieve the level of success and wealth that seems appropriate to you, so you will often worry about the path to that future rather than your old age. You don't mind cutting back, and can often do it cleverly via flea markets, thrift stores, or even beside dumpsters in tony neighborhoods where many good household finds can be acquired for less— or nothing. Those parental hand-me-downs are a treasure you'll happily keep. You also hold onto your clothes pretty much forever, and that can be a huge savings over time.

Aquarius is the third Air sign, along with Gemini and Libra, and as you know, Air is all about communication, and is not exactly focused on practicality. The most eccentric of all the signs, you tend to do what makes sense to you, whether or not anyone else can concur about your choices. There's no question that you have a charitable ethos and will often dig deep when anyone is in trouble. That could deplete your resources, but you will usually say it's worth it. You also see yourself as a mentor and if someone is in trouble, you might want to give advice that would turn their life around, whether or not the person in question agreed with your plan for their future. You are often technically savvy and enjoy your toys so sometimes you will splurge on top of the line, just-off-the-presses gadgets which in six months will cost half. Delayed gratification is not really your strong suit, because you have what could be described as mental urges to experience the things you deem worthwhile. You can cut back if you have to, however, and usually that will be in areas that seem less important. You're more than willing to live communally with one or more roommates if necessary and sometimes even if it's not, because you like being in group situations. You're happy to wear the same clothes often, and even to borrow items from roommates or pals. Likewise you will be very pleased to share cooking chores with friends so that you get a good meal and don't have to bother with the work every single day. While you might not always be focused on saving for the future, you do find investments interesting and will usually have the intelligence to know what is the best approach with your money in the current climate. Or as an Aquarius client told me, this is the time to buy houses for cash and eventually they will be a great resource for the future. Who has that kind of cash? Aquarius—sometimes!

Pisces is thought of as a creative, sensitive, artistic sign. While many Pisces types can make a bundle doing whatever it is you do, you don't tend to focus wholeheartedly on money, neither spending it nor making it. To you, it's just a resource you have or don't have, and either way it does not define you. Obviously that's a good approach because those who feel their superiority (or inferiority) is determined by a bank balance are almost always inferior rather than superior! Usually you're not as flaky as the Pisces clichés would indicate, and thus you don't lose a wad of cash tucked into your shoe, but you do tend to forget about bills and life's annoying little responsibilities. Thus if you reach for your cell phone and it's silent, you know why. Oops! The good news is generally you're charming and appealing and can call whoever it is that has turned off your service and manage to get it restored. It doesn't usually occur to you to make responsible fiscal choices. When you hear something is great, you want it, like a marginally-employed Pisces I know whose cell phone for a month costs what mine does for half a year. It did not occur to her to say hmm, I might not have the money to pay for this down the line and maybe a more economical plan would cause less angst. Perhaps that's because you Pisces don't have that much angst over practical things like phone bills. But if you're without your phone and Hollywood calls, you could miss your big break, so why not take a few minutes to go over your expenses and look for ways you can trim them if need be. Perhaps you don't need every premium channel on your DVR box, particularly if you're out every night and seldom watch TV. Don't let things slide—take care of them once, and you won't have to worry about them again. You are a sweet-natured person, and if someone is in trouble, you are willing to help. That could mean you have a buddy conked out on your couch for the third month in a row. Be a helpful person, not a patsy, and make that buddy pull some of the weight. It's the fair thing to do.

We're all in this mess together, and even though they don't call it a depression, it sure seems to be one. At the very least, we're all depressed over the national—and the global— economy. But the first step is honestly to assess where you stand personally in this mess. Are you still employed? Even if your income or assets have been reduced, if you still have an income, give thanks. And look around you. Chances are someone close to you is either unemployed or in difficult straights. This is the time for you to pitch in. Share the blessings you have. Help a strapped family member with some bills. Take a neighbor a casserole. Put off buying that fancy item and give the money to someone who hasn't had any for a long while. It will make you feel better and it will help everyone when you help someone.

If you're the one in need of help, take heart. Maybe things will be improving soon. Like Kevin Bacon, take a little time to list your blessings. Then get a little creative. Consider how your own situation can improve—perhaps by doing something outside your professional or financial comfort range. Downsizing can be a good thing. Asking for help from someone who loves you can be hard but it can bring you closer together.

Here's hoping that sooner rather than later, we'll be thinking not about tightening our belts but about building a secure and hopeful future—with confidence and wisdom.

3
COPING WITH LIFE

Life has its problems, that's for sure. And some of us handle certain types of problems more easily than others. Sometimes it's a matter of observing a friend and how he or she approaches a situation that you find daunting. We all have different perspectives on life, we all have our strong suits, and all have our Achilles' heels.

In *When Life Gives You Lemons*, I look at problems and discuss coping mechanisms. You might be good at one irksome situation and more frustrated by another. With a little thought and a few tips, you can sail through life and vanquish whatever is getting you down.

Lazy? We all are sometimes. Just getting up and getting going can be daunting some days. So I took a little survey online from some friends and did some research to find helpful approaches that help you *Motivate Yourself.*

Work is a four letter word, not just metaphorically, but literally. We all have our burdens to bear, the things on that to-do list, the jobs that must be done to earn our daily bread, and the various other things that we must tackle. How do you cope with *The Responsibilities of Life*? Can you cope a little better by examining this process? Of course you can!

On the lighter, and infinitely more fun side, there's shopping. Some of us love it. (Me! Me! Me!) Some of us would rather do almost anything else. (Really?) So what's your approach to shopping? You certainly have to shop for other people at some point, those greedy so-and-so's, and in *The Zen of Shopping*, I cover ways to approach this task from the perspective of your own sign *and* the best approach to shopping for any other sign. Learn about yourself and tackle those gifts on your list right here.

WHEN LIFE GIVES YOU LEMONS

Okay, I do admit it! I can be a cranky person. I'm not always cheerful and I don't always accept disappointments with the most positive of spirits. Sometimes I just want to shout and scream and be cranky for a while. Sometimes I like to lie on the couch and eat candy and watch television when I know that I should be meditating. That's because I know that I'm not always ready to deal with a problem head on when it occurs. When something goes really wrong, I have the tools to fix the problem. I know how to go inside and meditate and get to the source of the problem and to release whatever it is. Sometimes all that's necessary is getting to a place of realization where an insight so small creeps in, and that insight helps all the dark clouds roll away. Eventually I always do get to that point. And then I cheer up again. It's just a matter of getting to the point of readiness to accept the healing.

It's important to develop some sort of coping mechanism of your own. Chocolate is the answer for a lot of us, but it somehow doesn't provide all the healing necessary in a real crisis. Life can be wonderful. It can be pure and purely beautiful. It can resound with heart warming energy that generates a feeling of genuine happiness to be alive. But it can also be a load of crap. Things do go wrong and at some point you will be down and out, miserable and ready to blow your brains out. That's a given! How are you going to cope?

ARIES: Your nature drives you in the opposite direction from most people who spend time confronting their issues. You are someone who likes to keep active and generally you follow your instincts, act on impulse and do basically whatever the mood inclines you to do. On the whole, that leads to an exciting life. But problems do set in, and usually they're as a result of that act first and think later mentality that has for so long been your modus operandi. At some point you are going to stop and face the fact that once again you are neck deep in crap, and that you have caused your own internment. Once again, your inclination will be to flee. You will want to just go race your car or shoot something or punch something or destroy something. The only problem is that once this fateful moment arrives, you'll realize that these are the behavior patterns that have gotten you into the mess you now face. A new tack is needed. And that approach involves generating more self-awareness. It's the time to do something that doesn't come all that naturally for you—seek help from a therapist, have a heart to heart talk with a friend who is adept at behavior analysis, and in general do what you have to do to make sense of who you are and why you make the choices you make. Then you'll stop feeling badly about yourself and once again life will be exciting, fun and an experience you want to savor.

TAURUS: You are someone who understands only too well the chocolate approach to problem solving. Your love of pleasure and of food is well documented, and you may already have spent years medicating yourself with food as a way to evade your problems. Unless you're one of the six skinny Taureans on the planet, you see where that has gotten you. The real issue isn't about life's minor crises—you have the tools to handle them. It's about your own determination to maintain a death grip on the status quo. And when the here and now really is threatened, you feel as though your head is about to explode. That's when you doubt your sanity, fear for your future, and worry that Western civilization as you now know it is ending. Perhaps you give in and suffer a migraine. A better tool for crisis management is letting your mind wander. Start first with the problem. What is it that you're so afraid of losing? Face it clearly—is it a job, a lover, whatever. Then let your mind roam. Envision your life first as it is now so that you're clearly in touch. Be honest. What is the life you're now living? Then take the risk. Say ok, what would my life be without X—whatever the thing or person is. Life without X. Let your mind open up. Create the scenario. Let it be bad, if you imagine that's all that's possible. Your life without whatever and all the tragedies you can imagine. See them in your mind. Then keep going. What are the next developments? Soon enough your mind will surprise you. Your mind will begin filling in the blanks. And you will see something amazing. There *can* be life after X, pretty good life too. Once you do that, you'll start to calm down and life won't feel so scary. Only by actually confronting your fear of loss can you let go of it and feel more in charge of your destiny.

GEMINI: Throughout the Zodiac, one sign seems to handle potential crap from the universe better than any other—and take a load off Gemini, that sign is yours! Other people stress and worry but you go with the flow. Perhaps that's because you live most strongly in your mind and enjoy your intellectual pursuits anywhere you go, so the external realities don't affect you or threaten you when they change. Change is something you crave, not try to avoid, so you're mellowness personified. That's not to say that things don't go wrong in your life—sure they do—after all you *are* human. But you don't worry too much about them. You understand the power of positive escapism. You're happy enough to retreat into a TV show for a few hours, to read a book or to talk to a pal, and even if you're dealing with the crisis of a lifetime, you feel that you can get through the day without submerging yourself in the pain. That's a very good approach. It means that you have faith in the universe and figure things will work out while you're busy with a book, and chances are they will.

CANCER: Tears and emotional terror are your normal modus operandi. Other people are blocked emotionally. Not you! Not you! Your emotions are a river that runs through you, offering you the opportunity on a constant basis to enjoy a catharsis whenever anything goes wrong. You don't hold back—you let go and you give in to those feelings, weeping when necessary. Food is another comfort zone for you. In fact, you may be too at home with the idea of sucking down that quart of ice cream whenever a crisis occurs. You weep, you consume so much ice cream that you have excellent biceps from hefting that comfort-laden spoon. Yet none of that is enough to make you completely better. What you need when things go is the concern of other people. You need to be held, petted and loved. You're not shy and you're not emotionally constipated. You're rarely proper. And all that is to the good. Because when something goes wrong, you speak up, you reach out, and when you're enveloped in arms other than your own, you begin to feel a bit safer. Even if that means you break down in line at the supermarket and share a touching moment with a stranger, you know that's what it takes to make you feel that life can once again be managed.

LEO: Your pride is very important to you. You care about your dignity and you don't enjoy the idea of wallowing in your misery in front of other people. If you're going to be miserable with an audience watching, you want to be in control. It's one thing to perform a satire about the crises in your life before a standing-room-only crowd and quite another to get all sloshy in a public place. Shopping is always a positive and pleasant diversion unless you have money management issues and find yourself accumulating too many trinkets and the bills to go with them. There is always something about luxury that calms you. Even if all you do is stroll through the best jewelry store in town, seeing all those twinkling gems makes you feel calmer. There are quality things out there, available to give someone pleasure, so the world can't be as bad as it seems right now. Shopping is great, that's true, but a better way to gain a boost is to spend time with someone you trust and to hear how valued you are by that person. Being appreciated is validating for you, and it gives you the boost you need to get out the in the world and to conquer whatever fire breathing dragon is threatening to incinerate your world.

VIRGO: Life can be so frustrating for you because since yours is the sign of perfection, you constantly face disappointment, and are then burdened with a sense of failure. Nowhere can you find evidence of the perfection you're trying to create. People have problems, and heaven knows they're not capable of handling them. So it's all up to you—all of the time. Feeling this constant sense of problems being dropped in your lap is exhausting as you run around trying to help everyone everywhere you go. Of course, on the up side, you're used to coping with problems, so it's rare that a crisis seems insurmountable. It's just the humdrum of being bombarded daily with mini tragedies. What do you do? Work even harder? Drive yourself into an early grave? That is your tendency and your inclination but it's not your best solution. When you really get bogged down and overwhelmed by problems, there is only one real answer. Stop immediately and resign from Virgo for a while. Go to the mall. Go to the movies. Be a hedonist. Don't believe any of that crap that advises you to clean out a closet. As if your closets aren't already perfect!   Find something simple, something good, something pleasant, and escape there for a while. You can rescue the world after you've had a little break.

LIBRA: Although Virgo is the sign of perfection, yours is the sign of prettiness. You want things nice, sweet and clean, and that pretty much tends to preempt your indulgence for a crisis. When friends get involved in those nasty old tacky life situations, you want to run in the other direction and take another ballroom dancing class.   You certainly don't want to be involved in anything messy yourself, and that's just why you go off the deep end when a real crisis happens. It's as though some etiquette monitor in your brain is mocking you and accusing you of becoming irreversibly tacky. Now this may sound harsh, but I'm sorry it's true—your first step in dealing with a crisis is to say to yourself "Get over it already." Okay so you are involved in the town's messiest divorce—or whatever.   Who cares? That's life. Somewhere there are people with leprosy whose skin is molting like snakes. Somewhere far away from you! Take some time to review the really horrible tragedies happening all around you. And then life gains greater perspective. Then spend a day volunteering time to people less fortunate—give some time to the hospital or a shelter or whatever needs to be done. When you confront genuine crisis, it will give you a sense of empowerment to deal with the chaos in your own life. And once you dig in, soon enough life will be pretty again.

SCORPIO: The greatest problem you face is your own imagination. Other people are dainty and proper, but you don't suffer from those debilities. You can imagine anything, right down to the seamiest consequence of any action. You're not squeamish, and there in your mind are the most disgusting potentials that you fear could mutate into your own horrible reality. A small problem begins, you work on it in your mind, and suddenly you've been plunged into a horror movie. As all these imaginary but truly heinous consequences begin to plague you, you have to confront the one thing that most frightens you—losing control. The truth is you want to have power but you know how much power you really have—none at all. You're at the mercy of the winds! That is the fate you most want to avoid, but unfortunately most of life requires us to be at the mercy of the winds. It's scary. One thing you can do to calm your imagination is to remember back over your life. Review the other catastrophes that have befallen you. You're still here. You survived. Remember back to the fears you had at the time, to the truly awful things you expected to happen. What percentage actually did occur? It almost doesn't matter because no matter how bad it was, you got through it. Here you are today, reading this paragraph and blushing at the thought of your own paranoia. The whole point of the crisis is to help you find a way to trust in the universe and to feel that you've been taken care of before and will be again.

SAGITTARIUS: Like your opposite number, Gemini, your motto echoes that of your hero and mentor, Alfred E. Newman. "What, me worry?" No, your inclination is not to worry about anything. You live in the here and now, you spend time outside with your friends and your pets and when you arrive at home to discover you've been evicted, you pack up your stuff and adios in your Jeep. That's the life and I have to say I envy you. Does that mean that your life is easier than mine? Probably not—as a "perfect" Virgo, I just worry more. But problems do occur, real problems and you do have to deal with them. Simply because you'd rather pursue escapist activities and chill out, it doesn't mean that crises disappear. And the only way for you to deal with them is to get out of that hammock and get going. Sometimes you do have to dig in your heels, be responsible and meet life head on.

CAPRICORN: As serious people go, you are the most serious of all. You want to live a good and orderly life and that means managing crises before they occur. Damage control is your specialty. You can't quite fathom how people can stumble through life failing to see the writing on the wall, when you spend time crunching the numbers and making sure that things will indeed work out. Things do work out fairly well for you, it's true, at least in the business world. If only two plus two were as easy to calculate in your personal life, you'd probably be crisis free forever. But human interaction is more difficult for you. There is a bit of irony here. The skills that make you so perfect professionally trip you up personally, and that's why you can't solve your most intimate problems. It's not impossible, however. You simply need to toss aside your calculator and tune up your listening skills. Learning to listen to other people and to respect what they tell you enough that you don't scoff at their point of view will help with most of your crises. Put aside your need for logic and neatness. Life is messy. People are messy, but that doesn't make them bad—it makes them interesting. The other approach to crisis that also benefits you is to take some time for pleasure. You're not a fridge and you can't be on and running for years at a time. You need a break, you need sex, you need chocolate—just like all the rest of us!

AQUARIUS: One of your natural abilities is to look at life and see how much better it could be if only the world would change according to your visionary ideas. Other people pass a slum and avert their eyes. You stop, take it all in and come up with a plan for transformation into something good, something useful, something rewarding. It's great to have such a visionary mind as yours. The only problem is that the rest of the world rarely conforms to your better vision. It's frustrating to see what life could be and to be unable to make it happen. Other people get bogged down in what you consider nonsense, and once again you feel powerless to dislodge them from the crapola, no matter how hard you try. Of course that doesn't keep you from trying. In fact, no matter how badly your own life is going, you never stop trying to change the world. It's a good thing you're doing, and you want to take quantum leaps to do it. Is it possible, though, that this form of commitment, albeit saintly, is also some form of escapism? It's always easier to fix the world than what's in your own back yard. Is it also possible that your all or nothing mentality is holding you back and preventing you from accomplishing the very growth you so dearly want? Could be. If you resolve to work on some small problems of your own for a while, to see solutions that are not huge or world changing, but are helpful nonetheless, you'll make some progress. And that's a good feeling. Commit first to doing what you can do, particularly to solving your own problems before everyone else's.

PISCES: Your tenderhearted nature gets you in a lot of trouble. You feel things deeply and whenever anyone has a problem, you feel you have one also. That's a lot to worry about. Because you're such a people person, you feel constantly bombarded, surrounded with and overwhelmed by the day to day problems of life. How can you help it, when you have the weight of the world on your shoulders? That's a huge problem for you and sometimes when it gets too upsetting you decide to flake and not keep promises made to other people. You just can't take it any more and absenting yourself is your form of self-preservation. It's understandable, of course, but it may be hard for the people who love you to forgive. It's hard to be let down, particularly in a time of intense need. First of all, you need to give careful thought before making a promise. It's better to say no in advance than to flake later. It's also important for you to clear your energy using psychic techniques. Do a visualization and see the problems of other people slide off you as though you have a magical Teflon coating. You can offer sympathy and love to the people you care about but you can't take their problems as your own. One side effect of accepting too many problems of other people is that you neglect your own life and discover what was once a tiny problem has escalated into a crisis. So also remember to handle your own problems first. Then go ahead and be the good listener, loyal friend, and loving person you were meant to be. After all, you can do only so much, so do what you must then do what you can.

Life has problems—we all know that. Some—like a life-threatening disease—are very serious indeed. But most of the problems we face are relatively minor. What makes them seem worse than they are is the attitude we bring to them—and to life itself. I'm not saying we should all be positive, happy-go-lucky Pollyannas who are cheerful to the point of nausea no matter what happens. Go ahead and whine a while. Let yourself be miserable. If you have the flu, lie down and moan loudly, curse your fate and cry, "I'm sick," for as long as necessary. But at some point you have to take the reins of your life once again, and that's the time to muster your courage, revel in your faith in the universe and to find whatever well of joy remains inside you. Life can be wonderful, and it's nice even during a crisis to remember this fact. Something as simple as noticing a pretty flower bed can be enough to lift your spirits to the degree that once again you find the strength to go on. Give that a try—admit you're miserable, find something to cheer you up, and then charge back into the fray and slay that dragon!

MOTIVATE YOURSELF

Lazy, I want to be lazy
I want to be out in the sun
With no work to be done
Under that awning, they call the sky
Stretching and yawning and let the world go drifting by
I want to peep through the deep, tangled wildwood
Counting sheep 'til I sleep like a child would

Irving Berlin

Although I know it's not particularly fashionable for a woman to champion Ernest Hemingway, his economy of prose always appealed to me. Much of his way of looking at the world is now out of sync, but some of his comments had a down to earth quality that still applies. One of my favorites of his was a statement about writing. He said that when you're about to write a new book, first you go wash your car. To many people this could be viewed as a wry comment about writers' notorious tendency to procrastinate. But in fact, I believe he meant something else. Hemingway was a Cancer, but with his Moon in Capricorn and Mars in Virgo in the first house, he was practical at the heart, and action oriented (no surprise to those who've read his books). To him the act of washing the car was physical activity that generated mental stimulation. That may have been one of his tricks to get motivated. And of course the water also helped— Cancer is a water sign.

For years people with whom I work have said to me, "Well, you're a fast writer," and this is meant to be a compliment. I don't bother to correct them because in my mind I write no faster than anyone else, although I do type pretty well. My trick is to sit there 'til it's done, to surrender myself, to just do the work. That's not speed, it's determination. Once I begin, it moves forward. Beginning is another matter however, for often I find myself sitting at the computer in a kind of a stupor, shopping online, doing searches for improbable diseases or gadgets I don't need, or posting on social media. A war then begins between me and the other me, the stern taskmaster inside my head. She nags and nags. And nags. It doesn't help. I sit there until the spirit moves me and finally I begin. Virtually everything in my world happens via what seems like whim, passing fancy, or just a kind of floatiness, but really it's a matter of my energy being revved enough to get going. But that doesn't stop that bossy inner voice from nagging.

In the fall I began an arduous project to re-release my first astrology book, *Love and Sex Under the Stars*, something I'd resisted for years because the book didn't exist in a file and had to be typed. Ultimately I decided to do it, and launched forward slowly, with many interruptions because of other projects. Frequently during those floaty moments when nothing was being done, my inner superego would nag, "Will you get going already." The outer me usually replied, "Oyy." Or "Blurg."

By Thanksgiving, it was well underway, but there was cleaning and cooking to be done, and my expectation was to resume work immediately after. Instead, like a pile of butter-soaked sweet potatoes, there I sat at the computer, barely able to pull the keyboard toward me. Finally my fingers began the work, but it wasn't the book they were typing, it was a Facebook post, "I'm 64 and I'm tired." Sometimes you just have to face the facts: when you're tired, you need to let yourself rest. I relearn this constantly. Somewhere in the back of my mind must be a fear that one day I won't make a deadline or something equally wacky.

Like Hemingway, when faced with a big new project, or a pile of things to write, my first step is to go out, go shopping, or to lie and daydream. Washing my car, no, I'd just get wet, not inspired. Maybe it's about building momentum. Sometimes it feels as though on an inner level I'm connecting with my guides, who'll provide the inspiration. Once when a cousin, knowing I don't drink coffee, asked me how I got all perky in the morning, I just shrugged. I drift around in a blur until I feel awake. Or ready.

When contemplating this article, I looked online for some quotes about getting motivated. What surprised me was that most of them were about achieving success. In my mind, that wasn't the issue. The issue was getting motivated *today*, not for the twenty years it would take to build success. I did find some pithy comments about laziness, which seemed more apropos, and you'll see them below.

Then I wrote a post asking friends how they motivated themselves: *What's your sign and your way of motivating yourself—either to achieve big-time or just to clean that pesky bathroom...* Many of the answers provided good insights.

I was interested when people suggested going out in nature as a way to rev their gears. In my world, if I leave the house, then the day is devoted to fun and no nagging occurs. And also no work. But Pam in Oklahoma, an Aquarius, says sunshine energizes her and makes the world look better so she can work. Sandye in Florida, a Taurus, concurs. Susan in Connecticut, who is a photographer and a Cancer, goes out for a drive to a nature spot and becomes part of the environment for as long as it takes to feel the inspiration kick in, then she makes a game of getting things done, as though she's playing "beat the clock." She feels it's inertia she's defeating, and by making a game of it, her chores are more rewarding—and more manageable. That's something I share with her. It's the getting going that's hard, not the getting it done. Because Susan has a condition that enervates her, she has to use the time she has, and so sometimes she sets a clock for ten minutes, feeling that's a manageable interval in which to make some headway. Next hour, another ten minutes. I too like that idea and find if I'm on hold on the phone, or waiting for something, instead of being trapped in limbo, I use that time and because it's finite, I actually get more done than while waiting to get my oomph back. Then instead of being annoyed that my time is being wasted, I'm rewarded with an accomplishment. Imaginary gold stars are always part of my life, and days in which I lie like a slug on the couch and do little are sad indeed.

Rewards are a tool used by other people as well. Melanie, a P.R. ace in Canada, has a to-do list, and when some items are crossed off, her reward is an hour of reading time. Nina, a Leo, blazes through her chores with the plan of having extra television or reading time, and likes to combine both pleasures. If you ever read the book about efficiency expert Galbraith, whose work was chronicled by one of his kids in *Cheaper By the Dozen,* (the original version), he said he was efficient because he liked having the leftover time.

List making is a big deal for many people, and that helps because it's so satisfying to cross items off the list. Kelley in Virginia, a Pisces animal activist, feels she's a little OCD about the satisfying act of list completion, but it makes her feel like she's accomplished great things.

Many people mentioned music as a way to get through chores that feels energetic and fun. Capricorn Rosinda in Canada, a food blogger and mom to two young girls, is an early riser and she has get up and go from dawn onward. Her house stays spotless because she lets the music move her. Penny in New Jersey, a Libra writer of beloved romance novels, also uses music to motivate her to clean, but like me prefers to write in silence, where she says no motivation is required. Les Mis writer Victor Hugo took a very novel approach—he had his valet hide his clothes so he'd write naked and not be able to wander from the task. His wardrobe must have been lots smaller than mine!

Sandy, a Pennsylvania Pisces, who is a jewelry designer and a total dynamo, says she is unmotivated lately, but when you hear the list of her daily accomplishments, you're put to shame. Okay, *I'm* put to shame. She agrees with Cancer Joann, an aspiring innkeeper, who says company coming provides motivation to deal with housework. Household chores are hard. You do the dishes and what—two or three days later it seems the sink is full again. My high school friend Mike in Wisconsin says he just helps with the chores, but the truth is this Gemini never misses a day of work, not even when the snow is higher than an elephant's eye. Jacqueline in Australia, another Gemini, who hilariously keeps trying to fix me up with her gorgeous tall sons (completely against their will we both acknowledge) offered this pithy tip: "What is this cleaning thing you talk of...."

We all have those days—or those chores—we really don't want to tackle. And we have the day to day that can't be avoided. Whether you're working at a job or self-employed like me, there's stuff that must be done, even if you're not in the mood. How does your sign handle these situations?

My whole comic persona is that of a guy who explores the id: I romanticize gluttony, I romanticize laziness, and people identify with that. **Jim Gaffigan**

The great thing about being an **Aries**, is that you have an unlimited supply of get up and go. That why you're usually gotten up and gone, which leaves little time for chores of the mundane variety. While other people feel guilty about this situation, you don't give it an instant's thought. Nobody is better at living in the moment than you are. Life brings you opportunities for fun and excitement, and you take them. Unless you've won the lottery, you obviously must work, like the rest of us slobs. So that means most of the week revolves around dancing to the tune of your alarm clock. You may be a morning person, making the clock unnecessary, but even in a career you love, there are many days you'd rather be doing something else. So what do you do? Building in rewards helps, but you're not as big on delayed gratification as most people. The idea of work now, get a fudge sundae later doesn't always work for you. It might be possible for you to treat yourself first, then do the chore after. Like my friends who need a nature kick to kick them into gear, you might allow yourself a walk, a drive, or a ride on your motorcycle as a way to blow out the cobwebs in advance of tackling that big work project. Even if you have to rise a bit earlier, you might not mind. Household and other chores are more difficult, but nobody can avoid those dishes or laundry forever. Making an appointment with yourself can help. Between seven and eight, you plan to do some housework, knowing that after eight, your life is your own. Obviously you prefer it to be your own all day long and all night long, because let's face it, that's who you are, but you also see the value of clean underwear, so that's a compromise you might be willing to live with.

Laziness is nothing more than the habit of resting before you get tired. **Jules Renard**

Although **Taurus** has a reputation (not entirely undeserved) of being lazy, indolent, and food obsessed, you do value hard work because it brings in the money. Being an Earth sign, you like things pretty and neat, and that takes some effort, which you are usually willing to expend. Like my friends, company coming is a good motivator for you, but also you just take pride in your home and want it to be nice for your own comfort and enjoyment. Where work projects are concerned, you tend to immerse yourself in tasks that take a goodly amount of time, not the sort that can easily be completed in an hour or two. You don't really mind this because continuity has a certain pleasant ring to it. Each day you arrive and see the progress you're making and that gives you satisfaction. When I first began writing books, I'd always print out the day's efforts, because what made me able to keep going was the sight of that pile of pages, growing taller by the day. This is something you understand very well. You don't mind delayed gratification because you see life as a slow process and you're happy to know that if you plant a seed today, in a few months you'll be eating a tomato. Patience is a wonderful attribute, and it's one you naturally possess. Because your natural pace is slow and determined, you don't really see exhaustion as a reason to stop, and generally you're good at modulating your energy. If you find that you dread going to work or dealing with a household situation, it's time to take stock. Perhaps it's time to consider a new job, or to divest yourself of that knick knack collection. Because continuity is so important to you, it's wise to be certain that where you immerse yourself is where you want to be.

Well done is better than well said. **Benjamin Franklin**

One word comes to mind here **Gemini**, and it's a word

we've discussed before. You've heard it, you know it, you've lived it. *Bored*, the word is bored. Yup, it's a big problem. You're a good starter because you have no absence of whims, but every whim does not generate the kind of follow through necessary to make a project work. *Maybe we should catalog all our....* You fill in the blank. And it's a great idea and will make your work much easier. And you lurch forward, seeing that it's a good idea, but then you're in the middle of it, and it's no longer an idea, but a reality. And you're sick of it, but you're stuck. Obviously a good solution here is to delegate. If you can be the idea person with an army of grunts to carry them out, you're totally content. The other positive is if you're working at tasks that take a reasonable time to complete. Writing *War and Peace*? You'll leave that to the Virgos, for they don't mind suffering. You'd rather pen a novella—or a greeting card. You like variety in your day, so having a to-do list to cross off is a good thing, because it allows you to pick and chose your chores—and your battles. Maybe today you're in the mood to deal with the piles of stuff in the garage and to mount a garage sale. The weather is nice and you can immerse yourself in those boxes of old toys. Or if you have twelve things to do, allowing a small chunk of time to each can result in some gold stars, even if only partial completion is the result. As long as you find a way to manage your activities and achievements to suit your temperament, you can make it happen.

My weak spot is laziness. Oh, I have a lot of weak spots: cookies, croissants. **Anthony Hopkins**

Being a Cardinal sign, **Cancer**, you're a self-starter and usually you have a plan for success that requires a level of commitment you're willing to provide. Yes, you may have a stash of candy bars and Twinkies in a desk at work, like Brenda, the sweets-intolerant-but-obsessed policewoman played by Kyra Sedgewick on *The Closer*. Her job was stressful, and a spoonful of sugar made the medicine go down. Tiny little happiness breaks are definitely the fuel that moves you forward. That could include moments spent on your smart phone pawing through pictures of loved ones, and brief conversations to check in. Smuggled ice cream cones in the dead of winter may also be involved. Love is a big motivator for you, and often you work for the knowledge that you're providing for your family, even if you don't enjoy the job you're doing. At home you're usually more mellow. Your preference is to have a big immediate and extended family, and to have them dropping by as often as possible. How neat it is—that's another matter. This doesn't bother you as much as other signs because you know that life is messy and if you don't clean it up right away, who cares. You don't judge yourself by the tidiness of your garage. On the other hand, you do like your home to be nice, and a dinner party can provide excellent motivation to vacuum up those dust bunnies and to polish the antique silver. And then you do what you've always done—reward yourself with some version of a treat, which if it's not edible could be something like a massage, a mani-pedi, or a new thriller for your e-reader.

The reason laziness is rarely pushed as a lifestyle option is down to one simple reason: money. There are fortunes to be made out of active lifestyles. Gyms charge fees. But no one is going to make money out of sleep. It is free. **Tom Hodgkinson**

As a **Leo**, you know only too well the accuracy of the quote above—it seems that all of life comes down to a balancing act between making money and using it to fund the life you want to live. You might laugh and say people do make money out of sleep—those who sell those divine, luxury beds and the thousand-thread sheets that cover them. These are items you're more than willing to pay for, and that returns us to the idea of making money. Nobody is more aware than you are of the role money plays in life, yet you also admit that there's a cachet to having a good job, and it forms part of your identity, adding other layers of chic and cool if it's the right job. Who doesn't want to be Anna Wintour or Paul McCartney? You can even see the coolness of Donald Trump, if not in his hairdo. The good life is what you aspire to live, and part of it is making a splash in the working world. That to you means bringing your own special panache to whatever job you do. Obviously you prefer the more glamorous jobs to the dull stuff like dusting your Oscar. If you can afford it, you'll say you'd rather hire people for that. Having a maid not only keeps your home party-ready, but it makes you feel more successful, so that's a win-win. There are things you must do yourself, and when you're in the mood, you don't mind going through your wardrobe to find items to donate to charity, or rearranging your jewelry. As long as you can feel a boost of self-esteem, then any job brings emotional rewards as well as those gold stars we all like to earn.

Periods of wholesome laziness, after days of energetic effort, will wonderfully tone up the mind and body. **Grenville Kleiser**

Welcome to my world, **Virgo.** There are no lazy Virgos, but that doesn't stop our inner selves from name calling, now does it. We'd never whip an animal, but easily we whip ourselves with accusations and demands. It's tough and I sympathize with you. You can be about ready to drop, and then your inner voice says, okay do one more. It's like being in the grips of one of those wiry, muscle-bound young athletes on *Dancing With the Stars*, who no matter the level of exhaustion say, "Okay, do it again." One good trick when work must absolutely be done despite fatigue is to cut the project down. Maybe you can't do it all today, even if you usually do. So decide to do just half. I like this approach because it seems to allow me to work without falling dead on the floor. The only problem is when the inevitable shouting match begins with your superego, who the moment half is done, whispers, "Okay now do the rest." It doesn't make you a lazy slob when you whine, "But you said I only had to do half." The best approach is to be kind to yourself. You know your history. If you're not a flake and never have been one, realize that you, unlike Superman, are sometimes tired. Respect exhaustion, and allow yourself the time you need to heal. Would you lift something heavy with a broken arm? Forcing yourself to work when dead beat is the same lack of respect. If normally you're a dynamo, know that you will be again—perhaps after a nap. Otherwise, you'll end up with a cold, which is a physical ailment resulting from a need to take it easy for a while. Remember also that chores considered in advance give you the emotional tools to manage them when you actually begin. Make a plan, then follow it. Do as much as you can, then don't regret relaxing. You've earned the rest and tomorrow is another day.

My laziness is really profound. I'm really interested in where it comes from - it almost feels chemical. And we've all got ADD now, short attention span and all that. **Hugh Grant**

The **Libra** issue isn't a short attention span, but the tendency to change your mind, although if you think about it, maybe that is the very definition of a short attention span. The ability to complete any task stems from the commitment to stick with it to a reasonable conclusion, and if you decide to change your mind mid-stream, that could lead to incomplete work. The severity of this tendency depends on the nature of the work involved. If your job is relatively menial, such as attaching a nut to a bolt on an assembly line, you have to keep on attaching those nuts. If you are a creative type doing a project with many steps, changing your mind slows down the project. Decades ago I worked as a photo stylist on a book with a famous Libra needlework expert. There were a certain number of shots scheduled per day, but each day she would flip-flop and change the elements of the shot. It put us vastly behind, slowed down the project, irked the publisher, and increased costs with the photographer. Everyone was annoyed, but ultimately the book did get done. Being able to make a decision and move on to the next one is your challenge, and that requires you to force yourself to do so. There may not be one perfect choice but many equally good ones. With annoying household tasks, you're more willing to move forward because you do like having people around you at home, and even if you wait until the last minute, their imminent arrival helps speed your progress. You're also one of the social types who'd happily pay a maid to keep things ship shape, if you can afford it. With things that only you can do, such as weeding through those out of date handbags, you see it as a trip down memory lane and employ a team approach, inviting your best pals over to vote yay or nay on each possible choice.

Run away from laziness; work hard. Touch intuition and listen to the heart, not marketing directors. Dream. **Alber Elbaz**

For sure **Scorpio** is a bossy sign, and you like to do things your own way. If you're your own boss, the buck may stop with you, but that appeals to you. You'd rather have your own screw up than someone else's and your own triumphs as well. You certainly have plenty of stamina, so normally you're willing to stick around long enough to finish a task, and even something arduous like making sure all the commas are correct in a huge tome can be a pleasant endeavor. You have the ability to keep your eye on the ball, to know what sort of success you want to generate, and to know just what you need to do to make that happen. You seldom feel obligated to take anyone's advice and keep fast to the course you set. Obviously this is a positive trait. Being a substantial person works in your favor where any chore is concerned. If you want to do it, you do it. Routine appeals to you, so maybe that's why. You might have it all organized that once dinner is over, the dishes are done. That way nothing piles up. If you don't want to do something, you're more likely to stick to the schedule than ignore it, and it's also possible that granting yourself a reward here and there makes it a sweeter prospect. Perhaps you delay your dessert until the dishes are done. Life is filled with various obligations, and you know this only too well. But it doesn't bother you as much as it does other people, for somewhere in the back of your mind you see yourself as a workhorse, able to plow through obstacles and meet all challenges with stamina and determination.

Know the true value of time; snatch, seize, and enjoy every moment of it. No idleness, no laziness, no procrastination: never put off till tomorrow what you can do today. **Lord Chesterfield**

Sagittarius, have I lost you already? We can look up procrastinator in the dictionary, and usually there is your picture. None of this bothers you at all for you are the universe's true free spirit who's wise enough to grasp life's thrills, chills, and joys without a backwards glance into the realm of responsibility. You realize that the moment is the only important time frame and you live your life without guilt or remorse. It makes for many exciting tales of adventure and a steady and uncompromised heartbeat. The question is can you make a living that way? Sometimes you can, particularly if you focus on doing something that you love, making your job part of your favorite hobby, like my Sag nephew who works for an athletic company which makes and sells snowboarding equipment. His business is his pleasure, nobody cares about the tattoos and the piercings, for he's a cool dude (or whatever kind of dude they say now). Believing is a part of the process, and if you can believe in the career you have, there's no stopping you. Or if your job has great perks, like some California mail carriers who enjoy the perfect weather and an outdoor stroll. Little chores are easier to put off. There's sunshine to contend with, and sometimes that trumps the laundry. If going commando bothered you, it might be problem, but nothing much bothers you. You may even eat full time on disposable plates. Because you have so few rules weighing you down, your life is fun on a daily basis, so who am I to offer you advice. Okay, I can't help it. Do your laundry, please. Wrap those gifts instead of waiting until the last minute and using an old map, which might, yes, maybe, be cool. By making a game of chores, you get them done. You can sing and dance your way through those scrubbing bubbles in the bathroom.

I'd be more frightened by not using whatever abilities I'd been given. I'd be more frightened by procrastination and laziness. **Denzel Washington**

If anyone is terrified of the prospect of procrastination and laziness, it's you, **Capricorn**, and of course Denzel is one of you. You seldom need motivation to work, you need a friend who's well armed to pull you away from work so you can indulge in frivolous pursuits like dinner. I may deal with a slave driver superego, but you and your superego are one. And you like it that way. "Yes, Ma I'll come open my birthday presents in a minute, soon as my homework is done." Yikes! While you may not be in need of tips to vanquish laziness, you do love tips on increasing productivity. Being efficient appeals to you and if you can do more with less effort and less time, it means there's more time left to do more. Unstoppable! Just like the efficiency expert in *Cheaper By the Dozen*, you want to fill your life with perfectly orchestrated moments. If you can engage in what I call a two-fer, even better. That means if you're doing laundry, there's the down time while the machine does its work, time you can use to clean a bathroom, or do your work on the computer. It's like magic, because work you'd be doing anyway is getting done while some other work is also getting done. What can be better than that? You are a well-oiled machine, but I do have some advice for you: take a moment every day to do nothing. Let your thoughts and feelings flow and you'll discover that you have more inspirations and new ideas that might never have surfaced if you hadn't made the time for them to be born.

I don't think necessity is the mother of invention. Invention, in my opinion, arises directly from idleness, possibly also from laziness - to save oneself trouble. **Agatha Christie**

Without a doubt, **Aquarius,** the quest for efficiency has at its core a desire to champion laziness, the idea that at some point there will be a lake of unused time in which we can happily float without a care. You tend to have intense focus and the ability to stick with something as long as it seems rational to do so. You don't always care if a plan of action makes sense, because you're immersed in it and it seems like a good idea to keep going. What might be a better alternative, is to stop now and then and take stock. If what you're doing is getting you to the destination of choice as efficiently as you'd hoped, it might be time for a left turn. Checking your progress against possible improvements is always a good approach when seeking success. You're an innovator and you adore following new ideas, but you're not always someone who wants to stick with the old ideas or the chores that bore you. Organizing by type and alphabetizing all your books is a fantastic idea, but somewhere around the letter H, you might shrug and move on to the next good idea.

If you're by profession a librarian, however, you must learn to make it all the way to Z. Household chores can benefit from innovation, but bathing in your clothes as a way to clean them while simultaneously cleaning yourself might be more annoying than efficient. That doesn't mean you won't try it. In your world, it's always about balancing innovation and discipline, and you have the ability to do so rather easily—as long as you want to.

My block was due to two overlapping factors: laziness and lack of discipline. **Mary Garden**

It's not so much that you're lazy, **Pisces,** but rather that you tend to become distracted rather easily, floating from one task to the next, doing a little here and there, and completing none. This is where discipline comes in. As many people have said, having that to-do list and being able to cross items off is very rewarding. It makes you feel as though you do indeed have accomplishments. Washing half the dishes is as bad as washing none, for you still have dishes to wash. If you decide to paint a room and only half a wall is done, that is a difficult choice with which to live, for there is the motley wall, staring accusingly at you as half a sink of dishes waits in the corner. The I-can't-do-this-'til-I've-done-that system is your friend. It may not even be about rewards, although that too is good. Once the dishes are done, then you can bake the cake. Of course new dishes will be created in the process. You may be yawning, but if you say, yes I can take a nap, but not until I've completed one thing on my list. That way you waken refreshed from your slumber with one less thing to tackle. There's also the need to balance what you want to do with what you must do. If you have work to complete, then the deal may be struck that once whatever manageable chunk is completed, then you can have a candy bar—or whatever else you want—such as the chance to sketch uninterrupted. It's difficult to be a creative person as well as a disciplined one, but with discipline, more of your inspirations are likely to come to fruition.

I leave you all with some more quotes, notable advice from notable individuals, those which made the most sense to me: *With the new day comes new strength and new thoughts.* **Eleanor Roosevelt.** *Even if you fall on your face, you're still moving forward.* **Victor Kiam.** *In order to succeed, we must first believe that we can.* **Nikos Kazantzakis.** *The secret of getting ahead is getting started.* **Mark Twain.** *Motivation is what gets you started. Habit is what keeps you going.* **Jim Ryun.** *Learn from the past, set vivid, detailed goals for the future, and live in the only moment of time over which you have any control: now.* **Denis Waitley.** *If you can dream it, you can do it.* **Walt Disney.**

THE RESPONSIBILITIES OF LIFE

In 2002, when Jennifer Aniston won her Emmy, she said it was just the icing on the cake, and then she went on to rhapsodize about what a delicious cake it was. She had a happy life, and she loved her work. In other words, life to Jen was sweet! We all have a number of influences in our lives, and they coagulate into a complicated mix. We have the workday world in which we must function to eat. That's pretty straightforward really, even if our careers are as delicious as Jen's. But there are other responsibilities in life—something as simple as mowing the lawn to something as complex as looking after an elderly relative who has nobody else to be involved.

For some people, these are the things that make life rewarding. Almost everyone looks back fondly on the days when the kids were small, although that was a tremendous amount of work with very little free and personal time. Children are a huge responsibility, one which most parents find tiring, but also life's greatest thrill. In the old days, before women's lib, housewives took great pride in their sparkling homes and considered the responsibility of taking care of their families—and keeping their homes pristine—not just a job but a calling. Now with most women working outside the home, we tend to let things slide much more, or as I heard on an old *Roseanne* rerun, "You'll have to excuse the mess, but we live here."

Sometimes life tosses responsibilities on our heads—like jury duty, taking in a vacationing neighbor's mail, helping a lost child at the mall find his way safely back to mom, and a million other little distractions. Sometimes we willingly make the choice to be responsible, like the people who do hours of yard work weekly, those who polish their cars by hand, or their shoes, or their silver.

It's all about the same thing, ultimately—the desire to function in the world and to create a life that seems appropriately orderly to you. We're all different in that regard. We all accept or embrace—or reject—responsibilities to a greater or lesser degree, depending on our makeup—and tolerance for crap! I used to tease my Aries sister that her vacuum sat so untouched—right in the middle of her floor no less—that the vacuum itself had a coating of dust on it. She didn't care at all, because her priorities were elsewhere. In those days she was a stay at home mom, but even so, the laundry was often undone and the household awry. When she entered the workplace, she was much happier and she did work quite hard. It wasn't that she was lazy—she only put effort into things that genuinely seemed important to her.

What does your Sun Sign have to say about your own approach to life's obligations? Read on!

ARIES: The trouble with work, in your opinion, is that it happens every day, every week, every month, year after year. You almost always dislike a schedule and the more constrained the routine, the less pleasant the job. Beginnings are always your favorite aspect of anything, so the first few months of any new job are always the most exciting, perhaps because you don't know what you're doing and a challenge is fun. After that, you feel yourself slip into a downward curve, popularly called boredom. It's hard for you to justify punching that time clock day after day, just to collect a pay check, because to you it feels more like enslavement than employment. Clearly you must be completely involved in your work, and when that feeling diminishes, you start looking for a new way to earn your daily bread. Of course what you miss with this approach is the achievement of expertise that can come only with time and experience. One Aries I know says members of his sign have a different sense of completion than many other people. That is true, but it's also often too convenient and leads to so many careers that the only status achieved is one of dilettante. You would always rather be having fun than working, so it really helps if your work is fun, something you might do for a hobby if you didn't do it for money. You take a similar approach to life's other responsibilities. If you have money, you hire people to do the chores you'd rather avoid. If not, you procrastinate. Of course, there's only so long you can put off doing your taxes, the dishes and the laundry, and calling your mother. Otherwise the IRS will haul you off to jail, naked and hungry, and mom won't be there to bail you out!

TAURUS: As much as Aries hates routine, you adore it. You can wake up in a good mood, feeling secure, as long as you know there's work to do and a paycheck coming. Although you love money and need the security it brings, it's not just about the cash. To you, a job well done is often its own reward, and more than that you enjoy the feeling that you have something to do, somewhere to be, and a schedule that feels stable and comforting. You have what might be called a Zen approach to work—you immerse yourself in the moment and remain positive as time passes. Work that features known elements and routine tasks can be quite comforting to you and you don't even hate manual labor, or as Cancer Harrison Ford said, you can see the value in moving a pile of rocks. You take a similar approach to the other responsibilities of life. You don't want to live surrounded by chaos—or dust, so you do the housework, keep the car neat, and you mow the lawn. As indolent and sensual as you can be, there is still a great deal of the puritan work ethic in your make up. Lying around for days at a time on a rumply couch while the newspaper (and pizza boxes) pile up and gather dust is not your idea of a good time. You feel happiest when things hum along, and that means putting a little effort into life. Just like older generations, you realize that nobody guaranteed each day to be nothing but fun and you're willing to work hard at whatever you do. Even if a task can be completed quickly, you often prefer to take more time so that it's done to your satisfaction, and you will recall that job in your mind, and feel content. Taking shortcuts has the opposite effect, and you hate that nagging feeling that comes when you haven't done something you should have.

GEMINI: When my Cancer daughter (who has Venus, planet of pleasure, in Gemini) was in grammar school, I asked her what her favorite subject was. She considered the question for a nanosecond, then chortled with gusto, "Free time!" That is a point of view to which you can completely relate. You like the freedom to come and go, and you need a continuing sense of involvement and interest to justify any pursuit. Like Aries, this could mean that you engage in a number of serial careers, but you don't mind at all, because you're seldom focused on what you achieve as time passes. Instead you prefer to live in the moment, enjoy it, and then move on. Although you realize you must make money to live, it's very hard for you to focus on that fact if you're at a job you don't enjoy. Unless you have many planets in fixed Taurus or sentimental Cancer, you'd just as soon be out of work now and then and surviving on ten cent packages of Ramen noodles (as did Libra Matt Damon before his ascent to stardom) than to feel you're selling your soul just to survive. Your values are otherwise. You need human interaction, intellectual stimulation, and as long as you have a bed (or someone else's couch) to sleep on, you feel that you're doing all right. Nothing annoys you more than a responsibility you didn't request. You don't really want to have to set your watch to feed a neighbor's gerbil, and being pressured to do so doesn't sit well with you. Sometimes you have to play little tricks on yourself, promising future rewards, to accomplish unwanted chores. Like my old Gemini school chum used to do, you say okay do your homework now and then after that you can read that hot new novel. That system keeps your eye squarely where you know it belongs—on pleasure, even if the gratification isn't as instantaneous as you'd prefer.

CANCER: A Cancer child I know complained to me about playing house with her best friend. "She always makes me be the baby but I want to be the mother. She should be the baby sometimes!" That's Cancer in a nutshell—you like responsibilities, particularly those of a personal nature. Even as the tiniest child, you know one day you will grow up to become a parent, and you look forward to that, not because of the glamour of being an adult, but because to you, that's the normal way to live. If there are elderly members of your family, or even your in-laws, you're the first to reach for the phone, make a casserole, offer an invitation. You willingly pet set, baby sit, and if a friend is sick, you will stop by with chicken soup. It's no wonder everyone loves you so much! You take a similarly proactive role where work is concerned. You don't mind pitching in, and you are always focused on getting ahead at your career. If it's the sort of job that demands years' apprenticeship, you don't mind, because you know that success equals security, and you always want to be able to afford the loving family and cozy home that matters to you so much. Work to you is more than productive labor, and more than just a paycheck. It's your way of building a family away from home. Just like those television shows set in a workplace where everyone is like family, you try to create warm and enduring relationships with people around you at work. It just feels comforting to have a history with the people with whom you spend your time. It doesn't mean that you're all work and no play, though, but you do take life seriously and the things that matter most to you—personal connections—are the most serious aspects—and the most rewarding—of daily life.

LEO: Although you love fabulous parties and all the frivolities of life so much, you also take work seriously, and you're at your best when some aspect of your creativity is being used to maximum effect. You don't want to trudge through your days. In fact, trudging is not something you ever want to do. You want to be engaged, involved, inspired, and so you must seek a career that feels interesting to you on a daily basis. And even if you rise to stellar heights, you're still always seeking ways to keep life and your work interesting. Look at megastar Ben Affleck—he was doing great, working at least as much as he wanted to, but what did he do? He and pal Matt Damon got together to found *Project Greenlight*, so that aspiring filmmakers would have a chance to see their movies made. Just like Ben, when you love something, it's more than a job, it's your life's passion, and you'd do it just as willingly on your days off as when you're on the clock. You're definitely goal oriented, and you try to keep rising to the level where you envision that you belong. If you can't achieve what you know you should, you consider leaving your current job and finding a more hospitable environment. This would be a tough choice for you, because like Cancer, you enjoy turning your workplace into a mini-family, or a group of pals. You take responsibility seriously and would consider yourself a bad person if you didn't. When you make a promise, you feel obliged to keep it. That doesn't mean you want to spend every weekend babysitting the neighbor's pets, because after all you have your own life to live. So you don't mind saying no when it's warranted. That way you keep your life in balance and there's time for work—and for play!

VIRGO: It often seems that your raison d'etre is turning chaos into order, and because of that, you are very comfortable with responsibilities of all sorts. Work appeals to you because it feels good to be productive. As Adelaide said in *Guys and Dolls*, "Let us not conduct ourselves like a slob!" That's pretty much your motto. You like being neat, organized, and productive. Of course you like money, but it's almost never about the money. You have to feel that you're donating your time to a worthy cause. Nothing appeals to you less than spending your days at a job for which you have no respect, and without losing too much sleep over the decision, you will change to a less well paying job if it feels more rewarding. Look at Virgo Mother Teresa of Calcutta— she worked all her life to help those least able to help themselves. She turned a calling into a career. You take that same fervor and apply it to everything you do. You have hobbies that are more work than many people devote to their jobs! I (a slightly less noble Virgo), have been making a cookbook for my daughter for more than a decade. I record favorite recipes, add family photos, food photos, and classic illustrations, then print out the page and insert into an ever-growing notebook. It's a lot of work, but so much fun and will be a hobby that lasts me all my life. Like me, you enjoy the sense that you're working at something meaningful. Maybe you're organizing the garage, cataloging your magazines or videotapes, indexing your cookbooks. It doesn't matter because to you it feels better than lying in a hammock in all your leisure moments. You're also willing to pitch in when other people need help, and because you're generally so organized, it's no problem to bring in the neighbor's mail, give the cat a bath, or help a friend assemble that giant swing set. You always feel that soon you'll get done and then maybe you'll give the hammock a try!

LIBRA: Good manners and gracious behavior are such a strong part of your code of living that you tend to approach all responsibilities with that ethic. It doesn't hurt you to put yourself out now and then for other people because that's the only mannerly thing to do. You reach out to people wherever you go and you make friends easily. That way the part of your life that really matters to you—the social, sparkling, fun part—always has plenty of fun companions. Of course, that also means that people are everywhere in your life and you're the first person they think of when something needs to be done. Often you would prefer to remain blissfully uninvolved—like when the neighbor's basement is flooded with sludge, or your best friend needs you to become an amateur therapist in some romantic struggle, or when a sibling's mannerless child is dumped on you for the weekend. But somehow you manage to get through it, a courteous smile on your face. When it comes to work, you recognize its importance, but it's seldom the number one priority of your life. You may be famous or extremely successful, but you admit readily that it's the people in your life who really make a difference to you. You like to befriend coworkers, and you agree that if you had to spend the day in the company of crass, annoying people, you would not be content in your job. Yet often you also feel that if you won the lottery and could play full time, nothing would please you more than that. If you're the artistic type, and many Libras are, then self-expression is very important to you, so your work is an extension of who you are. An opera singer doesn't wish to win the lottery but instead to sing and be applauded for hitting all those tricky notes. A fashion designer doesn't want to dress only friends, but the whole world. And so on! So the best approach for you if you must work is to find a career that is so strongly a part of your nature that you would feel a great loss at its absence rather than the burden of having to do it daily.

SCORPIO: Like your opposite number, Taurus, you enjoy stability and being immersed in a life filled with known quantities. If you've been at your job for many years, that to you is a badge of pride and contentment, even if that job no longer inspires you. There's a great deal of comfort in knowing that tomorrow will be much as today and that you will seldom be threatened by the unexpected. It's not that you lack ambition, because you may be at the height of your profession, but you seldom have itchy feet. The grass is always greener is not a syndrome that afflicts you. Instead you feel happy to think that you've been going to the same job for a long time and you want to maintain that comforting sense of continuity. It's nice to be with friends you've known for many years and to know that the same people will be in your life for years to come. You feel similarly about other responsibilities. You would lay your life on the line for a friend and you consider loyalty one of your best qualities. You're always there for the people you love, just like those guys who were Tony Soprano's "goombas," well okay maybe not quite to that extreme, but you admire that sort of fidelity. You feel a strong personal connection to the people who really matter in your life, so if someone needs you, you are there, as much because you're so totally immersed in loved ones' lives as because it's the right thing to do. You like your privacy, but grow close to neighbors over time and willingly pet sit and gather mail. Plus it's sort of fun for you to be in someone's house when they're absent because it feels like you're privy to some special secrets—whether or not you ever open a closet.

SAGITTARIUS: Responsibility isn't really a four-letter word, but work is, and often you have quite a distaste for both. You enjoy being a wil o' the wisp, and it's much more fun for you to be schedule-free than to be forced to punch any clock. Does that mean you're lazy? Sometimes it seems that way, but in fact you mostly have other priorities. You care about conversation and ideas, and are seldom so driven by ambition that you want to become a millionaire. It's not that you have a distaste for wealth, but rather that you have no particular compulsion to live that sort of life. Outdoorsy and relaxed, your happiest moments are when you're just hanging out with pals somewhere in a park. You do have interests, though, and when you can turn a special interest into a career, then you can blaze a trail to success that is both rewarding and fun. If you're an avid surfer, open a surf shop, or run a stables for the horses you love so much. If you're a pet groomer, you're quite content because nobody loves dogs more than you do. That's the key to job success—keeping it low key, with flexible hours and plenty of personal satisfaction. Other responsibilities are just as annoying as the workday world. When your old auntie calls and leaves a message, you truly mean to return the call, but you might have other things to do, so it slips your mind. Now and then you remember, but you're not driven to take care of it immediately. You're lucky—few signs have as little guilt and inner nagging as you do! You're often happy to pitch in and help a friend, but it's better if you're asked right on the spot than expected to circle the day on your calendar and remember to show up. Planning ahead is more of a burden to you than doing the chore.

CAPRICORN: Yours is the sign of work, so there's no question that during nine to five (or perhaps seven to nine depending on your zeal and stamina) you're in your element. Nobody gains a greater sense of satisfaction than you do from building a career from the ground up. It means something personal to you when you can achieve success, and you gain great validation from what you achieve. Of course you recognize that a job well done is its own reward and you try very hard always to do your best, but you'd seldom want to work without compensation. You always like to feel that you're moving onward and upward, and that sense of growth and reaching toward your potential is what keeps driving you. You care about the field you enter and choose something that does have growth potential. You don't want to feel you're stagnating or that you've entered a profession with a glass ceiling—or any sort of ceiling. It's just natural to you to keep looking upward toward what you might achieve next. Ambition feels normal to you and you're always quite baffled by acquaintances who lack it—how do they live that way? You can't imagine! You're responsible and have been since your youth. You're the one who babysat the siblings—even if you weren't the eldest, and the neighbors trusted you to mow their lawns or take care of their parakeet. To you that is a very good feeling. It just seems that there's a right way to live and a wrong one, and you take greatest satisfaction in making the right choices. Of course you are someone with your own priorities, and although you enjoy doing the right thing and helping others, you don't want to let anyone take advantage of you, and you make that quite clear. You're willing to say yes, but have no problem saying no.

AQUARIUS: There is no question that you're a serious person and that you regard life as an opportunity to exercise genuine responsibility. Does that mean you love working? Not always! You like being involved with matters that seem worthwhile to you, and are an ardent crusader for just causes, but sometimes it seems that the workday is filled with meaningless tasks and long, idle periods. It helps a great deal if you have a career that is rewarding to you—your own business or some other pursuit that makes you feel your time is well spent. Otherwise you get very cranky and wish you were anywhere else. You will seldom work just for the financial rewards, and if a job annoys you, you opt to quit despite knowing that you'll lose out financially. No matter what you do, your intelligence shines through, and thus you feel most comfortable making rational decisions about every phase of your life, including your work. You do like stability and enjoy the sense that you're progressing within a comfortable atmosphere, particularly when there are compatible people at work who become close friends. But you would never stay in an unappealing job just to maintain continuity. Even if you were scared, you'd take a risk and make a change. You enjoy new things and look forward to job changes when they happen. You like sharing your life with friends, and hope you're always available to lend a helping hand when need be. But you do have a very, very busy schedule, and often it's difficult to make time for the little chores that other people put upon you. Instead you'd choose to help by organizing a neighborhood group. You're always interested in improving your world and to you that's the ultimate responsibility.

PISCES: Work. It's something that most usually happens every day at the same time—often early in the morning. These are big drawbacks to you. You do recognize that discipline can be a good thing, even if it's not something you enjoy. You're much happier if you can make a living in a way that suits your freedom-loving spirit. If you can be a movie star, well okay there are schedules and obligations to movie making, but the perks are pretty nice too. That's the sort of thing that appeals to you. The humdrum daily working world almost never does. If you're creative, and often you are, you very much enjoy doing something to express yourself. Even as a child, you could envision a carefree life as a musician who works nights and sleeps all day. Being a yoga instructor could be a great career—even if it didn't pay well. The thing that matters most to you is feeling happy in the moment, and for that you'd be willing to sacrifice some cash. There are many careers that appeal to you, but you're not always happy even when you have work that you like. Some days you just want to loll around at home, or play hooky with friends. Thus a job that affords freedom to come and go really works best for you. There are many people in your life about whom you care quite deeply, and you want to be there for them in any way you can. Often you let friends cry on your shoulder for days at a time. But you don't like having to pencil in special favors because you're sure you will forget, and having to care for an absent friend's pet is a very big responsibility—one you're not sure you'd want. You try your best to be helpful, though, and your heart is always in the right place. If you can't carry through on something, you're abjectly sorry, but sometimes you just need to crash and get away from people, from life, and from all its many burdens.

THE ZEN OF SHOPPING

I earned my black belt early in life. The members of my family shared a passion which we practiced ensemble or separately, most weekends of the year. Many times I've told people that my happiest childhood memories were set in malls, and in a way that's still true. There was always a heady spirit of anticipation, of happy exploration as we set off in the car to visit our local mall. Who knew what treasures awaited us, what fun we might have, what fabulous delights we'd consume at the food court. As I think back on my childhood, there was so much adventure, so many amusement parks, so much laughter—and so many wonderful trips to the mall. My family was all about fun, and it wasn't really the greed of acquisition, but the excitement of unknown potential that tantalized us all.

As a young adult, I fell in love with New York City—and with Bloomingdale's, saying facetiously only in part to all who'd listen that upon my demise, I wanted my ashes scattered over that venerable institution. To me, Bloomingdale's and other fine stores were "the museum of what's happening now." I could spend hours happily strolling around, looking at what was for sale, at the people meandering beside me, and it seemed there were things to learn about what was going on in our society, in the world at large, viewed through the microcosm of a shopping spree.

Here in Los Angeles, the narcissism capital of the world, shopping is a way of life. Nowhere else will you find a couple of men strolling through the women's departments and discussing what—not a drag revue, but clothes for their wives! And here when I go to the mall, it's quite possible that it will be a movie star browsing next to me. If I want exercise, I go wander through a mall, and there's nothing I enjoy doing more—and if no purchases are made, so what. It's the thrill of the chase that appeals to me. When I actually need to acquire something, that's the best fun of all because it leads to many adventures, much searching, bargain hunting, price matching, and ultimately coming home with my prize, assured that it's exactly what I needed, wanted, and that there was no better choice—or deal--out there.

Shopping for myself is fun, but I love shopping for other people just as much, and because of the shopping black belt, I've been known to buy gifts for strangers—well relatives of relatives—and usually hear that the item in question instantly becomes a favorite. That makes it all worthwhile.

When the holiday season is upon us, for me it's the malls, not Disneyland, that are the happiest place on earth.

What's your approach to shopping? Your Sun Sign tells the story—and if you're out there, desperately searching for the ideal holiday remembrance, keep reading, because there are plenty of clues right here in this article to help you hone in on what to offer to a loved one as the perfect token of your affection.

ARIES—There's no question that at any given moment, there are several items you desperately need and should acquire. The problem is you get distracted by the things you like to do—and your life is always busy and active. That means that you're out scuba diving, playing golf, drag racing, or rototilling the back forty on the weekends, so where's the time to get to the mall? An Aries friend of mine moved to a new city and for months complained that he needed to go buy a TV, but did he? No time! That's not to say that once you manage to hit the stores that you don't enjoy the experience. You have many interests and hobbies and you adore looking at all the paraphernalia that goes with them. But you don't really love following a friend or spouse around on a shopping spree not directly related to your own interests. Well you're not the me-me-me sign for nothing! The key for you when shopping for another person, is to do something that doesn't come all that naturally to you—pay attention to someone else. That doesn't mean buying your oceanophobic pal the surfing gear you've been yearning for.

It does mean listening and taking notes. People drop hints about what they like and need, and once you have that info, the shopping becomes easy. Note what they already have, what they could use, and then do what comes naturally—buy a gift certificate so you don't have to spend all day in a store. But just remember, a little effort will certainly pay off, and if it's a gift for a lover, you'll probably receive so much shocked gratitude in return for actually paying attention to someone else that you'll feel it was all worthwhile.

If you're shopping for an ARIES: What could be easier? Aries talk all the time about their interests, their wants, their needs, and their desires. You need only about three minutes of conversation and you've heard the shopping list. There's no point in trying to introduce this person to something new. Just buy what you know they want. Every Aries has some sporty hobby, some unusual pastime, something that makes them cool. Cater to that! This is also a good sign for gifting of trips, baseball camp, time at the shooting range, and so on. Anything that leads to an adventure is a good Aries present.

TAURUS: You're my hero, Taurus. You know what's important in life—beautiful possessions, fine dining, and being massaged. You love to shop as much as I do, and you're just as picky, but if you spot a gorgeous cashmere something or other, you will snap it right up, because let's face it, you deserve it. If it's on sale, you're even happier, and you'll snap up two! For you shopping is like big game hunting, and you take it quite seriously. You skulk through the aisles, looking for perfection, and you don't rest until you've bagged your prey. Move out here to Los Angeles, why don't you—they have sales here that would make you orgasmic! Seventy-five percent off the already-reduced price! These are mantras that appeal to your music-loving heart. There are many things you love, and those are the items you shop for again and again, and of course for clothes because nobody enjoys looking nattier than you do. You take gift buying as seriously as you do shopping for yourself. There's a fine line between something you'd love to own and something you need, and that's the tightrope you walk when gifting. You want your present to be loved, but not to be frivolous. After all, what's the point in throwing money down the drain on something that will be used once just for the novelty. Better to buy something of quality that will be well loved and well used for years to come.

If you're shopping for a TAURUS: Remember, this person has good taste and is picky about what's suitable to own. It's not just the thought that counts. If the thing is ugly, not their taste, or poorly made, forget it. You might get a very heartfelt thank you but the item will never see the light of day. Taurus people appreciate fine workmanship, like all the earth signs, who have a natural affinity for things made by hand. A craft show is the perfect venue to find a treasure that can't be acquired anywhere else. Just envision what sort of things your friend already owns, and buy something in that style, whether a hand painted scarf or tie, a piece of beautifully painted pottery, or a funky little chotchky. Taureans love to eat, so a gift basket bursting with gourmet delicacies is always a treat, as are tickets to a concert, or to a class they've been wanting to take. For the most part, earth sign people love stuff, so something you can wrap is better than any sort of subscription.

GEMINI: Most Geminis don't really have the patience to shop, though you do love a good stroll. You'll happily walk through a mall, stopping at the bookstore to browse and maybe buy the latest whatever, assuming the line isn't too long. But shopping with a friend can give you the heebie-jeebies, because there you are, stuck in the girdle (or sporting goods) department for an eternity while your friend debates the merits of latex (or $42 hand-tied flies). If it's not an interest, you don't want to be stuck shopping for it. Besides, it's your theory that shopping causes physical ailments, because you've noted that when shopping with a friend for an agonizingly long period (and anything longer than 2 minutes can agonize you) your lower back begins to ache and the pain quickly spreads downward. You do enjoy catalogue and internet shopping, and find it relaxing to buy things that way. Shopping for other people is as annoying as shopping with them. If you're old, you can use that as an excuse, like my mother did after she hit ninety, "I just can't shop for anyone any more—I don't have a clue what they want," she says. Well hey, Ma, pay attention! But nope, that's not the Gemini way. You'd rather send a check or buy a gift certificate than try to put yourself in anyone else's shoes. Chances are though, if you're trying to impress a lover (or get one in the sack) a check tucked into a greeting card won't do the trick. And you can't give them software, books, or a magazine subscription either. The personal touch means a lot, so if you start early, perhaps you can subtly weasel out of this person a hint about a longed-for item. Then when you buy it, you've touched their heart—and might get a shot at touching a few other places too.

If you're shopping for a GEMINI: As my mother used to say, books are the perfect gift. Geminis like the media, so more of whatever they most like to read is never too much. And if it's something already read, they don't mind returning the books for different titles. Magazine subscriptions are much appreciated—and that's the gift that keeps on giving—every single month. Geminis also like tickets to special events, though you might have trouble tying them down to the specific date in question. Gadgets are another good choice for your special Twin, because they love those Fitbits, Gameboys, Playstations, and electronic chess or backgammon games. Games in general are a fabulous Gemini gift. No matter how old they are, this sign loves to play. My mother gave herself carpal tunnel in her nineties from too much time with the joystick!

CANCER: The great thing about shopping is how it jogs all those sentimental memories. "Oh look at that doll—I had one just like it in 1941!" Other people live in the here and now, but for water sign Cancer, you're always floating through time. Let's not get too confused here, though, because no matter how emotional you are, you definitely love stuff, and acquiring more is a favored pastime. Perhaps that's why you're the worst pack rat in the Zodiac. You buy it and keep it—forever. It's not just about clothes and those snuggly sweats you love so much, but about every little knick knack that strikes your fancy. If it touches your heart, you haul it home in a tote bag. Shopping for other people is no less fun for you, and since you tend to adopt the world, there's a huge collection of friends, relatives, and even ex's for whom you're constantly acquiring the odd gift now and then. Sometimes your psychic powers are down right eerie, like my Cancer daughter, who has many times given me things I adored. Your presents are never about practicality or what's absolutely needed. You want to wrap up a sentimental treasure which will bring tears to the eyes of the recipient and become an instant memory piece.

If you're shopping for a CANCER: Think sentimentality. Last Christmas, I sewed both a throw pillow and a cocktail top for my daughter Xandy—out of remnants from her wedding gown. She says that every time she snuggles the pillow it brings back memories of the wedding. So go for the heart—and the gut when gifting Cancer. A picture album or framed photo is a fabulous gift and there can never be too many of them. The "gift of time" as Xandy says is a great choice, and it doesn't matter that your Cancer is only one member in a group; they'll be delighted by your gift of tickets to a special event which you can attend all together. Food is another Cancer favorite and you can never go wrong with a gift basket, or a deluxe ice cream maker so they can churn out their own. Cancers with favorite hobbies love gifts that add to a collection (they all collect stuff), and they never mind if you give something of your own (or from a thrift store) as an heirloom. To a Cancer that's the best treasure of all.

LEO: Can I, a mere Virgo, dare to give advice to the 18-karat sign? There's no question that Leo and shopping go hand in hand. The Leos who dislike shopping are very few in number, and even they can get into the spirit of it at holiday time. You adore the best of everything, and lore has it that the credit card people had to up the odds to platinum to satisfy a status-seeking Leo who felt that too many of the hoi polloi were flaunting their gold cards! Clothes, jewelry, flashy cars, the list is endless when it comes to your passions. You don't just shop, you blaze through luxury boutiques the way rebel armies retake their homelands! There's no question that you adore shopping for other people, and not only do you like giving gifts that are just what your friends want, you're determined to give what you think they should have. Nobody should lack shirt studs for a tuxedo, or a fur-trimmed (please, Leo—you're the sign of the cat—faux only) cashmere cardigan. These items are more the staff of life than bread to you. It was probably a Leo who devised those incredible gift baskets given to movie star Oscar presenters. We're not talking mere beluga and sturgeon here—we're talking Rolex and Cartier!

If you're shopping for a LEO: Yes you do get credit just for the thought. No matter how elegant is your big cat, even a tiny budget can do justice to the holidays if you're creative. Leos love pampering and if you can't afford a certificate to a tony spa, you can make a booklet of coupons for the same services given by their devoted slave—you, you, you! Obviously where Leo is concerned, bigger is definitely better, so if it's in your budget, buy that fabulous item you've noticed your loved one eyeing. There's no mystery to it, Leos are easily dazzled and will give you many hints during your strolls along Main Street. Something small can still be elegant—like a fake fur scarf lined with dupioni silk. I sewed a bunch one Christmas for relatives in different places, and all responded with delight because it was the height of fashion and looked more expensive than it was.

VIRGO: I may be the exception that proves the rule, because most Virgos don't love shopping all that much. You know the importance of getting a good deal, but it just doesn't make sense to you to fill your wardrobes to bursting with yet another temporarily-fashionable item. Your heart is tried and true, and that's your approach to shopping. Because your taste is classic, the things you like never go out of style so you don't really regard updating as something you need to do. But you do have your interests, and many Virgos have hobbies reflecting their skills with their hands, and such pastimes require shopping. You have to buy the fabric, get the wood, or the precious metals—and of course all the tools that go with your sewing, building or jewelry making hobbies. Sometimes you're just too busy, and boy oh boy do you love the internet. A push of a button, no lines, no waiting, and before you know it, a package is at your door. You take a similar approach to gift giving. You have no respect for people who put off until tomorrow what can be done by yesterday. You're often done with Christmas before Halloween. And it's not as though you're hasty either. You spend a good deal of time thinking about your loved ones and exactly what they need. Yes, need in your world usually supercedes want, and if you can give someone a present of an item they really do need, it makes your day. Because you're so analytical and observant, you usually know exactly what that is, what color it should be, and from what store they'd most like to receive it.

If you're shopping for a VIRGO: Adorable knick knacks are most emphatically not the way to go. Something whose sole purpose is to give the feather duster a workout will rarely inspire more than disdain in a Virgo heart. This sign likes stuff that makes sense, is well made, and speaks to their interests. I, for example, would always rather have a kitchen gadget (well one that's useful to me) than something more sentimental because I love to cook. So know your person. Even if you're their lover, your Virgo might be more thrilled to get a new Kitchen-Aid or sheepskins for the car than something frilly from Victoria's Secret or flashy cufflinks. That doesn't mean Virgos like only boring, dowdy stuff. We like the things we use because on a daily basis, so we'll get more enjoyment out of owning this item.

LIBRA: In an ideal world, your life would be all about pleasure and refinement, and shopping is most definitely part of this picture. Staying up to date with the latest fashion is important to you because you care what people think. You love buying just the right thing for a special event, and there are many of those in your life. Clothes are probably the number one thing for which you shop, but you also enjoy choosing scents, body products, and accessories. It's just as much fun for you to buy something for a loved one as for yourself, and your specialty is giving them the thing they wouldn't necessarily buy. It's a great pleasure for you to wrap up a bottle of the nicest cologne because not only will your friend love it, you'll get a whiff now and then when you're together. Of course if your pals are less dainty than you are, perhaps it makes more sense to think about what they actually might like. Sometimes a set of socket wrenches makes a better impression than Chanel.

If you're shopping for a LIBRA: There's a world of elegance out there, and even if neither of you has managed an entrée, your Libra would really like to pretend to be part of it. This is someone who'd love satin sheets, lace or silk scarves, and of course jewelry. Libras don't want or need a practical gift, and if you're shopping for a lover, forget about most of those down to earth ideas. Do something over the top romantic. Get a series of ballroom dancing lessons. Or tickets for sunset hot-air ballooning. Frilly—but tasteful—undies work well as do those satin boxers. If you do give such a gift, you must also give something else because that way your Libra knows you want to do something actually for them, that you're not focused on turning them into a sex object for your own gratification. Sexy items are great, but Libra has to have all the hearts and flowers too.

SCORPIO: My dad was a Scorpio and perhaps he was the exception to the rule because he loved shopping, when most of your sign would rather do other things. Even as an adult we shopped together and one April we passed a new fangled crepe pan and I mused idly that it should have been one of my Christmas gifts. We went into different departments, then reconnected and he held out a wrapped gift, saying, "Merry Christmas." That was my dad—he loved to make other people happy. And perhaps that's your approach to shopping too. You buy what you need for yourself with little fanfare, but when it comes to the people you adore, it's a great thrill to tantalize them with things they love. You have a second sense about people anyway—like all the water signs—and thus you can easily stumble on a present that will forever be cherished. You also love big surprises and will go out of your way to build a big fake out. Oops I forgot your birthday—and then the person opens a closet and finds the gift of a lifetime.

If you're shopping for a SCORPIO: Focus on what

you know. This person doesn't want you to dig deeply into their psyche. What you need to know is right there for you to see, and the rest is off limits. I took a pottery class one year and made my dad a giant bowl for soup—which he treasured—not just because his daughter made it, but because he loved soup. Even a small present like that can be a huge hit if you focus on what they love. Some experimental tie-died t-shirts also went over big because he loved big, goofy prints. You can't tell a Scorpio what to do or what to like. There's no point in giving them what you think they need, because nope, they won't use it. Give them more of what they already love and do it from the heart.

SAGITTARIUS: Shopping? Who's kidding who here! Of all the signs, you probably despise shopping more than any other. Nobody is less material than a Sag (unless of course you have lots of earth and water planets). You seldom care about fashion, are content to live with furniture you find on the street, and if you remember someone's birthday, it's probably because they reminded you a dozen times. Does that mean you're an unenthusiastic gift giver? Not at all. You love doing nice things for the people you adore—and you'll contentedly spend money you can't afford to part with. But often that means you'll take your pal out for a meal, or say here's a bunch of money, buy something for yourself. There's no shame in doing that because to you it's always the thought that counts. Helen Hayes' husband met her by offering a dish of peanuts and saying, "I wish they were emeralds." That sort of sentiment will get you a lover, but you need more than peanuts to keep one. If you need to mark your calendar months ahead to be sure you're prepared with a nice present, then do it. It's easier than hitting the singles' bars after you've been dumped.

If you're shopping for a SAGITTARIUS: This is one person who's seldom greedy, will probably never complain if you get it wrong, and who appreciates the thought even if the gift is sort of paltry. That means it's pretty easy to shop for your Sag. Clothes are always a great option, and if you choose similar prints and styles to what your pal often wears, you'll get extra credit. Outdoorsy things are also a good choice for Sag. Usually they have pets, so you can always buy an adorable dog collar, riding crop, or iguana hideout. Gift certificates are another option that this sign will actually appreciate. Even if it's just to the local supermarket, your Sag will love it. And if you go all out and book an African photo-taking safari, you'll be hearing praise for years.

CAPRICORN: Of all the earth signs, you probably like shopping the least. You realize that a penny spent here and there adds up to dollars lost by the end of the year. You don't want to overdo on your wardrobe but would rather have a small collection of classic, serviceable items. And your hobby is usually working hard, and they pretty much give you all the staples and post-its you need at work. In fact, you wish most people had your sterling attitude about shopping because in your view, there's too much consumption in the world anyway. But the problem is that people you know don't really appreciate your promises to make donations to worthy causes in their names. They seem to want something personal, wrapped up with a curly little bow. What can you do—people are shallow but they're necessary. It can take years for a lover to teach you the requirements of gifting for special events—as it did my daughter for my Cappie son-in-law. Now he starts early and acquires presents in advance of her birthday. Otherwise she demotes him to Sag and moves him into the doghouse.

If you're shopping for CAPRICORN: Just because a person doesn't shop willingly, don't assume they don't like presents. Capricorns love to receive nice things. They adore beautifully wrapped presents, and it makes them feel good to know you care. Clothes for work are a great choice as are leisure garments. Maybe if your Cap had a casual sweater, you could finally get them out of the office on a weekend. Gift baskets filled with elegant food are another favorite and it means they won't have to eat beefaroni on New Year's Eve. Remember to note any special interests and cater to those things. History buffs appreciate coffee table books. Movie lovers adore those box set DVD collections. Practical presents that have a useful purpose most appeal to Cap.

AQUARIUS: It's not that you don't like to shop—you

just don't like to shop for the usual things. If you order all your clothing from a catalogue, that's perfectly fine with you. It means that on the weekend you can haunt the aisles of Best Buy in search of the newest innovation in technology. Or you can get some exercise by strolling through a flea market, where admittedly they have mostly junk, but hey you meet interesting people. You also love book stores, record stores, and hardware stores—if you can find them any more. Shopping for other people wouldn't be so hard if they would realize that what you're choosing for them is exactly what they should learn to like. You will put tons of effort into choosing just the right gadget—something really, really cool. But what a disappointment to bestow it on your bewildered techno-phobe girlfriend. But that's one of those horrible life lessons, isn't it. You can't really change people and that means giving them stuff they already might like, without buying one of those such and such for idiots books.

If you're shopping for an AQUARIUS: The cooler the better. Anything new and cool is bound to catch this person's fancy, even if only for a short time. It doesn't matter if it's useful or practical, or even if it will remain intact for a while. It should just be interesting. Gadgets are a great Aquarius gift. Just focus on what you know they like and get them a gadget that goes with the hobby. They even have electronic crossword puzzle gadgets that look sort of like a kid's etch-a-sketch. In fact, buy the etch-a-sketch itself because who wouldn't like one of those. Something that can be used with a group of people is a great choice, like a board game, a DVD, or a host it yourself mystery event. The idea is to provide some diversion, not something for their hope chest.

PISCES: You'd probably be my ideal shopping companion. You love drifting along through stores, just absorbing all that energy through osmosis. You're easily distracted by the people around you, and it's fun to see what everyone is wearing. To you it's more an event than a property search. There's no telling what you'll buy, whether some exotic item for your closet, the newest fragrance, or one of those crazy gadgets that twirls an apple around a spoke and peels it in one frighteningly long spiral. As much as shopping for yourself is a fabulous adventure, you adore buying gifts for loved ones. You seldom plan—except perhaps how to afford it—and just use intuition in choosing gifts. You feel if it strikes your fancy as something they'd love, then it will go over well. This approach has garnered mixed results, but the odd thing is that some people who've squinted and wondered *what's this* about something you've given them eventually confide that they've come to love the frog statue, little cloisonné box, or tickets to the opera.

If you're shopping for a PISCES: It doesn't have to make sense. This person would rather have something you feel they'd like than something absolutely necessary. So don't worry about being practical. Give something extraordinary, something with flash and pizzazz—like a magic 8-ball. Then again, this is someone who often neglects the necessities of life, and if they're suffering along with a broken clock radio, that might be a very nice present, particularly if you can find a funky looking one. Hand-made jewelry is a very nice Pisces present, and even the guys like a shimmery shell on a leather cord. Pisces will often mention things they want—like a set of CDs that teach a foreign language, and will much appreciate it when you buy them. But don't get upset if your pal never gets around to using it. Life is kinda short and there's a lot for a busy fish to do.

I hope I've given you some useful tips that will make your shopping a little easier and more pleasant. Here it's Friday night, and I'm going to check out the mall!

4
LOVE AND SEX—SERIOUS AND SILLY

Did you know that most people consult astrologers about love? It's true. Of course in these times, some also want to know about their finances, but few don't also ask, "What about my love life?"

I love writing about love, whether I'm trying to be serious or to make fun of the quirks inherent in each Sun sign. Even in humor, there are germs of truth.

There's a lot to be learned about yourself by examining your own approach to sex. Maybe there are some tricks of the seduction game you can borrow from another sign as well. In *Celestially Sexy*, I look at each sign's approach to sex, and use some celebrities and their infamous roles as examples. Not only can you gain insights into your own approach to sex, you can learn about your mate's. And if your mate is just a date, well, better forewarned than ultimately mired in regret.

Are you an ace at wooing? Sometimes we all need a little inspiration, and *Isn't It Romantic* gives you the tips you need to make time with any sign. Having some insight into what someone might like early in a relationship—or even in a marriage—helps you provide the sort of romancing to which your partner will most respond.

On the lighter side, I decided to write a pair of articles making gentle fun of the signs from the perspective of love. You know the flaw and quirks your guy or girl presents, but maybe it's all a little fuzzy. In *Your Hunka Hunka Burning Love* and *Your Lady Love* each sign gets roasted, but it's all in good fun. And it might even give you some insight into the craziness that is your special someone.

CELESTIALLY SEXY

In 1972—or there abouts—a lovestruck chanteuse attended a glittering Hollywood gathering, and dazzled by a future superstar, returned home and penned the words, "You walked into the party like you were walking onto a yacht...one eye in the mirror...all the girls think that they'd be your partner." Everyone knew Cancer Carly Simon had fallen hard for Aries pretty boy Warren Beatty, and the words, "You're so vain—you probably think this song is about you," seemed to sum it all up.

That's the thing about **Aries**—they're hot and they know it. Maybe it is a bit shameful to be a shimmering sex machine, but they wouldn't have it any other way. It's quite comfortable for Aries to feel that urge and to chase it—completely unapologetically. Aries is easier to recognize than any other sign, perhaps because they're so direct and straightforward. Why make life—or sex—complicated? They just know what they want, and feel entitled to get it.

To Aries, love is about one-third romance and two-thirds the hots, and often when occupied in pleasurable fulfillment of the hots, the idea of romance flies completely away. They're not a fire sign for nothing! Does that mean all Aries want to play the field forever and avoid commitment altogether? They might just agree with the great Mae West—a Leo—when she said "Marriage is a great institution. I'm not ready for an institution."

When we think of Aries, we think of seething passions, uncontrollable ardor, and raging energy that is impossible to quell. Remember Aries Marlon Brando in *A Streetcar Named Desire*, standing at the bottom of the steps of that seedy but sensual New Orleans set, squalling for Stella, his lady love. "*Stella! Stella!*" His energy was as raw as pure sexuality, and Brando displayed that passion in every role.

Aries is a vibration that particularly suits men, and so many hunks in the movies display that he-man vitality that keeps moviegoers swooning. They represent that raw, animal passion, and that is the heart and soul of Aries. In the forgettable flick *Proof of Life*, the only genuine response from the audience came when a supporting player said to heartthrob Russell Crowe, "Do you think she's going to leave her husband and run off with you?" Everyone in my theater laughed because that's what had just happened—Scorpio Meg Ryan had run off with Crowe, leaving hubby Dennis Quaid heartbroken. The irony of it all was that Meg had simply traded in one sexy Aries guy for another! That's the thing about Aries men—they can be positively addictive to women who like to be swept away on a tidal wave of ardor.

Remember Adrien Brody at the Oscars? So moved was he by his win that he raced on stage and swept presenter Halle Berry—one of Hollywood's legion of Leos—into a rough and joyous—and news making—kiss. That's Aries for you—a little selfish, very impetuous, completely unself-conscious, and equipped with a grin so seductive it could melt the resolve of a confirmed celibate!

Aries women are just as lusty and passionate as their male counterpart. They may not be macho, but are surely macha! Dainty is not a word that appeals to them because they prefer that sexy, larger than life persona. Remember Aries Bette Davis and Joan Crawford, considered red hot mamas by the men of their day, but vilified as Mommy Dearest's by their children. It could be the times or the social strata from which they sprung, but these two Aries women were tough broads, and that's often how modern Aries women feel. They call the shots, they make the rules, and nobody tells them what to do.

Who better than Aries Sarah Jessica Parker to play Carrie Bradshaw, sexpert columnist on HBO's *Sex And The City*? We watched her antics for years on the beloved comedy, and by the end she'd slept with just about every man in Manhattan. She was spunky, she was clever, and she lived as she pleased. Carrie was smart enough to agree with

Mae West's quip, "It's not the man in your life that counts. It's the life in your man." Does that make her a slut? No, ma'am, it makes her an Aries!

Jack Nicholson seems like an Aries, doesn't he? He's edgy, pushy, demanding, fearless, and more than a little scary. His killer grin is legendary. But, no, he's a **Taurus**, a sign known for sensuality, elegance, romance, and good food. For a Taurus, good lovemaking is an art worth developing into a hobby. They love to touch, and a proclivity for endless foreplay earns the admiration—and exhaustion—of every partner. Indolence is part of the Taurus lifestyle and they're never in a hurry to move any situation to its conclusion, a philosophy that lights more than a few fires in the bedroom.

Consider the case of Rudolph Valentino, the silent screen star who was one of the first true sex symbols. So beloved was he by a legion of female fans, that decades after his death they continued to visit his gravesite and bring flowers. Early in his life he was a gigolo, and his ability to perform the tango made women swoon. He was elegant and sensual, and many men of the era considered him too effeminate to be a genuine male sex symbol, but his female fans worshipped him. Valentino's life was far shorter than his legend, and he summed up his philosophy with the remark, "To generalize on women is dangerous. To specialize in them is infinitely worse."

A pretty voice is another Taurus trademark, and Renee Zellweiger was teased by her brother about her singing while growing up, but this Taurus managed to capture an Oscar nomination for her musical turn in the megahit *Chicago*. Most of the time we see Renee as a sylph, but look how she gamely agreed to expand her girth to play British chubette Bridget Jones. With sensuality comes a love of food, and many a Taurus is a bit overweight. No Taurus will ever reject you for being a little too plump—"There's more of you to love," they'll say!

George Clooney has an unmistakable voice, but as he rose to prominence in a number of televisions shows, he was chunky and lacked the muscular physique we expect of our movie stars. It didn't stop George from reaching the top, and his seductive voice and insouciant demeanor earned him millions of adoring fans. Now significantly thinner and more buff, he's a bigger star than ever. Who knew he was so hunky? We all did!

We seldom think macho when we consider Taurus. That touchy-feely personality seems a little feminine. Tony Danza, a former boxer, made a huge success on television playing a housekeeper—a macho guy who was completely in touch with his feminine side. He could cook, clean, and he was a nurturer. Although we never saw him in bed with a woman on this family comedy, his skills as a lover were renowned. He had it all and who wouldn't kill for such a guy! As Mae West said, "Too much of a good thing is wonderful."

Nobody ever really thinks of **Gemini** as a sexy sign. Gemini is all about conversation, ideas and intellectual interaction. Perhaps it was Gemini who invented phone sex! If laughing turns you on, then look for someone born in June. Clever, educated, good with a turn of phrase, Gemini is stimulating—intellectually. Phylicia Rashad, who played wife to now-beleaguered Cancer Bill Cosby on not one but two hit television shows, exemplifies the Gemini charms. Classy, intelligent, and wise, she is a woman who knows what she's doing but never loses her sense of humor. She's sexy not just because she's beautiful but also because she's smart!

Marilyn Monroe had the opposite problem. Somehow we'd expect her to be a sultry Scorpio or lusty Leo, but Monroe was a Gemini and it was her lifelong disappointment that she was never granted the respect her intelligence deserved. The greatest sex icon of film history, Monroe expressed more the opposite of her sign's qualities. She seemed sensual, sexual, desirable—but dimwitted. Marilyn described the situation clearly as Lorelei Lee in *Gentlemen Prefer Blondes*, when her future father-in-law commented that he'd heard she was dumb but she seemed quite intelligent. "I can be smart when it's important, but most men don't like it." That was a long time ago and nowadays there's nothing as sexy as an intelligent woman.

Gemini Helen Hunt is smart and she always plays a man's equal, whether she's an uneducated waitress or an ace ad executive. That's part of her charm—she's pretty but there's more to her than mere looks. Annette Bening is another Gemini whose intelligence shines through. Director Mike Nichols said of working with her that it was like driving a Rolls Royce. And it was this tall, much-younger beauty who did what none of the more overtly sexy stars of his own generation could do--tame legendary lothario Warren Beatty. Gemini Angelina Jolie considers herself quite typical of her sign, but her daredevil persona and white hot sexiness is more in the Monroe tradition. These days, with a marriage to Brad Pitt and a bevy of kids and kid-related causes, it's almost as though Angie has morphed into a Cancer! Beautiful Nicole Kidman tried to amp up her sagging career by emphasizing the sexiness in some of her roles, but not until she donned a fake nose and played an intellectual writer did she gain an Oscar.

Legendary singer Dean Martin was a Gemini, and perhaps that how he kept up his on stage patois so successfully between songs. That's the thing about Gemini guys—they love to talk. Colin Farrel did an entire movie from inside a phone booth, being taunted on the phone and surrounded by cops. Mark Wahlberg always seems calm and reasonable—in fact he seems like a Taurus, but he's a Gemini, and you can see the intelligence shining from his eyes. He began his career in a word-dominated music field— as a rapper, but with that physique, was it any surprise he was hired to strip down to his Calvins for a Times Square billboard?

Gemini is changeable and hard to pin down, and sex often becomes a passing fancy, as it did for sexually infamous screen legend Errol Flynn, who put the word wicked in the title of his autobiography, not once, but twice. He summed up the Gemini philosophy on his deathbed, saying, "I've had a hell of a lot of fun and I've enjoyed every minute of it."

Tom Hanks seems like the quintessential Gemini. Facile, witty, conversational, and clever, he always has a bon mot at the ready, and his toasting skills are legendary in Hollywood. But no, the verbally adroit Hanks is in reality a sensitive **Cancer**. This is the cuddly, home-oriented sign, and every

Cancer wants a love to last a lifetime. Casual sex is anathema to Cancer; they want a secure partnership.

The very great thing about Cancer partners is they can fall in love with a slob. They're not shallow and, just like the best mother on earth, they see great things in someone they love. A Cancer will see your best inner self, even on the day you forgot to wash your hair, and you'll get a hug, just for being you. A strong emotional connection leading to a lifelong commitment is always the goal in any relationship. Moonlight and romance are never enough; there has always to be a promise of marriage, children, and a happy family.

Harrison Ford makes a real distinction between the type of action hero he plays and the typical one. In his movies, it's not just about the action; his character is protecting his family. That's the thing about Cancer—the emotional dimension is right there on the surface, shining tentatively out of sensitive eyes—for all the world to see. Cancer Josh Hartnett played a young stud on Ford's movie, *Hollywood Homicide.* He was a young cop, but taught Yoga and it was his sensitivity, not any sort of machismo, that attracted all those women to him.

Beautiful Sela Ward played a terrified divorcee on television's short-lived "Once and Again," but when she met equally beautiful fellow-Cancer Billy Campbell, they just meshed. Their interactions were so filled with emotion, their eyes so sensitive and vulnerable, that untold numbers of the audience burst inexplicably into tears each week while watching the show. Even when playing a villain opposite the tempestuous JLo, Billy Campbell brought an emotional dimension—perhaps an unnecessary one—to the role. You always know where you stand with a Cancer, because their feelings show so clearly in their eyes—even when they're trying to hide those emotions.

All the mothers in front of the television were happy when Gilmore Girl Alexis Bledel—a Virgo-- found Jared Padalecki, the most considerate boyfriend on earth. This Cancer was a mother's dream. I couldn't decide if I wanted to adopt or seduce him—he was that adorable. Tall, sensitive, kind, considerate, he embodied the qualities a mother seeks in a daughter's boyfriend. When Alexis's character fell for the snarling Milo Ventemiglia, every mother in the audience yelled "No!" Written as a bad boy, he seemed like a careless Sagittarius destined to cause heartbreak. But no, these two young actors have more in common than their unpronounceable last names—both are Cancers!

Leo is the 18-Karat gold sign, and every Leo loves to woo in as much luxury as possible. They're passionate, fun-loving, and uninhibited. Nobody enjoys setting the scene for romance as much as Leo does—they're all natural actors. Spectacularly good-looking, seldom modest, Leo is all about the splendor that is—well—Leo.

Mae West is, to me, the quintessential Leo. Unapologetically sexy, her Diamond Lil character was adored as the first woman ever to make racy comments on film. In one now-famous movie scene, after seeing Mae's jewelry, a coat check girl exclaims, "Goodness! What lovely diamonds!" Mae replies, "Goodness had nothing to do with it." She was the first cinema femme fatale, and as the writer of so many of those double entendres, she became the highest paid woman in America. She loved being a sexy woman and had her nude portrait painted yearly until her death.

Leo always brings personality into the bedroom and it's with flair and style that every romance is played out. Looking good and being fabulous is the Leo way of life—and of lovemaking. Look at Leos Ben Affleck and Jennifer Lopez, whose romance was documented not so much because of their tender love story but because of the many millions they spent while in each other's company. Of course now Ben is happily married to Aries Jen Garner, a girly girl who easily plays an action hero.

Leo is always the object of desire and they love being worshipped and adored. Perhaps that's why so many Leos are sex symbols. Look at Madonna, the material girl, who, no matter how many times she recreates herself, is always a sensation. Kim Cattral, the sex-loving p.r. girl on *Sex and the City*, turned amorous encounters into a one-woman cottage industry in New York City. Nobody turned down advances from her character—how could they—she was too sexy for words!

Robert Redford, with his blond thatch of hair, his startling blue eyes, and his California boy looks, is the male Leo icon of this century. Generations of women fell in love with him, and although his on-screen chemistry with female costars often fizzled, his Leo good looks kept him at the top of the sex-symbol stratosphere. In *The Way We Were*, Redford lay in bed asleep next to the adoring Barbra Streisand, who showed the intensity of her passion for him by brushing aside a lock of his hair.

That's the thing about Leo—they're quite comfortable being the object of desire. It feels normal to be worshipped! As Mae West said, "It's better to be looked over than overlooked!" But that doesn't mean a Leo won't return the same degree of ardor or make sure that you're just as fulfilled in the bedroom. It's all a matter of pride to be a good lover, and where pride is concerned, Leo is aces.

Nobody expects **Virgo** to be a sexy sign, perhaps because their symbol is the Virgin, but as an earth sign, Virgos tend to be just as passionate and lusty as anyone else—subtly—and behind closed doors. The Virgo energy is perfectionist, tasteful, and seldom inclined toward cheap or meaningless romantic entanglements. This is the most helpful sign, and a Virgo lover is always willing to work hard to please a partner, no matter how arduous the task! Skills of all sorts are important to a Virgo, and being good in bed is just another skill. Greta Garbo, long considered the world's most beautiful woman, had a famous penchant for solitude and remained single all her life. When asked why she hadn't married, Garbo quipped "There is no one who would have me...I can't cook." Virgos don't choose a partner solely for sex appeal but also for other just as important, real-life qualities.

Virgos are touchy-feely, and they are sensual, oral, and tactile, but they're also often rebels. Ingrid Bergman was a screen goddess who was idolized all over the world for her ephemeral Virgo perfection until she fell in love and had a child out of wedlock. The world was scandalized but Ingrid didn't care—she was spunky and independent enough to live her life as she chose. In later years Ingrid was restored to the public's good graces and she observed, "I've gone from saint to whore and back to saint again, all in one lifetime." Most Virgos know what it's like to be sexually liberated or as Mae West said, "I used to be Snow White—but I drifted."

Taste and class just go with the Virgo persona. Look at adorable Hugh Grant, practically a human confection, as light as air in his debonair roles, movie after movie. Yet in his private life he was involved in a scandal with a prostitute, which he handled with such refinement and grace that it caused barely a blip in his career. Hugh is exactly what we think of when we contemplate the Virgo male—dapper, precise, well-mannered, even sometimes a little dull, just like—James Gandolfini? Yes, mafia boss Tony Soprano was a Virgo! So is Batman Michael Keaton. Virgo has a way of producing people who startle us a little and some are cinema bad boys known for their snarling performances like Richard Gere, although in *Pretty Woman* he was the soul of Virgo good taste and austerity—until reining cinema queen Scorpio Julia Roberts loosened him up!

There are many sex gods and goddesses in Virgo—like Sophia Loren and Raquel Welch, saucy singer Beyonce Knowles, Cameron Diaz. Who among us didn't swoon when TV's Grace fell into the arms of Virgo Harry Connick, Jr., and Sean Connery has been on the sexiest man alive lists for decades!

Libra is the sign of courtly grace and beauty, and they absolutely live for love. Nobody woos as romantically as Libra, and sometimes it seems as though sex just isn't that important to them because it's all about the hearts, flowers, and violins playing in the background. Ask any Libra and they'll all tell you that there is one and only one genuinely important goal in life—finding true love, but in process of pursuing that objective, Libras often get distracted by the social pleasures involved. Dating is not as repugnant a task for a Libra as it is for the rest of us. They love to woo and be wooed, or as Mae West said, "I like two kinds of men: domestic and foreign."

We naturally picture Libras in formal attire, whispering tender sentiments by candlelight, while an orchestra plays in the background. That's the thing about Libra sex appeal—it's chatty and cinematic. Gwyneth Paltrow, a refined Libra beauty with an upper crust education, captured the world's fancy for so long that when she and then-lover Brad Pitt broke up, America's heart was broken. Then it was broken again when she called it quits with Ben Affleck. More recently we've been reading about her "conscious uncoupling" with her rock star husband. We all root for the Libra romance because it stirs our hearts and our tender sensibilities. More than any other sign, Libra is filled with the promise of happily ever after, and that pure romantic sentiment is what we all want—at least to observe from afar, if not in our own mundane lives.

The celebrated romance of much older Libra Michael Douglas ended in marriage to stunning Catherine Zeta-Jones, with whom he shares a birthday. He had seen her in movies, fell in love from afar and made the grand gesture of having his people contact hers. Romantic gestures are everything in a Libra romance. Tall, sexy Australian Hugh Jackman played to perfection the part of a time traveling nobleman, transported to current day New York to woo crusty career girl Meg Ryan. After seeing *Kate & Leopold*, every woman in the audience wanted to return to days of olde!

Charm is the essence of Libra. Think of huggable Fran Drescher, so adorable as TV's *The Nanny*. Because of her charm and ability to get away with just about any wild and unpredictable stunt, she won the heart of her priggish employer. It had to be more than her winning smile that did it—Fran is practically today's Mae West, always preening sexily for the camera. Matt Damon is another Libra with a killer smile—and a body to match. Libra is an air sign though, so communication skills are essential to this sign's sex appeal, and it was Matt's writing that won him an Oscar, not his muscles. Brigitte Bardot, the French sex goddess of the 1960's, is one of the world's most famous Libras, and her unself-conscious naked romps set a new cinema standard. "I have always adored beautiful young men, " she said, "Just because I grow older, my taste doesn't change. So if I can still have them, why not?" Who could fight logic like that!

Many signs have religion; **Scorpio** has sex. No other sign approaches sex with a fervor so intense it might better be associated with a religious calling, and perhaps that's because the level of intimacy regarded as normal for this, the sexy sign, verges on the transcendent. For Scorpio, sex is a way to connect with the infinite within—and without.

Scorpio knows only too well that a permanent relationship provides more opportunities for the best possible sex, but can sometimes be persuaded to dally with someone new. The lure of the tryst is hard to resist. This sign cares about devotion, and once a heart is given, it's seldom withdrawn. Scorpio expects love to last beyond death. In the bedroom, a Scorpio will do anything—and everything—to please a partner and will seldom say no to even the most outrageous sexual gymnastics. It was no doubt a Scorpio who invented the line about consenting adults.

Vivien Leigh won our hearts as the beautiful but determined Scarlett O'Hara, and about her sign she said, "Scorpios burn themselves out and eat themselves up and they are careless about themselves - like me. I swing between happiness and misery and I cry easily... I am part prude and part non-conformist and I say what I think and don't dissemble." When you're a Scorpio, you're willing to let the chips fall where they may. Rules are few and breaking the ones that exist can be lots of fun. If we were casting the part of Scarlett a few years back, it would probably have gone to Julia Roberts, a Scorpio who plays a bad girl so easily that no matter what she does on screen we love her and know she's perfect—just as she is. Or as Mae West said, "Good girls go to heaven; bad girls go everywhere else."

Perhaps it was her Scorpio subtext that helped Calista Flockhart win newly single, much older Harrison Ford, but would anyone describe Calista as sexy? She's more adorable. But don't forget, charm is a very strong dimension of Scorpio; not every Scorpion is a Svengali, ready to enslave you. Well, okay most are, but they're shrewd enough to be subtle about it!

Owen Wilson has the blond looks of a California surfer and he's so laconic and easy going, I was sure he was a Pisces, just a very sexy one. But no, he's a Scorpio and it's very believable that when paired with Aries Jackie Chan that he's the sex maniac. Nobody thinks of Goldie Hawn as a sex maniac as she has always played the blond, blue-eyed ditz, just like Owen Wilson—but that's the flip side of Scorpio— someone so relaxed and charming, *you're* persuaded to seduce *them*!

I thought that *The Good Wife's*, Chris Noth, was an Aries. He has those Aries eyebrows and crocodile grin, but although he's as hot as an Aries, he's a Scorpio, and no wonder he's the one we remember when we think of the beefcake on the HBO hit *Sex and the City*. Could Gemini Ron Livingston fill his—ahem—shoes? Not if you ask me!

The **Sagittarius** approach to sex is as easy-going as their approach to everything else. Why not just relax and enjoy life? Undemanding, playful, seldom jealous, possessive or suspicious, to a Sag, sex can be a rollicking good time. The concept of serial monogamy might have been invented for a Sag, or else they're willing just to play the field. Woody Allen, whom nobody regards as sexy, has made many quotable remarks about relationships including, "Human Beings are divided into mind and body. The mind embraces all the nobler aspirations, like poetry and philosophy, but the body has all the fun."

Sex should be a good time or why bother is the bedrock of the Sagittarian philosophy, although in fact this credo extends beyond sex to everything in life. Alyssa Milano started her career as Tony Danza's spunky television daughter but has graduated to one of TV's most infamous sexpots. Uninhibited and playful, she's known for quite a few daring moves. Said Danza, when she posed nude in the 1993 pages of *Bikini* magazine, "I worried about her, but it wasn't my place to say anything. I played her father, but I wasn't her father."

There is an innocence and unspoiled quality to Sagittarius and that carries over into sex. No doubt Adam and Eve were born under this blissfully amoral sign. Britney Spears took a lot of flack about being so young—and so sexy—and she was quite verbal in response. "Just because I look sexy on the cover of Rolling Stone doesn't mean I'm naughty." It didn't matter how suggestively she gyrated on stage, Britney wasn't ready to become a woman until it seemed right—on her own terms: "Who really cares if I've had sex? It's nobody's business...I'm no different than anyone else my age."

Frank Sinatra, who always did it "his way," was a Sagittarian sex symbol who had more than his sign in common with Woody Allen—they both had notable liaisons with Aquarian Mia Farrow. That's the thing about Sag—it's always on their own terms. Don Johnson refused to work on Fridays, and got away with it, because so many women swooned over his two hunky television detective personae.

Winona Ryder has a spiritual, ethereal quality on screen, but in real life she's been proven a tad too fond of shopping, and her romantic history reads like a Hollywood who's who—and very hunky. The Sag approach to sex is always the same—do it on your own terms. Or as Mae West said, "I wrote the story myself. It's all about a girl who lost her reputation but never missed it."

Does anyone think of **Capricorn** as a sexy sign? We expect Cappies to be serious, hard-working, and often a bit dour. With one eye fixed on success and the other on their pocketbook, Capricorn is considered the most practical sign in the Zodiac. Yes we know they believe in marriage, commitment, and sex, but really isn't that just to make life less complicated and free up evenings for more work? When Meg Ryan told Pisces Billy Crystal in *When Harry Met Sally*, that she had great sex with "Sheldon," Crystal replied that no, a Sheldon can do your taxes and drill your teeth, but he's not a great lover. That's pretty much the Cap rep, isn't it?

The only surprising thing is how many superstar sexpots come from this sign. None other than Elvis—called Elvis the pelvis in his day—was a Cap, and although his success was stellar, he was too sexy to show on television from the waist down. Olivier Martinez burned up the silver screen, and was he sexy—well hoo-ha! He seduced Aquarian Diane Lane in *Unfaithful*, transforming Virgo Richard Gere from the guy you cheat with to the guy you cheat on!

Look at gorgeous Gilles Marini, a favorite on *Dancing with the Stars* not once but twice. His sex appeal, beauty and grace as a dancer helped him transition from unknown to popular television actor. In real life, he's a mellow family man, typical of Cap.

Capricorn guys often have a quiet, masculine strength, and they seem very manly compared to other earth signs Taurus and Virgo. Denzel Washington is upright, forthright, and very sexy. He usually seems like the perfect husband and father, except in *Training Day*, where he played a sleaze to perfection and captured the Oscar. As Mae West said, "When I'm good, I'm very good, but when I'm bad, I'm better."

Dapper Cary Grant was the male role model thought of when Ian Fleming created the character James Bond. Tall, elegant, and roguish, Grant was adored by several generations of women—and men. But he never fell under his own mystique nor considered himself greater than Archie Leach—the person he was at birth. Of course that didn't mean he wasn't great with women—or that he didn't have a practical Capricorn side when approaching the game of seduction. He counseled, "To succeed with the opposite sex, tell her you are impotent; she can't wait to disprove it."

Capricorn gals often come across as serious, icons of style who show us how to live with flair, like Diane Keaton, whose blazers and neckties started a fad that swept the nation. Diane's dance card is pretty impressive too—she's dated many super studs but never managed to marry one.

Kirstey Alley seems like a flaky Pisces or distracted Aquarius, but no, she's a Capricorn too. Her *Cheers* Rebecca Howe character was so fixed on success that she only fell for rich men, but ultimately she ended up married to a sexy plumber, Gemini Tom Berenger. She probably proved Mae West's point, "When women go wrong, men go right after them!"

Aquarius is the sign of the absent-minded professor. We think of them as intelligent, outrageous, rule-breaking, trend-setting intellectuals, but we rarely see them as sexy. Romance is seldom the Aquarian frame of reference. They prefer to call a person a friend, and that way if the romance fizzles, they can be content to stop sharing a bedroom without a backwards glance as long as the friendship remains intact.

When you're involved with an Aquarius, it's hard to know where you stand emotionally because there's so little of that dimension in the relationship. All you know for sure is you're pals, and that's really all that matters to them. Aquarius will woo a partner with words, and for those not terribly adroit with words, another partner would be a better choice. Mere sex is never enough to satisfy an Aquarian.

Despite the above, one of the sexiest leading men of all time, none other than the King himself—Clark Gable—was an Aquarius. Every woman in the world was in love with Gable for a long, long time, and his portrayal of Rhett Butler still stands as one of the American icons of masculinity. Gable married many times, often for the wrong reasons, prompting a friend of his to say, "Of course, Clark never really married anyone. A number of women married him; he just went along for the gag." The hard, mental, masculine edginess of Aquarius can seem very sexy to women who want to tame the guy.

Paul Newman was not just an enduring sex symbol, but a multi-million dollar philanthropist as well, quipping that his salad dressing out grossed his movies. His famous remark about adultery, "Why fool around with hamburger when you have steak at home," made quite a few women swoon—except for his wife, Joanne Woodward, who somehow found it unflattering to be compared to meat. Joanne is a Pisces, so perhaps she's a vegetarian.

Farrah Fawcett was a megastar who decided to quit her hit TV series because she didn't enjoy playing a kewpie doll. Her pinup posters sold millions, but she was determined to be thought a serious actress and serious person. Perhaps she agreed with Mae West's comment, "I'm no model lady. A model's just an imitation of the real thing." Like Farrah, Aquarius Jennifer Aniston has not only set trends in hair and figure, she kept dating more celebrated guys until she hooked a superstar—sexy Sag Brad Pitt. At least Jen agreed to marry the guy; Farrah, once stung, lived with Taurus Ryan O'Neal for seventeen years but remained independent—and ringless. That's the thing about Aquarian romances—they always have an aura of individuality. Look at sexy Aston Kutcher, who burned up the tabloids not because of his pecs and delts, but for being the boy toy of Scorpio Demi Moore! Demi's no fool; she probably seconded Mae West's remark, "A hard man is good to find!" And she was heart broken when he left her and now is living with Leo Mila Kunis, the mother of his child.

Pisces is sometimes seen as ditzy, often seen as unreliable, but Pisces is always romantic. How can someone with such a tender heart not be a real catch? Empathetic, sympathetic, and liberated of all rules designed to constrict the heart, Pisces aims to please—in the bedroom and out. Although jealous sometimes, Pisces is often too understanding and will be there for you even if you cheat. Of course this easily distractible sign may stray on you as well!

Pisces really wants true love, and that means chasing it whenever the fancy strikes. With this tendency, it's a little hard to avoid a crash and burn type of romantic history, but Pisces is usually willing to get up, brush off, and love again. Setting the scene for romance is as important to a Pisces as to a Libra, but they're far less judgmental and demanding. It's the idea of the magic—and the music—that's as important as the actual trappings.

There's a real tender, soulful quality to Pisces and a very huggable personality. Freddie Prinze, Jr. appeared on the scene from a tragic background and became an instant, but unspoiled, superstar. Devoted to his Aries wife, Sarah Michelle Gellar, he stopped more than just her heart with this comment, "Make your girl feel special whenever you can. I'm a big big believer in surprises. You've got to be romantic all of the time." Freddie expressed the Pisces philosophy adeptly when he said it should be Valentine's Day every day of the year.

Sharon Stone, a completely uninhibited Pisces, became a

superstar when she provocatively uncrossed her legs and let the camera play peek-a-boo. She seems a lot like a Scorpio on many days. Always in touch with her considerable sex appeal she says, "Any man in Hollywood will meet me if I want that. No, make that any man anywhere." As her approach to life is quite intellectual and deliberate, she could just as well have been an Aquarius. Who can fault her counsel, "...Never have sex with anybody who has more problems than you do." But no, Sharon is a sensitive Pisces, and she must be a bit more emotional than she seems.

Pisces can often fool us. Look at Bruce Willis, who has said of himself, "Only a few guys can save the world as good as me." He looks and acts tough and plays characters who can shoot straight and take out the bad guys. He's as far from our image of the sensitive Pisces as can be—he seems more like a zany Aquarius. But Willis has a tender heart and has never said a bad word about TV co-star Aquarian Cybill Shepherd although he reportedly didn't like her, and when asked about ex-wife Demi Moore's dalliance with much-younger Ashton Kutcher, he said he loves Demi and wants her to be happy. Must be more to Willis than saving the world!

Much married Elizabeth Taylor, considered the world's most beautiful woman for decades, believed in true love—obviously. She kept chasing it, through husbands and the years. Her weight problem aside, La Liz believed in living large and she enjoyed a lusty, fun filled life. She didn't believe in being a slave to rules: "One problem with people who have no vices is that they're pretty sure to have some annoying virtues." Her view of life and love remained uncomplicated, and she summed up the Pisces approach to romance, "What do you expect me to do? Sleep alone?"

ISN'T IT ROMANTIC

They had been dating for a pretty long while when he said to her one day, "I told the folks I was getting married Saturday." She, rather astonished, replied, "You are? Who are you marrying?" And he, nonplussed, answered, "You, of course." Apparently it all worked out because a few years later, along I came. Yes, that was the goofy way my Scorpio dad proposed to my Gemini mother. He was clever and creative and you would have thought he could have come up with a better proposal. After all it was the only one he ever made.

I told this story to a favorite client and she said her reaction might have been more along the lines of "Well screw you," which of course is a phrase nobody ever uttered in the olden days when my parents courted. She often complains that her boyfriend isn't meeting her needs, and sometimes even when he does do what she's said she wanted, she's still annoyed because he doesn't do it in the precise way she envisions. She has a very definite vision of what romance entails.

My dear friend Kerry Prep, the creative mastermind behind New York's celebrated Preppygrams, has a solution for situations like this. He will create a better proposal, in the form of a singing telegram, to aid the potential groom (or anyone wanting to share the perfect sentiment). In fact, one groom went as far as having his girlfriend drop him off at the airport on a pretend business trip, then he returned to the city and hid out—not for an evening but for several days—and then there she was at a family lunch when Kerry appeared, singing a special song with details all about her. At the climax of the song, her suitor came in, kneeled, and proposed.

As much as that future bride loved her public proposal, I think I would rather have a more private one. But that's the thing—we're all different. What we do all have in common is the desire for romance, which is a different thing than love. Romance is the sparklers that we all light now and then for someone special. Love is the enduring flame that glows in our hearts when we've connected with that person.

I've been divorced for many years now, but the truly good thing about it is that when I think back to my marriage, it's usually mostly the good things I remember. One year for—gee I can't recall was it my birthday or our anniversary— my husband had said we were going out, but I didn't know where. Outside our New York apartment, there was a limo and the driver greeted me. Later I joked that I thought he'd gotten lost. But no, he was for us, and into the limo we went to a Broadway show, *Ain't Misbehavin'*, and then we went to dinner at my favorite Chinese restaurant. It felt like a really special evening, and of course the best part was that he had planned it with me in mind.

That is the heart and soul of romance—that someone thinks of you and plans something you would like—and you do like it.

Of course not all romance happens with people who are already a couple. It used to be that a guy would meet a girl and romance her until she said yes. What she agreed to could be as simple as a kiss, as sizzling as sex, or as sweet as a marriage proposal. A guy I know, who is better at making money than at being sexy, went a little crazy after his divorce, and when he met a hot girl, he'd take her out and on the first date give her a diamond necklace. Well, he probably didn't do that on every date but he did do it at least once. That wasn't romance but more like salesmanship.

As nice as diamond necklaces worth more than my car are (and I do believe they are very nice indeed) the key element in any romantic gesture is the heart and soul behind it. When my casual boyfriend returned from an extended stay in Hawaii to live with me, he got off the plane holding a bouquet of flowers. More than just the sweet gesture of bringing me flowers, was the idea that he had bought them in

Hawaii and had to hold them on the plane throughout the entire flight. That was romance. And when we'd had a fight and I came home to find flower petals everywhere, well gee, that too was romance. A heartfelt romantic gesture says not only that you're loved and valued, but reveals the sweetness of the heart making it.

Recently on Twitter, Chef Gordon Ramsay asked his followers for suggestions about a birthday gift for his wife. There were many good ones. Mine was to buy her a little silver box, and that he and the kids should take some slips of paper and write on them the many various reasons why she is so special to them. Then she could pull them one by one from within the box and enjoy those many moments of love. That's romantic.

There are several ways to view romance. It can be the expression of a sentiment, such as I love you, please marry me. Or it can be time spent together that is somehow special, out of the ordinary. With a good connection it can feel romantic, or special, or comfortingly nice when you're sharing ordinary moments with someone. It's a heart beam sort of thing—your heart beams to my heart and we both glow kind of energy. But if you want to focus on deliberate romance, on planning something to enjoy with someone special (or someone you hope will ultimately become special) consider checking out their Sun sign. That might give you a little inspiration about what to do.

If you've been dating or mating with an **Aries**, you've probably already learned something that's key: in the Aries vocabulary, *we* is a synonym for *I*. Aries look for significant others who go along with their ideas, their plans, their wishes, and who enjoy their pleasures. This makes it both difficult and easy to plan something romantic. If you want to be creative and come up with an activity to share on your own, be prepared to have your ideas—and your plans— edited, even if they took much time and effort to set in place. The safer choice is to be a good listener and when Aries says oh we should do this (translation *I've always wanted to do....)* keep it in mind. That dream could become the raw material for something you can plan to do together. The cool thing is that Aries says stuff like this all the time and might not even remember having made the wish and then you will get credit for a fantastic idea. Of course the flip side is that Aries says so much of this sort of thing that he or she may well have lost interest in it by time you turn it into a romantic event. Either way, doing is the way to go. Sensitive evenings that involve dressing up and candlelight are better reserved for opposite sign Libra. For Aries, something casual and fun, like a trip to an amusement park where you can play skeeball and ride a roller coaster is such a good time that it feels as though you two are in a special bubble of romance and pleasure, and that after all is the main idea.

Taurus is all about the food, and yes other pleasures such as massage, spa days, and sentimental food rubs. But really you can't go wrong with a good meal. If you're well-heeled, plan a special dinner and hire a local chef to come in and cook for you both. If you want to enjoy life on a lesser budget, cook a nice meal yourself or buy some easily re-heatable take out. Knowing that you have gone all out to make a special meal for your lover really pleases Taurus. You can also opt to dine out and enjoy each other's conversation while someone else does the work. The key is to focus on food as the centerpiece of your romantic event, and the conversation will be the parentheses. Even something silly and simple like a breakfast in bed appeals to this food-oriented sign. There's nothing as pleasant as waking to the smell of croissants warming in the oven while a beautiful fruit salad is assembled. This is a simple breakfast, but you can insert whatever morning treats you prefer, and your efforts will be much appreciated. If you're an enthusiastic baker, preparing a tin of nice cookies to give to your sweetie (either to take home or into work depending on your living situation) is a gesture that's always appreciated. Love and food intermingle in many situations, but with Taurus, they always do. And please—don't forget the trappings of your nice meal—the soft music, the candles, and something nicely tactile to wear.

Gemini is all about communication, and as we all know, the most potent sex organ is the brain. With Gemini, love begins in the mind, and even if there are a few hot glances to start the romance, it will soon fizzle if there's nothing to say. This is not a sign which wants to court someone who can't hold up his or her end of the conversation. You can go out and do something together, but something simple such as taking a stroll down a pretty street, hand in hand, can be the ultimate in romance as you walk and talk together. You'll joke and laugh, and share a few serious ideas too, and the time will float away into a beautiful memory. You can also stay in together and play some games. My ex and I used to play Scrabble all the time in bed, and once he accused me of trying to distract him from the game by the lingerie I was wearing. Was I? Or was I! I know a couple who like reading to each other in bed and they try to find romantic passages to share, although they are far from original because they nabbed the idea to do this from the movie *Bull Durham*, even reading the same poetry. Unoriginal as it might be, sharing steamy passages from *Lady Chatterley's Lover* or something more modern could be fun and lead to romance that is more sizzle than sentiment. Or you could go one step further and get necessary props and act it out. As silly as it may sound, that's okay because Gemini loves to laugh.

Cancer is a sign strongly rooted in the past. As with Taurus, food is important, but so are memories. If you're dating someone new, it might seem a little crazy, but a Cancer would love to sit with you and look at your childhood scrapbooks, your yearbooks, or other mementos of your life. It's a great way to get to know each other as you share those sentimental stories and look at pictures of times gone by. If you're already involved, it's an absolute that this guy or gal has memories involving mom and mom's cooking, so if you're planning to make a special meal, you might want to get some favorite recipes from his or her mom and then when you serve them, it feels as though you're offering to fit right into Cancer's life, from the past into the future. A simple stroll together—toward an ice cream parlor usually— is a pleasant way to end a date, and as you eat your ice creams, you can walk and talk about your dreams for the future. The whole point of efforts made to woo Cancer is to share in the dreams that make up a foundation for life and as you talk, you mingle ideas and lives and sooner rather than later a deep emotional bond is formed. Hearts connect and your romance becomes your everyday life.

I'm sure it's a relief to know that there are some signs for whom you can pull out the big guns and do something sparkly, and yes, **Leo** is it. Although most people would enjoy a sweetly sentimental dinner at home, Leo is someone who gives points for glitz, so take this partner out for a spectacular dinner at a place that is luxe and if famous people eat there, so much the better. Leo enjoys dressing up and chances are he or she already has something to wear. Leo also enjoys receiving nice presents, although a diamond necklace before the first date as my friend above offered is sort of creepy. Arriving for a date with flowers is always sweet, or if you're mid-romance and know of a little treasure that would make his or her eyes sparkle, wrap it up and say it's for our five-weekaversary. Of course that could suck you into buying weekly anniversary gifts, so beware. If you can, rent a limo. Make it a big gesture. Leo is never embarrassed about being the center of attention or people's heads turning—in fact that's the goal. Then as you sit at your nicely appointed table while wait staff seamlessly sees to your every need, take his or her hand and share what first attracted you and why you've stuck around. Leo enjoys hearing why you feel as you do, and never minds a list of his or her fabulous attributes.

Virgo is teased often about being the picky-picky sign, and yes that's true, but it's a rare Virgo who is impossible to please in the romance department. That's because we give credit for efforts expended. I always say that part of connecting with another person is learning to be a good translator, that you understand what is meant by what is said, even if what is said is different from what is meant! In short Virgo can read between the lines, so if you make an effort, chances are that effort will be appreciated. Something simple is often perfect. Dinner and a movie doesn't sound like an extraordinary gesture, but if it's your Virgo's favorite weekend pastime (as it is mine) then it's something that will be appreciated. Just choose a restaurant you know your sweetie likes. This is not the time to insist he or she try sushi again if you've heard repeatedly that raw fish is for cats. Sometimes a simple gesture can be meaningful as when a heavy tray is lifted from her hands by a suitor who knows how to be chivalrous. That's the thing about an independent, possibly feminist sign such as mine—we still like those old fashioned gestures. Don't forget though that Virgo is an earth sign, and as such touch is important. A gift certificate for a massage is nice, but a couple's massage is better. Sharing that sensation of being pampered is a great way to relax together, and once the kinks are removed, you can get kinky together.

Please let the violins begin to play immediately, for if you're courting a **Libra**, then all the classic moves are the ones to emphasize. This is the mate you take dancing. Or to a restaurant that serves excellent food by candlelight with a live band and roomy dance floor. Then you can eat, listen to a crooner, dance a little, and gaze into each other's eyes, made even sparklier by the candles. When you look at it like that, what sign wouldn't enjoy this sort of evening? It's true that we all would, but for Libra the classics are where romance is at! This is the sign you can bring along to that formal charity event, even if it's a first date, because Libra not only lives for this sort of thing, he or she is prepared with excellent wardrobe and equally perfect manners. A formal evening allows time to move in slow motion, and as you dine elegantly, dance elegantly, and woo elegantly, it all takes on an antique quality that feels as though you were lost in the courtship mores of the past, when life was more romantic. Then of course you won't want the evening to end, so off you'll go to an after hours place to hear some music or to grab some breakfast, returning home arm in arm under the fading stars. Oh it all makes my heart go pitta-pat and it will for Libra as well.

The great (and also scary) thing about **Scorpio** is how well this partner can get to know you. Forget about having secrets, because with him or her you're an open book. The question is can you return the favor and come up with a plan for romance that dazzles Scorpio, the sexy sign? It might be cheesy, but it could be fun to go to one of those murder mystery events, such as a dinner or a train ride. Or you could just book the train ride, to somewhere as near or far as you'd like, and if far, those private compartments are considered terribly romantic, and yet rather chaste as the beds are bunk—and very narrow. Doing something impromptu can be wonderful because the surprise element is potent with any of the Fixed signs, who usually prefer to know what's coming. Let the weather be your accomplice. If it's winter, you know there will come a point at which you're snowed in, so hide some goodies for the perfect moment and plan a picnic in front of the fire. Soft music and congenial conversation do the rest. Casual use of nature is meaningful, so if it's summer, find a place to share a cocktail and watch the sunset. All your cares melt away, and you have the opportunity to concentrate on only each other.

Outdoors is the logical setting for courting **Sagittarius,** a sign which is more known for a love of camping, dogs and horses, and very little interest in traditional romance. A Sag-Gemini couple I know took their honeymoon on Safari in Africa—a gift from his parents—who also came along—and it was a fabulous time. In a way, when I saw the pictures it seemed to me more like one of those tribal rituals in which a new member is accepted into the group than anything romantic, but then I don't see safari as romantic. Sorry, Sag! The thing about courting this sign is it doesn't have to be traditional at all, and it doesn't have to feel precisely like romance, but more like a rollicking good time to share. Planning a hiking trip and bringing along a picnic might be the perfect day, and perfect way to blend your hearts. You could go on a silly afternoon in which you stroll, and then stop at a deserted playground where you can enjoy riding on the swings side by side. A trip to a big amusement park like Disneyland is another way your Sag will enjoy the effort you put into creating fun. Or you could find a small amusement park, but the idea is that you are a couple of kids out in the world, taking advantage of the sights, the sun, and all the laughs you can create together.

Just because **Capricorn** is the serious, hard-working sign, it doesn't mean that this sweetie won't appreciate efforts to be courted. As with Libra, the traditional works very well here, because Capricorn appreciates both tradition, and things of value. Going to a fine restaurant with a great chef and genteel ambiance is something he or she will really appreciate, not just for the effort you expended but for the value of the activity itself. Dining on really excellent food is a treat, particularly if it's fare you can't as easily make at home yourself. But in addition, you can assume that Capricorn will also enjoy something a little wilder and crazier, like those Japanese griddle restaurants where everyone sits around a big table, and the cleaver-wielding chefs toss food at the diner's plates. As this is another earth sign, one which works virtually non-stop, a couple's massage is another excellent romantic gesture, as well as one that promotes good health. As much as Capricorn enjoys being wined and dined, small gifts of good quality are also appreciated, and if you do plan on offering a romantic token of affection, consider finding something antique such as an old watch or cloisonné box. You might also decide that taking a class together would be fun, so consider those skiing lessons, a hands-on cooking class, or even an afternoon of learning ping pong. Capricorn likes to work hard and a class is one way to work and to play romantically.

Virtually everyone acknowledges that **Aquarius** is the sign of friendship, but nobody ever asserts it's the sign of romance. That's because Aquarius is rarely focused on hearts and flowers, even while in a romance, and this amazing sign can be in love, break up, and still say well of course we'll be friends. So obviously the approach you should take is finding an activity so over the top romantic that you convert your partner to the joys of romance? Not! Easy camaraderie is a far more workable approach than candlelight and violins. That's not to say that you can't plan a nice dinner somewhere or cook one, but it's also not to say that he or she won't at the last minute decide to invite along a whole bunch of pals. If that happens, don't despair. It can be a very fun time, and you will be side by side, laughing together with this group of compatible people, and to Aquarius that is a very good time. It may seem crazy, but one way to get closer romantically is when you're apart. If you can online video chat, there you are one to one, and you're talking and smiling, and nothing can really interrupt because only two people can be on screen at the same time. If you don't live together, those late night phone calls are a way to say good night and to feel the warmth of each other's voices as you snuggle down beneath the covers.

Pisces, a water sign, is sweet and sentimental, and will always enjoy being wooed or snuggled. Sometimes all you need do is wrap your arms around this partner and sigh tenderly for the cloud of blissful romance to descend over you both. He or she is very intuitive, and feeling your heart open is pretty much the most important thing for Pisces. That doesn't mean you won't be rewarded for expending some effort. A walk on the beach together, or through the woods, or anywhere the birds sing and the sun glows, is a way to relax together and feel each other's vibration. If you can, assemble the fixings for a clam bake (or other outdoor food fest) and find a nicely secluded (and of course safe) spot where you can do it outdoors. While you wait, you can talk about anything and everything, enjoy the smells of the food cooking, and of nature all around you. If you're a baker, take a day and bake and decorate some cupcakes together. Even if you're just using those horrid tubes of colored icing from the market, you can take great pleasure in drawing a heart atop your cupcakes and writing *I'll always love you.* I did mention foot massage before, but as Pisces rules the feet, you might like to put a cushion beneath your sweetheart's head—and feet—and gently provide that service while you both watch a romantic movie at home on TV. Pisces is a very flexible sign, so pretty much anything you try will be greeted with enthusiasm—and romance.

YOUR HUNKA HUNKA BURNING LOVE

During the course of my long career as an astrologer, I've read for thousands of people and during that time I've developed some philosophies that are so true they reach right to the heart of the matter. There are a number of truisms I like to impart to my clients, most of whom are consulting me over love and its ills. The most important truth is deceptively simple, yet so comforting, so undeniable, so meaningful. Here it is: *Men! Can't live with 'em, can't move a couch without 'em.*

When confronted with this ineffable truth, most women smile serenely and nod. Great truths speak for themselves. An occasional female of the spunky variety will counter back to me: "I can move my couch," she crows. But I always have the last laugh. "Not onto a truck," I say. Then, spunky or not, she nods. My great truth has sunk in and we bond over our mutual womanhood.

Once I was chatting with a guy friend and, in a moment of weakness, I forgot to whom I was talking. I shared my truism with him. I waited hopefully, expecting him to bow his head in shame (or flex his splendid biceps) and nod, accepting the inevitability of the truth I'd just uttered. But his comeback surprised me and changed my life.

"I don't move couches," he sneered, "I call movers."

GASP! The realization hit me like a ton of barbells. I have a phone line! I have the internet! I have a cel phone! I can call movers too!

So what was left but to rewrite my interpretation of the deepest truth ever told about love: *Men! Can't live with 'em....*

Okay, we agree that's a given, so what's the next step? Hie thee to a convent? Sometimes it seems like the only alternative. But for those of you who know you can't live with 'em but still want to try, here's some inside information that will help you cope with that hunka hunka burning love.

Your Aries Guy is single-minded where love is concerned. He comes to the relationship already madly in love—with himself! His approach is simply to recruit you as a member of his fan club. He comes first, second and third in all his plans and if you want to be with him, you'll have to be willing to do what he wants, agree with what he thinks, and let him take the lead.

Your fondest memories will be of the first date you shared, in which he wooed you so assertively, so determinedly with non-stop tales about the person he admires most—himself. It didn't even matter that your lips were clenched from just having had root canal because the only word he let you utter was "Umm...."

Most women complain that men sit on the couch in front of the television clutching the remote control and never relinquishing it. One would think that your Aries guy is just that sort of person, and in fact he is, except for the fact that he rarely has time to watch TV. He's too busy clutching the stick shift of his racing car, the poles of his skis, or a surfboard. This macho man is outdoorsy, athletic and action-oriented and he doesn't mind at all if you come along on his outings. Somebody has to have the manual dexterity to unwrap the bandages—and that's you!

He's self-centered, deeply involved with himself and his priorities involve activities that leave lesser men requiring round the clock medical care. So why do you love him? Because his inner child is not only alive and well, but a sweet and tender being who never stops marveling at the wonders of life. His outlook is often innocent and trusting. His smile is enough to send shivers down your spine. And he's your only chance to feel as Scarlett O'Hara did when Rhett swept her up those stairs for a night of uncontrollable passion.

Your Taurus Guy is wealthy beyond belief. God knows *you* can't believe it—you see no sign he has a dime because he refuses to spend any of it. This is a man who knows for sure that a penny saved is a penny earned, because he's saved every cent he's ever earned. All those home cooked dinners at your house that he appreciates so much? They combine his two favorite pursuits—eating good food someone else pays for.

It's nice to be with someone very sensual. Other people have televisions, computers and stereos for entertainment. Your Taurus guy is too smart for them. Why does he need gadgets when letting you rub his feet by candlelight is so much more romantic? Yes, those rumors of marathon lovemaking sessions are true. What else can you do after dark when he's too cheap to spring for electricity?

Your Taurus guy is cheap, slow and stubborn, so why do you love him? He's stable—this is the one guy in the Zodiac who can make a commitment at age three and still be there at ninety-three. He loves to make love and will keep at it until you're really, really satisfied. And he doesn't mind if you're a bit overweight. Skinny women are too hard to lasso from the confines of an armchair. Plus you know that there'll be plenty of money in your old age—not that you'll be allowed to spend it, but maybe someday you can get his power of attorney after he's senile.

Your Gemini Guy is quite a talker. Perhaps that's why you're currently huddled in the bathroom trying to read this article while he stands outside the door chattering. Yes, that tape you made of yourself saying "Uh-huh, yes dear, and hahaha, that's a good one," was necessary and you need not feel guilty.

This is a man who is flexible, up to the moment and intellectually aware. He'd never bore you with the same old sentiments or insist you remain in a rut. He didn't do that with any of his five other wives, and he isn't doing it to you. He does like to keep up with current events, and the droning of his voice as he reads the newspaper aloud is an invaluable aid when you want to make that jump to alpha waves in meditation.

This guy is quite a traveler. Yes, he did leave his last wife when he met you on his honeymoon, but that was a freak occurrence. It's fun to go on all those trips, and that tracking app you secretly installed on his phone takes away a lot of the stress of wondering if he will reappear after a day at the dog track.

Your Gemini guy is a non-stop talker, he has a roving eye, and he sometimes gets bored in the middle of lovemaking, so why do you love him? He's smart. It's nice to be with a man who has ideas of his own, and he has a way with words that keeps you laughing. His natural intellectual curiosity keeps you surrounded by people who are interesting, and your life is never dull. He's willing to try pretty much anything, and he never complains about coming home to find your pals there.

Your Cancer Guy is capable of deep tenderness and complete devotion. If not for his mother, perhaps he'd lavish some of those sentiments on you. At least you know where he is—sitting in a rocker next to mom while you get a much-needed cardio workout hauling that hundred-pound bag of fertilizer from the car. This is a sensitive guy, who's not afraid to cry or show his emotions. That's probably because the only emotions to which he's sensitive are his own. When it comes to your feelings, he's as clueless as an Aries.

It's nice to be with a man who's even more sentimental than you are. It's endless hours of good fun to pore over his grammar school scrapbooks. Who could get enough of that sort of activity? Plus, since he saves absolutely everything, you know that whatever you might need—it's still right there in the attic. It's comforting for the children to visit all dad's old toys, even if they're not allowed to touch them.

Family security is always his number one priority and it's hard not to admire a man who keeps up with even his most distant cousins. It's not so bad having them camped out in the garage and once their still is repaired and they return home, you'll miss them—badly. Look at all the work he did building that extra bedroom with spa onto the house. If you ask really nicely, perhaps your mother-in-law will let you try it.

Your Cancer guy is awash in his own emotional turmoil, in love with his mother, and an ice cream addict, so why do you love him? He's a guy with whom you can build a family, he loves children and knows how to snuggle when the lights go out. If you're sick, he'll take care of you, and when you're old, he'll remain loyal. He has decades of experience loving an old hag, so you know he won't leave you when you wrinkle.

Your Leo Guy is the most splendid fellow on earth—just ask him. Go ahead and lie naked on the bed and say in your most sultry voice, "Someone's burning with sexiness tonight." He'll look away from the mirror long enough to beam and say "Thanks for noticing." He's hard to resist with all that thick, luxurious hair. It's remarkable how it grows all the way around his bald spot, across his neck, down his back, right to the bottoms of his feet! He's as furry as your cat, without the bother of a litter box.

This guy knows how to live the good life and he expects you to look as good as he does. It's fun to receive all those luxurious presents. Who else has chains that look like they were recovered from a sunken treasure ship? Yes, jewelry like that is heavy, but he'll hire a personal trainer to teach you to hold your head erect. If you can manage to do the same with your cleavage and posterior, so much the better. Being a glamour girl is the right approach with this mate. His motto is there is no such thing as too much make up, too much jewelry, or too much pleasure.

In fact, the words too and much do not pair in his vocabulary. More is simply better. Nobody is better at maxing out a credit card, and if they're yours, so what. Before he came along did you really know how many ways caviar can be eaten, how many places diamonds can be worn, and how many outfits a person really needs?

Your Leo guy is vain, a spendthrift and his taste is excessive, so why do you love him? He's gorgeous, first of all, and he constantly works at remaining attractive. Other guys sit around swilling beer in tacky undershirts. He sits swilling champagne in a silk dressing gown. He loves elegance, makes you feel like the most beautiful woman on earth and has a generous spirit as big as the sky. It's a larger than life existence with this guy, so why not enjoy it!

Your Virgo Guy is neat, precise and practical, and once he knows you a little longer, he'll probably stop making love wearing protective hospital gloves. You have to admire the way he organizes everything in the house. Who knew underwear could be alphabetized? A lot of novice astrologers say that Virgos have to have everything perfect but your guy is too smart for them. He's made it perfectly clear that no matter how you try, you'll never get it quite right, and he accepts you for the useless, flawed being you are. And once you come to realize he's a saint, things will go much more smoothly.

He is modest, cautious, and health conscious. It's inspiring to be with a man who rises well before the chickens, and begins his daily workout after cheerfully consuming a tasteless granola bar. But don't worry, dear, that guilt management workshop will help you deal with the feelings of inadequacy he inspires. Life really makes more sense when you look inside his closet. There in some precise order, comprehensible only to him, are arranged a dozen pair of identical, ultra conservative khaki pants and neutral button-down shirts. Yes, he *is* still a boy scout!

Your Virgo Guy is picky, persnickety and has to have everything done in his own perfect way, so why do you love him? This is a guy who never bounces a check, can change a tire without cursing or getting a smudge on him, is an excellent cook, and who will help you work through any crisis in your life, and have you sorted out without blinking an eye. He is selfless and giving and so skilled in many areas that you feel like you're on constant vacation. And because he's such a perfectionist, he will try, try again in bed until you are his happy, smiling love slave.

Your Libra Guy is a real ladies' man. He just loves women, and you shouldn't be jealous of his seventeen female best friends; he's probably been linked romantically with only sixteen of them. It's fun to be involved with a guy who's more romantic than you are, one who actually enjoys shopping with you for dainties and lipstick, and as long as he doesn't try them on, you're probably okay.

Most guys want to spend their time watching sporting events, belching, scratching and crawling under cars. Until he came along, you thought men were some sort of primitive sub-species. This guy wants to spend time dancing, attending cultural events, and crawling into your heart. So what if he talks constantly about the million women he sees. At least you know he has outside interests. He makes it perfectly clear that he wants a relationship, and the fact that he has said that to nearly every woman in town shouldn't be such a drawback. It's proof he's consistent.

He's a great companion, but is a guy really supposed to ooze charm instead of sweat? It's fun to engage this mate in an argument. Conflicts make him uncomfortable, and you can win while he's pretending to practice his cha-cha. Yes, he does make you feel a bit like a clod, but is it your fault that he's daintier than you are?

Your Libra guy is a woman chaser, he doesn't have a macho bone in his body, and he smells better than you do, so why do you love him? He is the heart and soul of romance, and he restores your spirit of magic. He makes you feel that love is alive and well and something you can enjoy again. He inspires you to buy new clothes, he leads you on a whirlwind of good fun, and no romantic sentiment is too gooey for him to share.

Your Scorpio Guy isn't really that secretive. He just refuses to let you in on what he's thinking, feeling, or doing. Except for that, he's an open book. Don't assume those rumors that he's an alien are true; there are good reasons why no record of his past exists—he doesn't want "them" to have access to his private life.

This guy has one hobby—sex—but don't worry—it really *is* safe to have that many orgasms a day, and no it doesn't make you a nympho—just a lucky girl. You can confirm this fact with any of his past lovers, once you get the CIA to locate them. It's nice to be with someone who's a comfy homebody; just insist that he unchain you from the bed long enough to get some laundry done.

There's something comforting about sharing all your secrets with him. You can look into his eyes and tell him all the shocking things you'd never dared reveal before. And it's okay to do so because chances are he will never use them against you except when he's really, really angry. At least he is capable of great emotional depth, and that's why he's so adept at understanding your feelings. Who else has manipulated you with such finesse?

Your Scorpio guy is a secretive, bossy sex addict who always has to rule the roost, so why do you love him? The sex addict part alone is enough to sell him, but he's also intensely passionate, emotionally liberating, and you feel as though your connection with him will last a lifetime—at least. Loving him is like flying without a net, and it's intoxicatingly exhilarating.

Your Sagittarius Guy loves dogs and horses and is most at home when in the company of animals. That's because his furry friends don't mind the fact that he owns only one pair of raggedy jeans and two torn T-shirts. Like Peter Pan, he's a playful sprite who enjoys a frolicking good time. This is one guy who will never expect you to put him through medical school; doctors actually have to work for a living.

Thankfully, his prejudice about signing onto a lifetime of career complications doesn't extend to you. He is ready, willing, and enthusiastic about offering you all the kudos you need while building your own career. Go ahead and work those long hours; this is a liberated guy who won't feel demeaned by your decision to support him. He's also willing to compromise about your living situation. He was perfectly content camping out on his buddies' couches till you came along. He doesn't need that big place you work so hard to afford, but considerately, he will live there with you. Other men might resent being put on an allowance, but he doesn't mind at all, as long as it's enough to cover the stable bills for his horses.

Your Sagittarius guy is a boy who never grows up, he rarely makes a dime and bathes only on demand, so why do you love him? His point of view is irresistibly honest, he sees the important truths of life and is unspoiled, genuine, and a fun-loving good time. Because he's so complacent and accepting of life, chances are he has a shot of bypassing the heart attack years and actually being around to share your old age.

Your Capricorn Guy looks, acts, and seems like a banker, whether he is or not. Ultra-conservative, this workaholic has only one priority; too bad it's never you. Don't worry that you have to contact his secretary to make an appointment for a date. His mother and children have to do the same thing. Working is his reason for living, his favorite pastime and his full-time preoccupation. This is one guy you may never see out of his three-piece suit.

This fellow has strong, traditional values. He believes in the sanctity of the family, and plans to establish one of his own—just as soon as he can hire a suitable bride. Everything about him is so traditional that his taste is so long out of style he may actually be fashionable again. He certainly doesn't expect you to indulge in the whims of fashion. He wears the same clothes until they are so worn out they fall off his body and so should you. Don't worry—he will be too busy working to notice that you're naked.

Money and financial security are very important to this mate. After all, he has absolutely no vices and no thrill-seeking tendencies, so chances are he will outlive his entire generation. Surviving that long requires a nest egg. There's no chance that you will one day be able to wrest from him his fortune. He'll outlive even you. Not that he'll retire, but he'll outlive you.

Your Capricorn Guy is a penny-pinching, competitive workaholic who has no need of a personal life, so why do you love him? He's ambitious, loyal, and you can pretty well assume he won't cheat on you, except with a calculator. He is witty and can keep you laughing. He's a stand up guy you can trust to remain that way. And he's a hard worker, so when he takes time off for your annual conjugal tryst, he will try to please you.

Your Aquarius Guy has a personality that's so quirky you prepare for your dates by reading Jane Goodall's groundbreaking research on apes. He may not be Simian, but you can't quite determine what species he is. Unquestionably brilliant, he has points of view that are so outrageous they have no relevance to life anywhere on this planet. He doesn't mind being off center; it's fun for him to challenge the thinking of the people around him with his shocking remarks. But honey, don't feel badly. Your great aunt Alice had the heart condition long before you introduced him at that ill-fated family gathering.

This guy loves technology, and he can do anything with electrical gadgets. Perhaps you can't fathom why he's interconnected his computer, the fridge, and your vibrator, but he has a plan, and you should respect him for it. It's interesting to live in his absent-minded professor-like world. It's abundantly clear that he's forgotten more than you ever knew. Never mind that you don't want to know that stuff, it's still an accomplishment.

This mate loves to befriend the whole world. Those people around him may look like a raggedy collection of reprobates, felons, and terrorists to you, but to him they're just the guys. Yes, it's true that you've been dating for twelve years and he still introduces you as his casual friend *whatsername*, but that's just his boyish charm. He understands gadgets intimately, but inexplicably, he can't hear your biological clock ticking?

Your Aquarius guy is distant, detached and seems to hail from a planet in another galaxy, so why do you love him? He's smart, really very smart, and it's always amusing to hear his outrageous ideas. Perhaps one day he really will save the world. It's nice to be with someone who absolutely won't make a commitment, because then you don't have to deal with your own fear of closeness. This is a man who dances to his own drummer, and if you can understand each other, it's fun to be surprised every day of your life by the clever things he says.

Your Pisces Guy is more sensitive than a twelve-year-old virgin. He doesn't mind crying, and he isn't ashamed to let you see his tears. That box of cereal was once a living organism and it deserves to be loved, not just eaten. He's willing to listen to your problems, and will always lend you a shoulder to lean on. Yes, he will too, once he's finished listening to the problems of every one else on the planet, all of whom have targeted him for their dumping ground.

It's nice to be with someone who has artistic sensibilities.

It's unfair of you to ask him to go out to work. Watching endless hours of television reruns of *The Brady Bunch* is an important cultural pursuit. He supports you in your career goals, doesn't he? How can you be so insensitive where his choices are concerned? This is a man with *feelings*—and everything has to be balanced for him to function properly. Chances are there will be a day or two in the next decade when he absolutely does feel balanced, so in the meantime, cut him some slack, will you?

You never have to feel weak or ashamed of your irrational emotions with this mate. There is nothing outrageous that you could feel to which he hasn't already succumbed. No matter how miserable, how depressed, how slobby you get in your chocolate-stained bathrobe, he will still accept and love you. Unfortunately he has the same standards for everyone else. Just take a number and wait in the den along with the rest of the world.

Your Pisces guy is a distracted, whiney, emotional wreck, so why do you love him? He is tender and loving, and although he's that way to everyone, you know that his feelings for you are truly unique. He is a special person who has deep feelings, and he really pulls hard for the underdog. You never have to feel that you're going to be overwhelmed by a macho man. In fact, if you want to, you can probably overwhelm him!

YOUR LADY LOVE

Some years back I received a humorous e-mail that proved to be very telling. It contained an anecdote about a fictional couple, Roger and Elaine. They were driving in the car when Elaine mentioned that they'd been seeing each other for six months. That prompted Roger to think that yes, it had been six months, because that was about the time he had last taken his car to that thieving weisel, the mechanic. As Roger went over the situation with the car in his mind, Elaine fretted silently about the relationship and Roger's reaction to her statement.

What did his silence mean? Had her comments put Roger ill at ease? Was he angry at her? Did he think she was being too pushy, that she was asking for a commitment? What was Roger thinking? Elaine couldn't let the matter go. She began to get teary, but hastily controlled herself. It must be something serious, something ominous, and perhaps their relationship was not on shaky ground.

Roger knew something was up, but he didn't know what. He was pretty sure he hadn't missed one of Elaine's remarks but it seemed like he had. What did it all mean? Something must have flown over his head—oh well, he would survive. Roger drove Elaine home and she promptly put in an emergency call to her girlfriend so they could obsess together over the situation. Roger went home and promptly fell into a sound sleep.

Roger and Elaine were not on the same page. But how could they be? Men and women love each other, they share lives and marry, but so often you guys regard us as creatures more exotic and incomprehensible than the ones at the zoo. Although women are referred to as the weaker sex, you guys live in terror of us, wondering what you dare say, think and feel, and knowing that women are simply beyond your comprehension.

When Henry Higgins complained, "Why can't a woman be more like a man," he echoed sentiments shared by all mankind. You men say what you mean and if someone doesn't understand what you're saying, you rarely weep, whine or sneer, "Well if you don't know, I'm not telling you." When someone gives you a present, you say, "Wow what a nifty set of screwdrivers." You don't tear up and wail, "Screwdrivers? Is that your idea of something personal?" Or, "So you think my fingers are too fat and I need to screwdrive some weight off?"

You're a *guy*! Of course you'd never think to behave that way. If something upsets you, you roll with the punches, you go with the flow, you smash a hole in the wall with your fists. Isn't that the sane way to live?

Being a woman myself, I am not quite on your side, but I do have sympathy for you, so here are some bits of information that could help you win the battle of the sexes.

Your Aries Gal challenges that complaint made above by Henry Higgins. She's a lot like a guy, and is one tough broad. She can change her own oil, race go-karts faster than a testosterone-poisoned teen, and if you annoy her, she isn't shy about applying those useful techniques taught in her karate class. This is a woman who knows what she wants and who isn't afraid to say so. If you get stuck with her on a desert island, she will have you following her plans and obeying her orders. She can't help it—this is not one of those females who regards herself as a delicate flower.

This mate is someone who has her own agenda and if you want to be in her life, don't expect her to join your team. Expect to join hers. She enjoys good conversation, as long as she's at the center of it, and as long as you don't expect her to listen to your tales of woe. She was not put on this earth to coddle you or anyone else. If you get sick, she's just as likely to sneer and say, "Get up off your lazy butt," as she is to squeeze you an orange.

Your Aries Gal is self-centered, macho beyond belief and you're a little afraid of coming up against her in a dark alley.

So why do you love her? She's lots of fun, she loves sports and outdoors activities, and she's a challenge in any competition. It's almost like dating a guy pal instead of a gal pal. And she almost never dissolves in tears at incomprehensible moments.

Your Taurus Gal is sexy and indolent. She loves to recline on the couch and munch on gourmet treats. If ever there was a mate for whom a gladiator kneeled and peeled a grape, it's this pleasure-loving woman. She seems to have no agenda at all, and she's relaxed and relaxing to be around. Plus there's the money. You've heard amazing rumors about all the money she has in the bank, and even if you never see a dime of it (don't worry, you won't) it's comforting to be involved with a woman who could buy and sell you. She doesn't buy much, and chances are she won't sell you as long as you keep popping those bon bons into her mouth.

This mate loves to be wined and dined, and as long as you're paying, she's happy to share the most ultra-deluxe meals with you. Does it seem that we're spending a lot of time talking about food? The way to her heart is definitely through her stomach. And despite her own wealth, this lady appreciates a gentleman caller with his own sizable bank balance. She is not the sort to dally with a gigolo—well not for more than an hour a day, that is. Yes, she does love to make love. After all, she's usually lying down anyway, so why not include some recreation with that posture?

Your Taurus Gal is lazy, probably a bit overweight, and she never lavishes a cent of her fortune on you, so why do you love her? She's sensual, and she reminds you of those old paintings of women reclining on a divan surrounded by angels and baskets of fruit. She is very womanly and she makes you feel even more masculine by contrast. And you know that once she gives you her heart, it's yours forever.

Your Gemini Gal is a multi-tasker. Who knew a woman could keep up a running monologue while reading a book and watching the television? She always has something to say and no, that's not why you bought those earmuffs and the radio headset. It's inspiring to be with someone who is so well-informed. How would you know every detail of your neighbor's lives without her? Who else would tell you the blow by blow of Grandma's hysterectomy?

The great thing about this woman is her many interests. Okay she has the attention span of a gnat, but at least you get to try new things. It's not as upsetting as one might think to hear about all the men to whom she was engaged, since after all, most of those involvements lasted only as long as a talk show. You used to feel like a very smart guy until she came along. She can fill in all the blanks of the crossword puzzle, use ten-dollar words, and feel at home reading any gibberish-filled book.

She's ditsy, uncommitted and talks nonstop—so why do you love her? She's smart and interesting. And she gives you your space. Other women are determined to rope you in and tie you down. This mate is too busy enjoying life and other people to worry about whether or not you'll be around tomorrow. It keeps you on your toes!

Your Cancer Gal is sentimental about everything. No, that's not just a pile of clutter in every corner—they are treasures and if you say one more word, she'll be crying again, and we all know whose fault it will be. This is one sensitive woman, and weeping seems to be her favorite pastime. C'mon buddy, everybody needs a hobby. In fact, she's a one-woman circus with a new emotion every twenty seconds. You just never know what you're going to come home to. A werewolf has less scary moods.

This mate loves children, and having a family is her main priority. Other people discuss the weather on a first date; she had you choosing names for the children. It's not hard to know what sort of mother she will be, because she is so attached to her own mother that you have to drag the old biddy along wherever you go. It's sweet to know that you will never have to be alone—her mother will be right there between the two of you until you finally give up and drop dead.

Your Cancer Gal is an emotional wreck, she's clingy, and she has never thrown away a single thing in her entire life. Her mother will always be more important to her than you are—so why do you love her? She's sweet and tender and nurturing and you know she will always take care of you. She loves to snuggle and she really cares about your welfare. Nobody is a better mom or better able to create a happy home.

Your Leo Gal is a natural beauty queen, and the sooner you can afford to buy her that diamond-encrusted tiara, the higher the esteem in which she will hold you. Other women go to ruin; she goes to the gym and the mall. Some men come home and listen to their wives complain they didn't know what to make for dinner. This will never be your problem. Your mate always knows what to make—reservations—and she has no reservations about telling you so. If you wanted a Suzy homemaker type, you should have chosen a Cancer.

Leo is the sign of royalty, so remain prepared to pay court. She is always supposed to be the center of attention, and you must always remain her loyal servant. Of course that doesn't mean she won't also need a maid, a chauffeur, and a cook. Living the good life is the Leo raison d'être, and you might as well surrender. This is not a woman who wants to spend time in cutoff jeans or gardening gloves. And if you have some sort of tuxedo allergy, better call it quits right now.

Your Leo Gal is a vain spendthrift who wants to party till dawn every night of the year. She needs a closet the size of a football field and her fingernails are so long she's virtually unable to do so much as scratch her own butt—not that she would ever stoop to such a tacky gesture. So why do you love her? She's gorgeous and sexy, and you're the envy of all the guys in your circle because she's yours. She's sunny and warm hearted, and she makes you feel good about being you. Life is fun in her company, and you enjoy yourself more when you're with her than when you're alone.

Your Virgo Gal is so pristine and organized that she makes you feel like a big, hairy, useless slob. It's comforting to know that she loves you anyway, despite all the many shortcomings you never realized you had until you met her. In fact, she's kind enough to help you work through your problems, and in short order, she will have you feeling organized and safe again. It's sort of like joining the army but a lot more pleasant. That's the benefit of being in love with a woman who is just like Mary Poppins—practically perfect in every way.

She has her schedule to follow, but don't worry, she will give you an appointment for sex as soon as you've done your chores. She's not the sort of woman who wants to be tossed onto the kitchen table. She can't make love to the sound of stuff dripping onto the floor. This is a woman who has a lot of requirements and rules about everything—that's why she's known as picky.

Your Virgo Gal is an order freak, she's never been wrong in your entire relationship (meaning you've never been right), and she sees germs in places other people don't even know are there, so why do you love her? She puts your needs ahead of her own, she goes out of her way to make you happy, and she keeps your world humming. Other people see her as a girl scout but to you she's a perfect, passionate goddess.

Your Libra Gal is the social butterfly of all time, but you don't really mind lining up to have a conversation with her—everyone else does it. It's all the black tie events, the concerts, the ballroom dancing lessons. She seems to live her entire life by candlelight and you wonder if your eyes will ever adjust to sunshine again. Other women do inhabit the real world occasionally, but this woman seems to float through a fog of violin music.

She's so sweet, and seems to expect so much of you that you don't really mind trying so hard to please her, even if you do suspect that all this meaningless romance will kill you. Yes, you've maxed out your credit card on the endless bouquets of flowers she seems to expect, and somewhere an activist group is forming to save endangered posies from groves denuded at your behest. But that's love isn't it? There are so many other guys seeking her company that you have to give it your all.

Your Libra gal lives in a world too rarified for a real guy like yourself, she's surrounded by people too good for you, and looks aghast if you should so much as belch, so why do you love her? She's sweet and pretty, and you feel that she changes your life for the better, gives you some class, and makes you feel that the world is indeed a pretty place.

Your Scorpio Gal is a woman, not a girl. In fact, you're a little scared of her because you feel that you could easily become her love slave, and you're pretty sure she held onto that collar after Rover passed on. She unleashes a mighty flood of passion in your direction, and you want to make sure you remain unleashed as well. This is a woman who knows what she wants, but she only reveals to you as much as she wants you to know. You can't help wondering about what she's not telling you, but hey, since most women talk too much about stuff you never wanted to know, her secretiveness is almost a pleasure—almost. On the days when you're nearly positive that she's not plotting your demise, you don't prod her.

This mate inspires you to reach deep inside yourself and to reveal those old secrets you never told anyone else. She seems pretty trustworthy, and since you see no sign she's keeping a dossier on you, it's nice to share more intimacy than you have in the past. And of course, there's the sex. Who knew you'd ever find a woman who wanted more sex than you do? Of course it doesn't make you a wimp when you sigh, cross your aching legs and plead, "Not tonight dear, I have a headache." You survived the military, didn't you, and she's only slightly more exacting than that.

Your Scorpio gal is an intense, sexually demanding dominatrix, so why do you love her? Who can go wrong with an intense, sexually demanding dominatrix?

Your Sagittarius Gal is a regular Daisy Mae Clampett. She's sweet and outdoorsy, and you can probably hose her down before you introduce her to your parents. They'll appreciate the fact that she's honest and unspoiled, and even if she doesn't own a dress, know which fork to use, and calls the symphony a hoe-down, she's still your true love. The folks'll learn to accept that mangy, flea-bitten—er beloved—dog who goes everywhere she does. If you can sleep with it, they can at least set a place at the table for it.

It's nice to be with a woman who is unpretentious and uncomplicated, and some day you can build a new room out of all the stacked up pizza boxes. She's willing to compromise—just let her know which fast food place you prefer and she'll grab dinner for both of you. So what if your last girlfriend laughed at your fishing equipment, refused to go to sporting events, and made you bathe daily. This girl has her own tent, and will teach you a thing or two about camping. And if you're afraid of big bugs, don't worry. She'll just catch them and set them free outdoors.

Your Sagittarius gal is not terribly feminine, she regards your mother as someone from an alien culture, and she has never been on time a day in her life, so why do you love her? She's warm and friendly, rarely makes demands on you, supports you in everything you do, and she has interesting ideas about how to live a happy, uncomplicated life. Plus she has all that sporting equipment.

Your Capricorn Gal is a good person to know. She shows you what you might have achieved if you weren't such a lazy, sniveling loser. Yes, she's too busy to waste time dating, and demands to see your family tree and your financial statement before agreeing to so much as a pre-date phone call, but at least you know where you stand—just like the other applicants in her life. If you manage to land her as a wife, you can rely on her to keep the home in order (she hires great people), the children well cared for (she hires great people) and the marriage long lasting—assuming you don't mess things up on the fifteen minutes per day you see her, the marriage could last your whole life.

This is a no-nonsense woman and she's not interested in seduction or in frivolity. So what if the word lingerie isn't in her vocabulary. It's not really in yours either, is it? It's nice to be with someone who decides she needs sex, calls you on the phone, and asks if you can spare some time at lunch. You can cuddle with your guy pals over beers after work. You understand what it's like to be building a killer career, amassing a fortune, and being a huge success. If only you could manage to do those things yourself, you wouldn't feel so inferior to her.

Your Capricorn gal is a strict, demanding, workaholic who is more successful than you are, so why do you love her?

An overachiever since birth, she can spring you from jail if you make a misstep, introduce you to the right people, or bankroll your internet business. Her values are solid and traditional, and she doesn't have time to notice if you're spending too much time with the guys.

Your Aquarius Gal wants you to be her friend. You don't mind that at all, but you'd sure like to know if she also wants you for a lover or a husband, but unfortunately she's never too clear in that regard. She has so many people in her life—and frankly they all seem so peculiar—that you are basically clueless about your relationship with her. That's ok, she'd be clueless too, except she's too busy saving the world to worry about something as frivolous as romance.

It's nice to be with a woman who is smarter than you are, and it's also nice finally to learn how to program your DVR, but what does it all really mean? She sends you ten e-mails a day, but you feel a little let down when each one contains jokes about stupid things men do. You know you're stupid, but hey does she have to remind you of it constantly? When she said she was going to take care of your cookies, you thought hey, she's going to come over in an apron and bake a treat, and that means she cares, but all she did was fiddle with the files on your computer.

Your Aquarius gal is impossible to understand, never acts demure or romantic, and makes you feel inept around anything electric, so why do you love her? She's smart and interesting, she cares about the rest of the world, and she never falls apart like silly women do. She's capable and competent, and she makes you feel glad you know her, even if you don't know what you're doing together.

Your Pisces Gal is as tender as a well-aged piece of prime rib, though don't you let her hear you comparing her to a piece of meat. You know how Paul Newman fared when his Pisces wife heard him compare her to steak! This is a sensitive and emotional woman, and no, you will never, ever understand her. What you can do is offer her your hankie when she begins weeping uncontrollably. She has the weight of the world on her shoulders and she can't help feeling the pain of just about everyone and everything, and that includes you. In fact she feels your pain more deeply than you do, but don't let her make you feel like a clod for not responding with tears to your own situation. She'll cry for you.

Don't expect to monopolize her time. She loves you but doesn't like to be hemmed in. She has too many people who want to share their tales of woe with her, and the word *no* is seldom in her vocabulary. Likewise don't be mad when she can't balance the checkbook—or can't even find it. This woman isn't practical—she has you for those mundane tasks. She is ethereal, an angel who came to fill your life with music (and wayward derelicts in need of some TLC), so be appreciative.

Your Pisces gal is too busy feeling ever to think, she has never been able to explain a single decision she's ever made, nor has she been on time once in thirty years. So why do you love her? She makes you feel big and strong, and you can't help wanting to protect her from everything out there in the cold, cruel world. She reminds you of what's good about life, and what's sweet in heaven, and even though you know you have no clue about what makes her tick, you enjoy the music that plays in your heart whenever you think of her cute, helpless ways.

5
RECREATION

Recreation isn't optional. It's a necessity. Some of us are more naturally pleasure oriented, and some are more focused, moment after moment, on achievement. No matter how strongly you need a long to-do list or how readily you check out of the world to do something fun, you need those moments in life that restore your spirits, bring a little fun, and allow you to decompress. Without recreation, it would be hard to be the best version of yourself the rest of the time.

In *Finding Your Bliss*, I address this very idea. What do you need to do in order to become centered and ready to tackle life's chores again? What is it that makes you happy and brings that peaceful smile to your lips? Seek your bliss, for it's your path to more well-developed self-expression.

In *Hot Fun in the Summertime*, I took a poll of friends near and far, and they shared favorite summer pursuits. Each sign is represented by friends who offer their unique sign-appropriate take on a fun way to enjoy the summer. Life is sweetest when it's easy and slow, and a summer vacation brings the sweetness to the forefront.

Not every vacation involves a suitcase, as I wryly recount in some tales of my own travel misadventures. Why go anywhere when you can have fun right in your own back yard? *The Staycation* offers sign-based tips on how to mount your own fabulous vacation at home.

FINDING YOUR BLISS

The other day my daughter gave me a very nice compliment. She said that nobody stopped to smell the flowers more than I do. Considering the fact that I'm one of those picky, hard-working Virgos, it's nice to be able to admit that my motto will never be all work and no play. I'm good at pleasure—I admit it. Something as simple as driving by a nicely landscaped flower bed, or feeling a breeze blow, or chopping a carrot can make me feel that life is wonderful, and I'm glad to be a part of it. Just as babies need love, tenderness and to be held, adults need pleasure. We all need something that makes us feel glad to be alive.

Recently a client came to me for a reading. She had been crying for days and had to take a leave of absence from not one but two jobs. She felt she had lost all sight of her spiritual center and was deep in the middle of a serious collapse. I'm used to working with people who are mired in very serious situations—in fact that's the norm. But in this case, the solution was deceptively simple. My client needed more fun. I felt a little like a quack saying go out, have some fun, and call me in the morning, but that was what she really needed. And despite the fact that she admitted joie de vivre had long ago lapsed in her life, the client found it very hard to see that a little fun could make so much difference.

Fun and pleasure are very important aspects of life. They are the way we regain our balance, rediscover our center, and most of all they're what keep us happy and willing to endure the travails of daily life that can be so stressful, trying or depressing. I'm not suggesting that it's a positive goal to toss responsibilities to the wind and embark on a spree of constant, wanton behavior. I'm just saying that pure pleasure is as necessary to life as food, water and air. And I'm saying that the better attuned you are to pleasure in all its forms, the more likely you are to have a happy life.

What do you need in the form of pleasure? Check out your sun sign for some insights into the ways you seek joie de vivre.

ARIES: Like everything else in your life, you like your pleasure hot, fast and exciting. Genteel, quiet moments are good for everyone else, but you want to feel your pulse race, your heart pound and your blood pressure elevate. If you find yourself so buried in work or other responsibilities that you can't take time for fun, you feel that some part of your nature is being denied. You need thrills and chills, and you need them on a regular basis, and when you don't have them, you tend to generate mini dramas at work or in your personal life in order to replace the excitement that's missing. Playing sports is one way you seek relief, and nothing is more thrilling than racing your car, speeding along on a motor cycle, or breaking the waves in a motor boat—speed being the operative word. As you get going, you generate those magical chemicals in your brain called endorphins, and enjoy the natural high that speed and excitement produce. Pleasure for you is all about getting in touch with the thrill of being alive—and your way of doing that is by enjoying the death-defying stunts that make lesser souls shudder.

TAURUS: Yours is definitely the sign of pleasure, and you are very often a hedonist par excellence. Pleasure is the undercurrent of your life and in some way or other an aspect of everything you do. You're a hard worker, known for your stamina, but you understand the good feelings of satisfaction that working hard provides—and of course you enjoy making money because of all the pleasure money can bring into your life. Even if you've worked killer hours at very hard labor, and are ready to collapse by the end of the day, you still have the capacity for pleasure. You eat your dinner and you savor every bite—it's just your nature to notice the food you eat and to enjoy it, whether it's something simple at home or a gourmet meal at a top restaurant. Physical pleasures come very naturally to you and those are some of the ways you restore your spirits—good food, the pleasure of sex, touching and being touched—you understand what it is to live in a body and to savor that experience. You're an earthy person, and that's why you're so good at pleasure. A simple walk through a garden can restore your spirits, even if you're very blue or dealing with a crisis. It's the miracles of life in all its diversity that drive you forward, that comfort and heal you, and nurture your body and your soul. And because you find your thrills in ways small as well as large, you're seldom at a deficit for pleasure, and that's one reason why you're usually calm and complacent.

GEMINI: Your overriding need is for intellectual stimulation. In many ways your life can be completely austere, and you will feel no sense of lack. You can live in a small room with nothing more than an easy chair and a television, dine nightly on pedestrian fare, and still feel content with your life as long as you have something to read, interesting people to talk with, and ideas to explore. On the other hand, you could be transported to luxury surroundings, with an army of mutes to wait on you, and deluxe foods to eat, and you'd be totally miserable if there were no books, no television and no conversation. You need a constant sense of movement, and the influx of ideas provides you with that antidote to the stasis that you find so mind numbing. If you have a job that is too routine but still demands your attention, you feel as though you're in a straight jacket, and you need to do something like running as a way of regaining that sense of flow. A duller, more routine job is better because it gives your mind free rein to daydream. Often you will travel as a way of focusing on fun. You're out in the world, experiencing new things, and your mind thrives on the constant changes and newness. So for you, joie de vivre is all about staying awake, staying involved, staying alive.

CANCER: As we've said many times before, you're a homebody and your family is the most important thing in the world to you. Even if you work yourself to death taking care of the people you love, there is no sense of a loss of pleasure, because for you, building a happy home is the greatest thrill you can have. You're an emotional person, and you tend to become flooded with emotions. When they're happy feelings, that's a good thing, but in the course of daily life, sometimes you feel overwhelmed by sentiments other than the happy and loving ones that are your stock and trade. When that happens, it's time to pamper yourself. You tend to use food as a treat, but being taken care of also feels good, and so getting a haircut, a manicure, a massage, or even talking to a sympathetic friend can provide the surge of pleasure you need. "Children are life renewing itself," as Melanie said in *Gone With The Wind,* and for you that's very true. Spending time outdoors at a playground hearing the happy squeals of playing children is enough to clear your head and your heart. Snuggling with a wriggling puppy or kitten is another warm feeling. For you, pleasure and warm emotions go hand in hand, and as long as you're doing something which literally makes you feel good, you're going to start feeling better.

LEO: You're another one of those signs for whom pleasure is a natural and normal part of life. You were not put on this earth to be a Puritan, and thankfully, you're completely aware of this fact. While you might sacrifice your own needs on behalf of someone you love, there's no way you will completely give up the good life—it's what you were born to live. Eating good food, living in a pretty environment, making love in satin sheets, and buying pretty trinkets, is the normal way to live, not some form of excess. You're in touch with the fact that this is the earth plane and here life is material—and the material realm can be pretty wonderful. That's just the way you like it. If you, like Madonna, are going to be a material girl (or guy) there's one necessary ingredient—money. If you find yourself lacking in ready cash, that certainly curtails your ability to live the good life, and it also tends to give you the mopes. Life is too fabulous, and there's too much pleasure out there ready and available for you to languish among the have nots. If that's the case, it's not the time to become a pleasure seeker. Lolling in front of the television is amusing but it won't help you now. Instead, you need to forget about the good life, get a good job, and then you can resume your normal, pleasure-filled life. If a lack of cash is a constant problem, and you feel yourself mired in an ongoing state of deprivation, there is a need to examine your life to see if you're giving shallow luxury too much importance. If so, you will need to build more depth into your life so that you can focus on what truly matters. Life, love, tenderness, and personal appreciation can't be bought and can provide cost-free pleasure when you learn to value them as you should.

VIRGO: Your nit-picky Virgo traits can be quite aggravating for other people. You can find flaws in everything, and an extreme need for perfection can lead to a lot of disappointments. In fact, it can put a serious crimp in your pleasure seeking activities because you can see what's wrong with that five-star meal, movie, or spot a loose button on that very expensive designer garment. Feeling that you're getting less than you should, even when you're treating yourself to the very best, is annoying. The reverse is also true, though, and it's one of your most special traits. You can see the tiniest details, and because of that your ability to find pleasure is magnified. You can get many thrills from the smallest of life's moments. You spot a dragon fly's odd shaped wings and smile; a flower with a tiny stripe catches your eye; food arranged nicely on the plate is worth savoring even before the morsel reaches your mouth. They say that God is in the details, and for you so is the pleasure. You do drive yourself too hard, and when you're overworked, you get cranky. That's the time when you need to stand back and decompress. You need to make that special dinner you love, devote time to that special hobby, soak in a bubble bath, or to let someone else look after you. And when you do that, and turn the full force of your detail-spotting ability toward the goal of discovering what there is to appreciate, you see how rich and filled with potential pleasure is every aspect of your world.

LIBRA: If social interactions are the stuff of pure pleasure, then your life is a veritable orgy of fun. There's no question that social activities are a very strong aspect of your life, but to you they're more like the air you need to breathe rather than any form of escapism. You're a people person, and you need contact to survive. Beauty and pleasure are important to you, and you try to make your life an oasis of happiness. If you lived a life that was all work and no cotillions, you'd surely wither and die. If the crush of a busy schedule starts to get to you, you will always take the time to get that much-needed personal contact, even if all you do is stop in at a favorite hangout so that you can spend time with friends on your way home from work. Pleasure comes in many forms to you, and it's always relaxing to shop for clothes, to go dancing, to stroll through an art museum, or to be around anything that's beautiful. Your strongest source of pleasure is romance. You need love or the possibility of love to keep you going. The nuts and bolts of life just aren't enough to make your spirit soar. It's romance, the sweet whispers of a new relationship, or the tenderness of a long-lasting one that remind you daily that being alive is all it's cracked up to be.

SCORPIO: Pleasure is a rather mild word where you're concerned. Although you can appreciate some of the finer things of life that are mellow, you, like Aries, also like to immerse yourself in thrills that are more truly thrilling. You understand the desire to be in situations where your blood is racing a bit too fast for your own good, and to live life on the edge. Speed and danger do sometimes appeal to you. And of course there's sex, but you consider that more like a holy fire of transcendence than something categorized as mere pleasure. The point is that you never do anything half way. In this life, you're an all or nothing person, and you don't want some dainty treat when instead you can have the thrill ride of a lifetime. Gusto is the word that applies to you, and in your life you have gusto for your work and for your fun. You are steady and stable, though, and sometimes you've been known to dig yourself into a rut. That's the point at which you have to take steps toward excitement in order to remind yourself who you truly are and what life can really be. Whether it's a trip to an amusement park with the kids, to the kinky sex toy store with your lover, or an attempt to join the Polar Bear club in darkest winter, you need to do something new to recapture your gusto.

SAGITTARIUS: Pleasure is something you understand very well, but not everyone's idea of pleasure equals your own. For example, the luxury-loving Leo way of life doesn't appeal to you at all. You don't want to eat gourmet food, dress up in designer clothes, and attend sparkling events. To you that sounds more like enslavement than pleasure. You have a mellow approach to life, and your need for pleasure is rather pagan. If it were possible, you might spend your entire life lolling around in a hammock, your trusty but smelly dog at your side. You like nature, and being out in the great outdoors, sharing it with friends or a pet, is the perfect way to live. If you could, you'd be a forest ranger, and that way work and pleasure would merge perfectly. Your need for outdoor activities is as strong as your need for food and water, and if you're involved in work that keeps you inside, you feel a sense of urgency at some point that drives you into whatever recreation appeals most to you. You like sports, but you don't care if your games are organized or more casual, like hiking through the woods. It's the call of the wild and purity of nature, yourself as an animal out in the wilderness, that you need in large enough doses to make your involvement with civilization bearable enough to continue.

CAPRICORN: You know that book of old sayings lying at the back of your bookshelf? Well, look up the adage *all work and no play,* and you will notice someone's picture right next to that phrase. No surprises here! The photo is of none other than yourself. You will also find your photo next to the *a job well done is its own reward* chapter. What you won't find is any mention of you in the fun is worthwhile section. Even when you have a hobby, it's more like a job. It's something you can work hard at and produce something worthwhile. If it relaxes you, that's a positive thing, and yes it can be qualified as pleasure, unless you give yourself deadlines and stresses about your hobby in addition to those you generate about your job. The problem is that other people tend to collapse when they drive themselves so hard that there's no pleasure in their lives; you thrive on it, because your work is also your pleasure. On the rare occasions when you feel blocked at work and that you can't take any more, you recognize the need for some recreation. So you add a room onto the house, reorganize the garage, polish all your shoes or your silver, and these activities, basically work of another sort, help you regain your center. If you've really gone over the top, and find yourself stressed and exhausted, you'll need to take the same approach to fun that you take to work. Remind yourself that you need to relax and plan your vacation accordingly: see movies, dine out, walk through nature and sniff a flower. Go home and have sex. If you make an entry on your calendar for all these activities, they will feel less like useless pursuits and you'll then accept your need to engage in them.

AQUARIUS: You are first and foremost an intellectual person, and you recognize your need to remain mentally stimulated. Many of your pleasures keep your mind active. You like your computer and can tinker happily for hours, video games enthrall you, and it's fun to hook up and program your various toys. There's a world of gadgets and you like them all. Friends are also so very important to you, and you couldn't imagine life without nice people to share it. Your life is your own and you don't follow the same path as anyone else, so you realize that what is fun to you may not be on anyone else's agenda. You are quite happy to spend endless hours chatting online with your pals around the world. To you that's a great source of pleasure. Your ability to focus is strong, and sometimes you find yourself immersed in a project which is so compelling that you can think of nothing else. It's a great thing to be able to concentrate so intensely, but sometimes you threaten to burn yourself out before you actually complete what you're doing. You need to turn your mind to other things in order to come back to the situation with a fresh approach. At that point, it's time for fun. You can call up some friends and go hang out together, or you're willing to try something new and different. As long as the idea is appealing, you're there. And once you get that little, much needed mental diversion, you're ready to get back to work.

PISCES: Feelings are your specialty, and because you have such well-honed emotional sensors, you can also feel pleasure quite acutely. So many things appeal to you that life can be quite sweet. You like socializing with friends, listening to or making music, experiencing art or movies, or even having a quiet drink at the corner saloon. Like me, you're good at pleasure, and you have a good sense of appreciation for life's finer moments. In fact, because you're so easily distracted, you find yourself involved in something you should be doing when something interesting and fun comes along, and because fun is so hard to resist, you're off in a flash having a good time and putting off till tomorrow something you were supposed to complete today. It's a rare Pisces who says nope, gotta keep working, instead of going with the flow and enjoying the temptation put in front of you. In a way it's a good thing, because to you life is an ongoing opportunity for pleasure, and your motto is carpe diem. When you get in a bad mood or find yourself surrounded by people who are sad or whose negative energy threatens to engulf you, you're often wise enough to know that this is the time to find some balance via pleasure. That's the time when ducking into a matinee for some escapist cinema is a healthy and wise choice. You know you can't do anything worthwhile when your emotional state is all frayed, so you use pleasure as the healing tool it's meant to be.

Pleasure isn't something frivolous or unnecessary. It's one of the many essential components of life here on earth. Each day should offer something of pleasure to us all. What fun will you accept into your own life today? Make it something special and you will feel that life has regained its sparkle.

HOT FUN IN THE SUMMERTIME

Something unusual happened this year in Los Angeles, something I don't recall occurring in any of the other years I've been here. We had an actual fall, followed by an actual winter. I'm an Easterner, an uneasily transplanted California girl. Before moving west, fall had traditionally been my favorite season, because I love the autumn leaves and blustery winds. Wearing a turtleneck and gloves by October never bothered me—I loved it. Brisk is beautiful. In California, there is none of that, and each year here I miss seeing the foliage and ask Eastern friends to report on the local color. To make matters worse, fall in Los Angeles is often peppered heavily with hot, dry, desert winds; in fact, it's the hottest time of the year. Summer is usually relatively cool until the end of August, followed by a hot fall and then suddenly it's Thanksgiving and you shake your head and say how did this happen. It's disorienting, like some weather-induced jet lag. It doesn't feel right, this a-seasonality, and nothing that we traditionally associate with seasons falls into place as it should. In fact, it can be in the 80's as the Thanksgiving turkey roasts. But this year we had a brisk, cool fall and a chilly, rainy winter. It was season appropriate, and now probably for the first time ever in the last two decades, I'm looking forward to summer. As Steinbeck was quoted in the movie, *Cannery Row*, life is spinning in greased grooves.

Looking forward is a process, which frankly, at my age, also comes with some rather nostalgic baggage—that of looking backward. My dad traveled a lot on business throughout my youth until he finally worked nearer home most of the time when I was in high school. He missed us and we missed him, and so our summers were spent on adventures, driving along with him as he conducted business on the road. My annoying little sister was packed into the back seat with me, her sweaty, floppy, sleeping limbs encroaching stickily on my personal space to the point where I'd sometimes take refuge on the floor of the car, undulating myself over the hump in the middle. There were no seatbelts in those days—and no air conditioning. Nobody was terrified that the unthinkable could happen, that you could crash and all be blasted to smithereens. Life was simpler and less worrisome—except if you were the older sister who didn't want to be leaned on. Ultimately, to make more room, my dad installed a wood platform in the back, extending the seating space all the way to the back of the front seat. That gave us more room for our books, games, and squabbles.

Despite arguments and constant (and justified) accusations of cheating at board games, we had so much fun on those trips, causing most people to marvel at my childhood, spent as it was at fairs, amusement parks, and pursuing whatever activities my parents could devise or stumble upon as we sped from state to state. We saw the Wisconsin Dells, a name I still remember, although I'm not absolutely certain it was an amusement park. We toured a cereal factory, something I loved, and perhaps why I still love factories to this day. Remarkably, after the tour we were served something I'd never before or since considered eating—vanilla ice cream topped with chocolate cereal—and it was fabulous. We visited friends in different states—once attending the wedding of an older guy on whom I had an early crush, and who wrote in my autograph book an inscription I still remember for the thrills and chills it bestowed on me. "Yours without a struggle." Cute!

I remember driving through states, and along the routes seeing those sequential billboards with their funny little messages, little stories often in rhyme, which culminated in some message about Burma Shave. And there were the endless collection of roadside shops selling exotic treats called pralines, and absolutely necessary, overpriced collectibles. "How much longer before we get there," was our constant entreaty, responded to by patient parents who knew the trip had just begun. Ultimately we ended up back home in Florida, splashing and playing in our backyard pool.

By the time I grew older, summer was spent at our house in New Jersey, lolling around the pool at the community center—or was it a country club? I can't recall, but it was a center and a pool, and I had a lifeguard boyfriend, and some kids for whom I babysat, and some days I earned the princely sum of five bucks, enough at that time to buy a bathing suit, a shorty nightgown—or some other item of substance. In those days summer meant a trip to the local farm stand for some just-shucked corn and big, tangy beefsteak Jersey tomatoes. I'd bite into one like an apple and it would bite me back!

In later years I lived in New York City, and summer was both a trial and a pleasure. Heat would rise from the asphalt streets, and there would sometimes be the acrid smell of steaming garbage, left open in cans on Amsterdam Avenue, before it was gentrified as it is now. But there was the pleasure of finding a seat at a crowded outdoor café and dining al fresco, still my favorite way to eat, and the fun of strolling out with my daughter in the warm evenings for an ice cream cone. Macy's put on the best fireworks ever, and I don't think we missed a display on the fourth, no matter how hot or how far we had to walk. Probably my favorite was the crafts' show at Lincoln Center over the fourth, and I attend crafts shows here as well. I grow older but my pleasures of choice never change. Every New Yorker knows the true point of summer—to find someone with a place upstate or a beach house, and to become a frequent guest. Getting out of the city is as much an imperative in the New York summer as going on a vision quest is in some parts of the globe.

Here my pleasures are less defined by the seasons than they would be elsewhere, for here most of the weather is mellow and beautiful. I don't always realize it's summer until August, when my number one summer favorite event occurs—my birthday. Who would reject the idea of being a total narcissist and the thrill of a holiday devoted only to oneself! In other places, locales where there are real seasons, summer is more significant. There are things that can be done in summer which cannot be done in other seasons, and people revel in those opportunities. I remember one summer recently visiting Florida cousins and going out on a boat into the tourmaline Gulf of Mexico. A species of determined and militant flies was out, and we were forced to flee the beach and bob in the water while eating our lunches—in order not to become their lunches! There summer is spent on the water, and no doubt it's one of my favorite pastimes; I love the sea.

When contemplating writing an article about summer pleasures your sign might most enjoy, because I live in the land of eternal youth—and endless springtime—I decided to poll friends old and new on Twitter and Facebook—people who reside in locations with more well-defined seasons. It was appealing to make some new discoveries about what joys other people look forward to as the days grow longer, and the livin' gets easier. One of the most interesting perspectives came from an Aussie—she said she loves summer because it holds "the promise of a fabulous New Year." I bet that's one you didn't consider if you live stateside. Of course as you think of it, you realize that because Australia is below the equator—making them down under—summer in OZ happens during the end of the year—and our winter—so perhaps a highlight might be seeing Santa in a bikini.

Aries is a fire sign, ruled by hot, sexy Mars, but did you know most members of this clan like the beach? New York culture enthusiast David Hughes and inland gram Janie Phillips both agree that summer means sunshine cooled by ocean breezes. California organizer to the celebrities John Trosko reports that summer life is made more special by a slice of watermelon and some iced coffee consumed with friends on the Santa Monica beach. The normal Aries life is fast-paced and non-stop, but in summer the chance to stroll along the seaside provides a rare moment to take a breath, indulge in some introspection, and to think about the future. An Aries former boyfriend confided in me that he'd rather be a water sign than a fire sign because after all he is a surfer. Can't fault that logic! The notion of relaxing on a dock with a cool drink appeals to Aries, but that probably doesn't mean you're going to spend the summer in slow motion. You might opt to go on a fishing trip—one of those deep sea charter adventures, where it's a little scary but in a good way. It could be the time in which you choose to get certification in scuba diving. Can a person drive up to Alaska and across into Russia in summer, or is the ice no longer frozen thanks to global warming? You probably know the answer to that question, and if that strait is passable, you can totally see making the journey. As much as you do love summer beaches, you might opt to fill some of this time with a little speed, perhaps on the back of a Harley, or on a jet-ski, which is in the water and probably a little safer if Mars prompts you to go a little faster than your skills can control.

Taurus, a sensual sign ruled by Venus, planet of love and beauty, surely relates to the slow and easy summer life. Laura Penny, a local here, suggested that her favorite summer pastime is the create a painting art parties thrown by her gal pal who has a lush back yard. She provides lots of paints and canvasses, sets up a still life along with a casual summer buffet, and a group of great friends sit around creating amateur art under the warm sun. There's no question that Taurus likes to combine food with pretty much every other activity. A painting party where walls are done would be a requirement for a good friend, but a back yard art party with a good buffet is far more fun. Does anyone love a picnic more than you, Taurus? Even if you work through the summer, chances are you will grab your lunch and head outdoors with it so you can steal a little summer air before trudging back to the salt mines. You like the simplicity of entertaining now, the group events in which everyone brings a dish and just relaxes with a cold drink as the hours while away. You also love the clearance sales and the chance to stock up on good deals before the season is gone. Comfort is number one on your agenda, and you're unlikely to go somewhere you must rough it. Leave the camping to less demanding signs like Sag. You wouldn't mind staying in a fine hotel in a place not too hot. That way you could enjoy the outdoors *and* the indoors with a minimum of aggravation. Those culinary tours that allow you to take cooking classes while exploring Italy or France would be a dream come true for you.

Gemini, speedy and smart, is naturally the sign of communication because its ruler, Mercury is all about travel and the sharing of ideas. A sweet Gemini high school friend, Mike Bischoff, told me how fondly he recalled all the parties he attended in summers at our house, where kids hung out seemingly every single weekend. Now, a sports enthusiast, he loves focusing on sporting events in summer when he's not outside working in his yard, or hosting cookouts of his own for a big, extended family. Summer reading is a big part of the Gemini life, and it might be the perfect time to organize a book club which meets outdoors. No doubt you enjoy those company soft ball games, picnics, and romps with the children in your life. It's a great time to take a class in something interesting, and perhaps something not all that intellectual. One of my favorite summer classes was at the local community college, where a Russian coach with little English taught me ping pong. I'm not a Gemini, but as a Virgo, we share the same ruler, and it was loads of fun finding the perfect partner whose rhythms matched my own, and sharing talk and laughter as we slammed the ball back and forth across the net. Travel of all types appeals to you, so do something interesting this summer—perhaps even take one of those cross-country bike trips. You'll have to be in good shape and train rigorously, but there's a huge sense of adventure and accomplishment if you pull it off. Volunteering with organizations such as the scouts is another great Gemini outlet, and you can make a difference in the lives of some kids who need more summer fun too.

Cancer is a home and family oriented sign, and when we traveled cross country one summer on what I thought was the opportunity of a lifetime, my Cancer daughter complained that we should stop taking the scenic route because there was "nothing to see." So much for my meticulously planned journey—she preferred being home with her friends. The sensitive Moon rules Cancer, and that is one reason why you're such an emotional group of people. You follow your urges and your hunches, and something usually appeals to you because of how it feels. Rich

Gillanders is married to one of my Twitter gal pals and she reports one of his summer favorites is trains. Rich loves to visit model railroads and museums and take rides on trains, a pleasure he has in common with my Gemini great-nephew, who's four. There is a rhythm to the trains, a gentle hum and a soft rumble, the sort of easy motion a mother may use to lull a cranky baby to sleep, so no wonder Cancer people like that sensation of being cradled in a rocking train. Consider taking a little journey of your own on the rails this summer, even if it's only to a nearby destination. Of course that won't stop you from sharing good times and good meals with your local best pals and devoted family members. You might like to take on a project or two in off moments, such as creating a nice scrap book of all those old family photos or even finding unique frames and making a wall display. Being surrounded by your memories really gives you a sense of place within time, and a comforting sense of belonging too, the most important of your requirements for happiness.

Leo, ruled by the Sun, is a gregarious and social sign, and you love looking good in the company of people who can admire you as you deserve. Why shouldn't they—most of the year you work hard at maintaining your svelte physical presence, and in summer the days are longer but the clothes are smaller. It's party time, whether at a beach club or in your own back yard. Schoolmate Marianne Drake confides that she loves the cool feel of flip flops on her feet in summer—something we can do here year round but in New Jersey, she can do only in the warmer weather. Her patio is a popular gathering spot for family and friends who share good food and wine, and enjoy together the slower pace. Venezuelan Oscar Cabrera loves the beach, but he often uses the summer to visit New York, where he finds time to explore the city and its many theaters and restaurants. Not only can that provide cultural and intellectual stimulation, but it can also allow a Leo to dress in summer finery. This year it's your turn—host a spectacular party all your friends will talk about for years to come. It's also a great time to make those improvements to your home that will help it to shine. Shopping is usually one of your pastimes, but you can't keep accumulating without divesting, so consider spending a few hours collecting no longer wanted items to donate, so you have plenty of room in which to store your new treasures. You might also like doing something that relates to one of your hobbies. If you're a wine enthusiast, go to wine country and taste the fruits of someone else's labors. Usually Leos enjoy culture, and no matter where you live, there is always some summer theater available. It could be your year—why don't you try out instead of being a mere audience member!

Virgo, one of the practical, hard-working signs, is ruled by Mercury, which in Gemini loves change and movement, but in Virgo is often more analytical. That could be why an astrologer whom I don't know very well responded to my online query about favorite summer fun saying it was a fifth house matter, not a Sun sign one. MysticVirgo67 is correct—the fifth is the house of pleasure and romance, things we do tend to focus on often in the summer. She also shared that as an earth sign, she loves to garden in summer. I'm a Virgo too, and other than the crafts' shows I adore and the fireworks I love, with the hours-long picnics and Scrabble games as we wait for darkness to come and the spectacle to begin, lemonade is a huge summer pleasure. Never one to appreciate coffee or booze, I have two drinks other than water and juice—hot chocolate in winter, a necessity to warm my hands, and lemonade in summer. Making ice cream is another fabulous way to enjoy the season and you can stock your freezer with the frosty results of your labors, as I did once with a collection of fruity, jewel-toned sorbets. Although most people like summer pleasures that involve less work, Virgos like me take some of those empty hours to work on hobbies, like my recipe collection illustrated with pictures of the food I've cooked and family photos, and reorganization projects such as various closets. We are who we are! Because of the more readily available fruits and veggies, summer is an ideal time to launch a new eating regimen, one which need not be a diet, but which instead is focused on ideal health.

Libra, ruled by Venus as is Taurus, is naturally one of the most romantic, most social of all the signs. You love the slower pace of summer life because it allows you more time to focus on parties with friends and time shared with a lover. Aussie pal Zakaraya loves spending time with his small daughter, and pointing out the various stellar constellations to her on a clear summer night. He also looks forward to the beautiful summer fruits his family can eat outdoors as a breeze wafts over them. Social gatherings of all sorts are your normal milieu, and much of the summer is spent with friends, perhaps in elegant, romantic attire. Because you're so social and summer is the season of weddings, chances are good that each year you attend at least one, and those sweet memories can tide you over during the colder months. If you married during the summer, you might opt to take a trip, perhaps even to recreate your honeymoon, or even to renew your vows. Cultural pursuits are another one of your pleasures, and you enjoy the various offerings available in your area. You might decide to learn to play an instrument this summer, particularly if you have more time to practice. You could add to your wardrobe, and perhaps take a trip to visit old chums who haven't had the benefit of your company in quite some time. If you have friends who decry their single status, who's better than you are at matchmaking, surely one of your favorite summer activities.

Scorpios are more in touch with the transformational energies of their ruling planet, Pluto, and perhaps that's why pal and devoted Scorpio gram Roxanne Donger says she can't wait for it to get warmer so she can speed walk daily during her lunch hours. She loves working up a sweat—and releasing toxins—and to her, the hotter the better. As a Virgo, my entire goal of life has been to avoid sweating, but I can see the benefits Roxanne describes. Sex is another Scorpio specialty, and who can complain about a summer in a nice beach location with the opportunity to be intimate on a secluded verandah or cove. Whether or not you're working up a sweat, you like the idea of having more time to yourself, perhaps to read a good mystery, or to explore little-known areas of your general locale. You don't tend to be the sort who craves a constant infusion of new activities, but you do like repeating old favorites. Perhaps you have a beloved vacation destination you visit yearly, and the familiarity is the reason why you go again and again. Like all water signs, immersing yourself in happy memories is the greatest pleasure of all. You also like visiting flea markets and thrift stores for little treasures that appeal to you, depending on your areas of interest. Collections can be enhanced at very little cost, and you gain both some exercise and the thrill of honing your bargaining skills.

Jupiter, the philosophical and beneficent planet of expansion, rules **Sagittarius,** and it would seem that Sagittarians have much in common with each other, whether they're on the same continent or not. Thus New York legal pro Kim Spencer agreed with British branding specialist Phil Dean that attending festivals and outdoor fairs is the best way to spend a lazy summer day. They were the only two people to mention these choices and of course both are Sag! Kim likes to stroll outdoors in the evening, while Phil is content to lie in the sun with a good book. Phil, an avid cook, will often host a barbecue, sometimes even cooking an entire pig. Phil loves traveling to hear music, and Kim will even board a plane several times a year to hear Depeche Mode. Amsterdam native Matt Lewenderste says he loves spending time in cities in summer, and he and his friends hang out on the terrace, sharing a cocktail and a meal. To Matt, summer is all about being in love. He must have some planets in Libra, don't you think! Adventure is part of the Sagittarian make up, so naturally you want summer to have a little flair. Go ahead and take that trip to an exotic location and meet some people who speak a little differently than you do. Try something unusual. The same ol' same ol' isn't your favorite approach, and you remember so fondly every adventure you make. If you've never gone camping, this could be your year. If, like many of your sign, camping is a favorite, plan a trip and invite along some novices who could benefit from your outdoorsy skills. Exotic cuisines appeal to you as much as any meal you can grab on the fly, so consider taking a cooking class and learning how to stuff a grape leaf or make a tamale.

Capricorn, ruled by Saturn, planet of hard work and

limitations, often gets a bad rap as the Zodiac's workaholic. But you enjoy summer as much as members of the lazier signs. College chum Jay Okun says he loves playing golf in the summer, something he could do here year round, but in Pennsylvania only in the warmer months. He loves the relaxing hours spent late at night on his deck, surrounded by stars overhead. Baseball is another favorite, but for some adventure, Jay loves to take a drive in the country. Canadian mom and fellow Capricorn Rosinda Antunes agrees that taking a road trip is a wonderful summer pleasure. She loves to stop in new spots with her family and to explore the shops, try new eateries, and stroll around at a relaxed pace. Why not do some research about a destination that really appeals to you, even if it's just a few hours' drive away and choose a weekend in which to hit the road. Those outlet malls are super destinations for there's always some bargain or other for the whole family. Petting zoos are great for Cappies with little kids—or grandkids, and although you are an earth sign, there's no reason you wouldn't enjoy a little jaunt to a nearby aquarium. If you have not so nearby family members, this could be the year of a big family reunion, whether in your area or theirs. Being part of something bigger than yourself is as essential to you as to opposite sign Cancer. You like the sense that you're building something that endures, and connecting with your heritage is a way to affirm this.

Aquarius is known as the eccentric sign, ruled as it is by Uranus, planet of sudden change and individuality, but Aussie Tina Nguyen says she loves the decidedly uneccentric balmy summer nights and sweet gelato treats after work. Like her opposite sign, Leo, Tina enjoys wearing something special in summer—a mini skirt. Summer is a time of happy anticipation in OZ, and for us in the States, that's true too, for we often look forward to the fall and the holiday season, even as we're floating on a raft in someone's refreshing pool. Trying new things is definitely part of your makeup, as is sharing good times with friends. You don't really care if your activities are well planned in advance, and living life on the cuff may in fact be preferable. Go ahead and hang out at an impromptu pool party, discuss that outrageous new movie or book, and plan a charitable event you want to sponsor. It's also a great time to access new skills, whether you learn to use some new gadget, stream video from the web, or find a way to speak a long-dead language. You're usually techno savvy, but if you're not, it's never too late. The ever-expanding numbers of gadgets that do cool things is mind boggling. You might like to use your cell phone to capture a video memory of some fun event as I did locally when they had some silly pig races at a mall. Or you could discover some wacky new fiction that you can download and read on your portable reader gadget. It's a brave new world and you're at the forefront, whatever summer pleasures you indulge in.

Pisces is a sensitive, creative sign, ruled by illusory Neptune. Sandra Gillanders says she loves going to Maine—a passion she shares with Leo Martha Stewart. There she can walk the beaches and pluck precious bits of sea glass from the sand. The quaint Maine towns are treasure troves featuring exciting antique stores, where she and hub Rich can while away hours in casual exploration that leads to a serene meal at newly discovered al fresco dining spots. A crafter, Sandy plans to spend some time this summer at her new hobby—jewelry making. That's the perfect Pisces activity, for it can be done indoors or out, while relaxing with friends, and the proceeds can even be sold on a crafts site to finance new projects. A seaside location is ideal for all water signs, for its relaxing energy is soothing and inspires new creative inspiration. If you live in a popular destination, you might find yourself at the mercy of all sorts of friends and family who want to turn your home into their own B and B. Perhaps you will enjoy that—but even if you do, set some rules and demand that they don't also turn you into their personal maid and chef. The summer is also the ideal time to catch up on movies you missed—and it's particularly comforting to be sequestered in your coolest room on the hottest day of the year, with a chilled beverage, some warm popcorn, and the DVD player humming for as long as you want to retreat. Exercise is always a good thing, and if you want to feel more fit, consider finding a pool and swimming daily laps. You'll be both refreshed and better in shape. If you're an ace swimmer, volunteer and teach a class so others can benefit from your expertise.

Whatever your summer holds, be it huge and scrapbook-worthy experiences or smaller, more mundane but equally notable fun, share it with people whose company is a pleasure. Set aside at least a few unscheduled days to diddle around on an impromptu basis, doing whatever strikes your fancy. Nothing is nicer about summer living than that.

THE STAYCATION

Ahh vacation. It's a word as hopeful as love, as sweet as candy, as magical as abracadabra. What is better than the blessing of having a stretch of time that you can fill any way you like? Who doesn't love the idea of a vacation, a little piece of freedom, and parole from your daily routine?

To most people, vacation means a getaway. There's the thrill of taking a trip to somewhere fabulous and everything that goes with it. Being able to indulge in a vacation getaway means you've done well, you've worked hard, and you deserve a break. You deserve something new, different, exciting, and fun. It's a reward you give yourself.

I've been on many trips and it's always quite a thrill to know I'm going. When my mother lived in Florida and I was in New York with my small daughter, so many times we hopped a plane and went to visit her in Panama City. And yes, that's in Florida. Unfortunately the airline didn't seem to grasp that fact and my luggage and I were always soon parted. Eventually it became a joke. The first time not so much. Wanting to look pretty to disembark, there I was, in a gossamer blouse, swirly flared skirt with a cinched waist, stockings (that's how long ago it was) and pumps. Then we arrived in Atlanta for the plane change. Have you been in the Atlanta airport? I felt like Forrest Gump in my pumps, trying to navigate across a vast stretch of space but within time constraints. Run, Forrest, run. In pumps.

By the time we arrived, my gossamer blouse was wilted, skirt was droopy, I yearned desperately to take a deep breath, uncinched, and to peel off those pantyhose. But since all my clothes were in Panama—the country, an actual foreign place, which had I been going there, I wouldn't even have embarked from the same terminal, and as nude beaches seemed no option at all, it was mandatory to remain cinched and pinched—and head to the mall for something loose—and fresh under things. That was the last time I dressed nicely to fly on a plane. And also the last time I failed to bring a carry-on with pj's, underwear, makeup, and a change of clothes.

This came in very handy the time we arrived at JFK airport in a raging storm, only to sit and wait. Then after that we waited. Then there was some more waiting. Outside it poured. Inside we waited. Eventually we learned the waiting was over—the last connecting plane out of Atlanta had left without us. Demand and you shall receive, and sure enough, the airline put us up at a motel at the airport. Was it magical? Sure, let's go with that. Finally we re-embarked. We connected in Atlanta, not walking down a gate that fed us directly into the plane, but climbing up rickety stairs off the tarmac into a tiny commuter thing that they said was yes, a plane. That was when the amusement park portion of the vacation began along with more rain. Up, down, and whoosh. Far as I know everyone held onto their lunch, but if you think flying on what felt like a roller coaster is fun, well good for you, smartypants thrill seeker.

Of course nowadays air travel is even more interesting. You can look online, perhaps for months, for the very best deal. You book your ticket. Then the airline inquires do you want to bring a toothbrush? That'll be extra. Of course you wouldn't want to transport a tube of toothpaste along with the tooth brush, because well, let's face it, that could be an incendiary device—and I don't mean your high-wattage smile. If you actually are going somewhere other than a nude beach, you might desire a change of clothes, and of course that too will be extra. Check your luggage? Really? Can that even be done any more? What's now being stowed in the part of the plane that used to hold luggage? Your guess is as good as mine. Sometimes you can wheel on a bag of precisely the right size—and ladies remember your purse is counted as a bag—and that means you can stand conveniently in a mob as two hundred other people try to find a place to stash their wheely bag too.

Or you can sit down and observe apprehensively

someone who hasn't worked their biceps in decades attempting to hoist a bag into the overhead bin, and wrangling precariously with it all the while you're praying they don't propel it onto your head. It's also important to remember that the yummy airline food you used to enjoy with such relish is no longer an option. That's right—they may go up and down with carts that will whack you on the elbow, but no trays of food will emerge. Don't worry, though, you can opt to buy a who-knows-how-old twenty-dollar bargain sandwich at the airport, and stash it in your bag, in order to enjoy a picnic that might not make you sick, right there in your seat. Soon enough you'll be about a third of the way into your journey, and the air will go off in the plane. Some agoraphobic in an office decided that only those in the front of the plane need an air flow, and those in the back can easily breathe in what those in the front exhale. This is your chance to pass out until you potentially can land. As far as I know, there are no extra charges to allow you actually to disembark so you can exit the plane, ka-thumping your wheelycase behind those same two hundred people, on your way to paradise.

There's a lot to be said for car travel as well. The last big car trip I took was between Florida and Los Angeles. Day one, the car was packed and I, with my trusty traveling companion, Mickey, a cat who loved to travel, set off for our first stop, New Orleans. The miles flew by, the music blared, and the air conditioner roared on that hot August day. Ka-chink, putt-putt, and suddenly the air conditioner, which had always been a bit of a lemon, died. It was maybe twelve degrees warmer than the center of hell, steamier than the belly button of the equator, and I was in a car with windows I could barely leave cracked open because who knew if Mickey would decide to leap out if they were open. First stop: car dealer for a new air conditioner, like twelve hundred bucks. I demanded and got a loaner car, headed with the cat to a mall, rented a stroller in that mall, and pushed him around (he was too heavy to carry for hours) and ignored the bemused stares of people who thought I was reenacting a scene from *Alice in Wonderland*. Eventually the car was repaired and we journeyed on, cool and comfortable, toward our appointed destination.

That was the goal of my dear friend Rachel, a Brit, who with her beloved husband, for months had been planning a vacation to spend Christmas with her oldest American friend in Martha's Vineyard. Daily for months everyone in our online group of pals would hear details of this exciting upcoming journey. Because of her business, Rachel had only the one week at the end of the year in which she could travel easily, and Christmas with her pal would be wonderful. But remember what happened? 2010 was a very snowy fall. Record breaking snows fell everywhere, as we all checked the weather reports and flight reports with apprehension. Yes, Rachel's flight was cancelled. You probably saw in the news all those people trapped at Heathrow as no planes exited for days on end. At least Rachel wasn't among them. She and Paul were sad their trip was not to be, and there they were, no tree, no Christmas goodies on hand, and no way to travel up snowed-in, rocky terrain to her parents' house where they normally celebrated. Rachel is spunky and she naturally mourned the loss of her plans, but then she recovered and reclaimed her holiday. Leaving behind her home in the English countryside, she and Paul hopped the train to their flat in London, and there together they spent Christmas in what turned into a sort of second honeymoon. They visited museums, ate at favorite places and some new ones, strolled ancient streets and some they'd never visited, and shared pictures of their vacation at home online with their friends, who were happy at their joys and still sad at their disappointment. Maybe they stayed at home, but it was a vacation and they both emerged refreshed and renewed from it.

There are many good things to be said for a vacation spent at home—a Staycation—the least of which being it costs not a cent to sleep in the world's most comfortable bed, your own. There are no worries about pet care, because you're right there available to give love and kibble to your furry friends. And nobody will lose your luggage.

Unless you're an extremely practical chore-oriented

person, please realize that a Staycation isn't the time to reorganize your closets. OK some people like doing this sort of thing, and if so, go at it. Some people like gardening, and if weeding your forty acres is your idea of a good time, go for it. Some people like do-it-yourself projects, and yes I'm one of them, so to me a Staycation in which I redo something at home would be bliss. And bliss is the point. You can find your bliss doing something at or close to home just as readily as you can go off into the wild blue yonder. You just have to choose something that is genuine fun. Don't confuse a Staycation with being under house arrest. You have many options. You can choose a pursuit that will last as long as your vacation, such as taking a seminar in an interesting subject. You can book all your days in advance, choosing things you've always wanted to do, and day after day do them. You can use the time to do a project you've always wanted to attempt, such as sewing that slipcover, assuming it's not something that makes you suicidal. Or you can spend the time day by day, on the fly, doing whatever strikes your fancy. Many times I've enjoyed this immensely and been sad when the time flew away. Impromptu pleasures are always my favorite, except, well okay I like the planned ones too.

I wonder if your astrological sign will provide some clues as to the best of all possible Staycations for you. Let's find out!

ARIES: You're definitely not one of the signs who wants to stay home and organize a closet or anything else. You do like to shop, and you could see visiting a mall to add stuff to your already overfilled and under-organized closet. But chances are you don't want to do that every day for a week or more. You want variety. Often when you say vacation, you mean adventure. You want the thrills and chills. You want the excitement. You might want that scuba certification, that trip through darkest Africa, or a journey Down Under. If that's what you really want, then a Staycation might not be for you. But, on the other hand, with the current economy, it might be prudent to consider fun available to you closer to home. No matter where you live, there's some form of adventure out there that would appeal to you. Here in Los

Angeles there are amusement parks of all sorts in every direction. Do we who live here go to them regularly? By we I mean me, and the answer is no, I don't. But you could. Or you could find some sort of amusement or attraction not too far from your home. There are natural wonders in every area and parks that can be camped in, rivers that can be explored, mountain paths that can be climbed. It just depends on your starting point. Even if you live in a city, there are environs beyond your city, and renting a car for a day or two and journeying a little beyond the borders of Gotham can still be considered a Staycation. Another fun option is to host a visit from a faraway friend. Then you can spend time as tour guide, showing your pal all the coolest places you enjoy close to home. If you really have wanderlust, and particularly if there's some rain during your vacation, rent some action movies or movies set in distant places. Even bad movies are made enjoyable by an exotic location you've always wanted to visit.

TAURUS: You can certainly get on the Staycation bandwagon more readily than almost any other sign. That's because you like the idea of one, saving money, and two, staying home. If you are forced to punch a clock daily and waken before your internal clock wants to see the light of day, you might say it's a vacation to sleep until you waken naturally. Nothing is as relaxing as having nothing you must do. Waking, puttering around a while, making a breakfast you'd normally not have time for, are all super enjoyable for you, even if you must fill your larder in advance to do so. Later on there's plenty of time for you to go out and do something. You might consider taking a cooking class. Even if you're an expert cook, classes like that are a true pleasure. You get to hobnob with other foodies, learn new yummy techniques and then you get to eat the food. They also hold wine and cheese tastings at stores and restaurants, and there could be one in your area. Dining is a big favorite of yours, and meeting friends to try a new restaurant, or sharing a meal with your sweetheart without worrying how late it's getting really does balance your energy. Small pleasures mean a lot, especially to you. That doesn't mean you don't enjoy pampering of a more elaborate sort. So go ahead and book that spa day. It costs a lot less than an airplane and a hotel. Or get the mani-pedi. Even guys love them nowadays. If you live in a place surrounded by nature—and everyone does because c'mon, nature is right outside all our doors—do something outside. Take a stroll. Have a picnic. Visit a zoo. If you have two weeks off, you can find different things to do every day. Or you can stroll through different malls, just to see the parade of shoppers go by. I'm not a Taurus, but that's one of my favorite relaxing pastimes.

GEMINI: You're a big time reader, but do you really want to spend an entire vacation curled up with a book? Sometimes! If it's summer, and you can lie outdoors on a chaise with your book, or EBook reader, you're pretty content, at least for a while. You might not know this, but many hotels will, for a very nominal fee, allow you to lounge around their pool even if you're not checked in. This can come in handy if you have no beaches. Even if you don't have an ocean, you do have a park, and you would very much enjoy hiking and exploring that area with some adventurous friends. Another fun adventure is to take a small child, whether your own relative or a friend's, to the library. Taking my great niece to the library for the first time was a riot. She thought my library card was a credit card, and didn't know why we read some books we liked and didn't "buy" them but "bought" the others we hadn't even read. You are a big spur of the moment person, and discovering an event in your area at the last second is no impediment at all to you hastening off to a grand adventure. This includes things like Renaissance Fairs, State Fairs, and even block parties. Because you so readily go with the flow, you're probably behind on some things you really do want to catch up on, such as correspondence. Whether email or snail mail, this is a good time to write a few cards, even if you stay up late doing it, because the next day you can sleep in. It's not terribly hard to manufacture your own zany adventure. You could conduct your own personal contest as to who has the best coffee—or ice cream—in your area, and day by day you can sample one or two offerings with a co-conspirator, and then decide who the winner is among yourselves. This can be translated into a blog entry and before you know it, they could be making a movie about you like they did *Julie and Julia.*

CANCER: You are of course the family sign, and it goes without saying that to you a vacation means family time. If you're of the age to be part of a young, nuclear family, there are so many things you can do with the kids, right there at home. One of my favorite at-home memories as a kid was the day my mom and I played jacks, right there on our kitchen floor. She'd never played before but soon became a champ. That sort of one on one time makes for treasured memories. You can set up the dollhouse with little kids, whether your kids, grandkids, or other youngsters in your life. Nothing's more fun than arranging that tiny world. And if you need things for the dollhouse, take a crafting day together and make those adorable items that every dollhouse needs. If you're a grandparent, you might enjoy a day off with one of your grown children, with or without the tots. This is the time to share those treasured recipes, and teach the youngsters your famous apple pie; they will always remember it. You might also like to go out in the world and see adventure—and stuff. Local thrift stores are everywhere, even in the sticks, and you could have a nice time looking through all the things you know you'll never need, but which provide clues into the lives of other people. You might even find a treasure to bring home—at a nominal cost. Water is a fabulous source of relaxation, and once again, there are Y's everywhere, and you could take a day and swim, or float, or just frolic. Another option where family is concerned is to invite faraway but still beloved relatives to visit you. Then you can make favorite foods, and enjoy boisterous conversations, filled with memories of the times you shared when you lived nearby.

LEO: Your love of routine is legendary and you're quite content to be nestled cozily in your nest. What you don't want is to be alone. Unless you have a yearly project you've turned into a ritual, like my Leo friend who always plants his veggie garden the same week every spring, you don't want to spend your vacation by yourself. You want to have glittering friends, twinkling on cue. If you do it right, a vacation can yield several social events, and you won't have to waste any food. If you have a party one night, you can follow it with a leftovers brunch a day later. You might also check the schedule for cultural events in your area. Did you know that movie theaters now offer opera performances on the silver screen? These are not creaky old movies, but HD affairs being broadcast not long after the live performance occurs in top venues in New York or other places. So you could sprinkle your vacation with trips to the opera, concerts, and that can be your excuse to look your best, always something on your agenda. Looking fabulous may be your specialty, but it doesn't happen only by magic, so a vacation is a very good time to take a couple shopping days to spruce up the wardrobe. And once you have the new outfit, planning a party is second nature. Like Taurus, a spa day appeals quite a bit to you—or you might opt for one of those doctors who provides a refresher without the nip/tuck. Or you might go whole-hog, pardon the metaphor, and do the actual nip/tuck. When people see you again, they assume the new glow is from the wonders of the vacation, not the surgeon's prowess. You love to dine out as much as you love to entertain, and this is the perfect time to enjoy lazy lunches with someone whose schedule is as lax as your own, such as an adoring spouse. A vacation with no must-do events is the perfect time to work on keeping the romance alive in your marriage or relationship.

VIRGO: Are you a putterer? I am. I love to do little projects. Taking a week off to sew Christmas presents is so much fun for me. I'm content to take off time to paint a room (and then to take off time to rest the muscles made sore by moving all the furniture and repeatedly climbing the ladder). It's satisfying. Sometimes a vacation is about work, but not the work you do for a living. If you have collections, you enjoy maintaining them. Dusting all those leather bound books, one by one, gives you a warm glow. A week or two can easily evaporate in the face of such scintillating pursuits. Not only is puttering around at home a great pleasure, going here and there with no objective at all is equally fun. You can go to one mall one day, another the next. You can spend a day driving around neighborhoods you've yet to explore, enjoying the architecture or the landscaping, and capturing some photos if you want to recreate at home anything you've seen. Although much of what I've described isn't what you'd call a lazy vacation, it's the sort of thing you enjoy. That's not to say you wouldn't enjoy a massage—and malls nowadays often have chair massages available, sometimes out in open air. For twenty bucks you can get twenty minutes of unkinking and kneading. Doing something outdoors restores the spirit. If you have a child, or one you can borrow, it's nice to go outside and fly a kite for a while. Not only is it a challenge, it's a genuine thrill to see it soar. You might also like to share some fun activities with a youngster, such as baking favorite cookies, or doing any of your hobbies which require skills that you could teach. The main thing with a Staycation is not to make it all about things that are labor, even if that labor is also pleasurable. Mix in some activities that are purely pleasurable, such as sleeping in with your sweetheart, and wakening with no reason to leave the room and each other's arms.

LIBRA: There's no question that to you a vacation should be all pleasure, and that includes romance. If you had to spend a fortnight alone with no tender glances or candlelight, well that would be more of an internment than a vacation. It's extremely rare for members of your sign to be without a significant other, so you would naturally want to do something fun with a romantic partner. Couple activities can be great fun, even if you just do something wacky each day, and completely out of character, such as a visit to the local arcade or a game of miniature golf. Strolling hand in hand pretty much anywhere can be all it takes to bring some magic into a day. Usually you enjoy shopping, not so much for the acquisition, but for the pleasure of the stroll, the fun of the little meals you eat along the way, the laughs you have when you try something improbable on your true love, and the great thing about shopping is it's entertaining and cost-free, assuming you buy nothing. Culture appeals quite a bit to you, so if there are interesting performances, even a high school play, you enjoy attending, and use it as a chance to dress up a little. You also might like to host a party for people whose company creates good cheer, and whether you're a cooking enthusiast or someone with good take-out available via speed dialing, you know it's the company more than the food or potables that brings the magic. As balance is one of the themes of your sign, you might consider taking a yoga class or even a meditation class. There's nothing like that sense of peace of mind such activities generate. Being social is your number one priority, and a Staycation should be a way to facilitate that. If, however, you find yourself currently single, use the time to find a new mate. Join those clubs, fill out the profiles on those online dating services, and tell your friends to host some parties with their nearest and dearest—and most eligible—so that once again you will be half of the best thing on earth—a couple.

SCORPIO: Like your opposite sign, Taurus, you too enjoy the prospect of being at home, particularly during those moments when there is nothing on your to-do list. You can be completely content to languish the better part of a day away by lighting a few candles in your bathroom, tossing something fragrant into the tub, and soaking until you resemble a contented prune. Why not—it's a vacation. Oftentimes there's something on your mind, something you're puzzling through, and a quiet period offers you time for contemplation, something you do enthusiastically. It's true that insights often come in a backhanded way, not when you're fully concentrating, but when you're thinking of something else. Call it your spirit guides' way of reaching out at a time when there are no walls to penetrate. Days can pass with you still in your cozy bathrobe, a book still warm from your hands, and any number of treats on your nightstand. This is a pretty quiet vacation for someone as sizzling as you are, and that's why you like it. That sense of being cocooned really restores your energy. Obviously you didn't get your sexpot reputation by spending all your time in a hermit existence, so on your Staycation, you'll want to share some tender moments, with a true love or a new love. You prefer the sense of familiarity that being with a known person brings, but there's also something exciting about unraveling the mysteries of someone new. Even a simple activity such as going to a movie, something goofy and cartoonish, where you can sport 3D glasses will do as well as a weightier offering. Sneaking a picnic into the movies is also sort of fun and you can eat your sandwiches side by side while everyone else munches on popcorn. You might also enjoy trying new cuisines. If there's an ethnic neighborhood in your area, this could be your chance to sample dim sum, huevos rancheros, or who knows what. The point is to mingle absurd adventures with some calming periods of doing little, and you will ultimately say it's the best vacation you ever had.

SAGITTARIUS: Like fellow Fire Sign Aries, you so often yearn for the wild blue yonder, that sometimes at work you can feel your eyes glazing over as you imagine yourself at the farthest possible point from your current reality. Still, you're usually rather a mellow person, and you can find pleasure in many silly pursuits. If there are farms in your area (and there are farms in every area), you and some friends might enjoy a day to go picking apples, strawberries, or whatever else is in season. You could order the fixings for a clambake and head to a beach or park, where you could turn it into a party with a bonfire, good food, and raucous humor. Life doesn't have to be organized to suit you, and you're more than content to follow the whim of a friend or lover who makes an impromptu suggestion about how to fill the day. You could do something as improbable as a visit to a religious service far afield from your own faith, just to observe what's going on from a cultural standpoint. You enjoy strolling through flea markets, just to see the array of stuff, to think about what that stuff meant to someone else, even if you buy nothing at all. Being outdoors is the most important thing for members of your sign. The last thing you would want is a vacation at home, indoors for days at a time, not even with the world's most interesting companion. Consider checking the phone book for some stables and going horseback riding for a day; you and horses have a special bond, and being out astride a horse in the fresh air will clear your head superbly. This is a good time to learn something new, whether you take a crash course in a language, and yes you can't learn much in a couple weeks, but it could be fun. You could learn a sport—or a new video game, engage in some sort of contest with willing friends, and of course spend quality time with your significant other.

CAPRICORN: Often you work but have another sort of work you also do, such as someone with a job but a desire for a career doing something else, such as writing. If that's the case, to you a Staycation is perfect, for it would allow you the time to stay home and pretend you're doing full time what you envision yourself doing one day. You can work on that novel, and although it's labor, it's thrilling. You could build that cabinet, and advertise it for sale. The point would be that you would be living the life of your dreams, and that's pretty wonderful if you don't get to do it full time yet. If you're already ensconced in a career, you work hard, probably harder than any other sign. Taking time off feels very odd to you, and it might be difficult for you to justify. You like being in harness, pulling your weight, but it would be a shame if you were one of those workaholics who can't focus on pleasure to the exclusion of all else. How sad to be on vacation and still logged into the computer at work, or on the phone with a colleague. Don't do it, Capricorn. You need a break, and one benefit of taking a break is it restores you to try harder so you can come up with new ideas and inspirations once you're back to the daily grind. Capricorn is the sign of the architect, and you might be a do-it-yourselfer who loves those household projects. Finishing the basement might be a great Staycation for you, or redoing that horrid old bath. To you this is work that is also pleasure. Just remember that even if you are doing something like that during your Staycation, take a day or two to do something that isn't work. Go out to eat. See a movie. Stroll arm in arm with your mate. Everyone needs to establish an ebb and flow in their lives, and so do you. It's the down time that restores you for the up time.

AQUARIUS: As the techie of the universe, you can spend endless hours—or even days—at those electronics stores which sell all the cool gadgets. A Staycation is your chance. Planning on getting a new computer? This is the perfect time because you can enjoy the process of setting it up without the pressure to be finished. Maybe you have a new smart phone and are raring to try all those cool new apps. How I envy you! This is the perfect time to experiment with apps and see which ones could really come in handy. Or maybe you have just acquired one of those fantastic Ipads or EBook readers, and now you can play with it, read stuff on it, or shop for accessories. Then it's time to show it off to your friends. Wherever they are, a gps application can smoothly and easily guide you right to their door. You're also the sign of friendship, and your pals are your greatest treasure. If you can coordinate vacation time, then a Staycation can be like a return to simpler times when you were in school, and you and your buddies could hang out without a care in the world. This is the time to try new things and to enjoy those experiences, whatever they might be. The crazier the better. Maybe you'll finally make that recipe that sounded good. Or use that cooking app to create a recipe of your own. You have more time now, so you can visit with friends all over the world via Skype and online chat to your heart's content. It's also a good time to connect with those people you've been wanting to know better. Arrange to have drinks or dinner, or host a gathering so everyone you know can get together. Remember those wacky scavenger hunts they used to have in movies from the 1930's? That could be a very fun adventure, one that could last for an evening or an entire Staycation. It's up to you and your excellent imagination.

PISCES: One of the greatest luxuries about being a Pisces is all the things that naturally appeal to you. There are so many interests, hobbies, and pastimes you enjoy, but sadly most days there's just not enough time. If you were off on a vacation, you'd be having fun, but you couldn't do most of your hobbies. A Staycation is your opportunity to indulge yourself in all the pleasures in your area. You can stroll through nature, taking a picnic and reveling in all the beauty that restores your spirit. A watery area such as a beach or river area is excellent for balancing emotions or stirring creativity. Back at home, you can enjoy any of the many hobbies you either do or want to do. Even if you try each one for just a day or two, to you it will feel quite magical. You also enjoy the moments you can steal to spend with your mate or family. Everyone leads such busy lives, that for you it's a treat to have some relaxing hours to share a meal, see a movie, or just spend a day doing this and that with no curfew. The arts are very appealing to you, so check out the local museum, galleries, or any other venues where you can see creativity at its best. Maybe sign up and take a class. You might not become Picasso in a day, but you'd have fun, and whatever you produce becomes a treasured souvenir. The idea that every day must contain an activity is one that sort of negates the floaty energy of the Staycation. Do as much or as little as you like. If you have a nice backyard, there's nothing wrong with taking a book or your laptop outside and just sitting and relaxing, while all around you the birds sing. If you're a city dweller, chances are in your home is one special, cozy spot where you go to relax and daydream. Go ahead and take advantage of this now. Nothing is quite as special as having the time to let your mind wander. Being a creative type has its perks. You can sit and enjoy all the images that float through your mind, and nowhere will ring an alarm clock.

Whatever you choose to do with your time off, let it feel like a gift. Life need not always be productive and it also need not always be fun. Sometimes the greatest gift is the time just to be, on your own, doing whatever your whims dictate. That is my favorite thing in the world and why the Staycation is such a great way to take time off.

6
THE LATER YEARS

It goes by so fast. Life at twenty seems endless. Between thirty and forty is a good chunk of time. But then you're sixty and it seems it happened while you were hunting for your car keys. One day you were forty, and the next your hair had turned gray. The question is, what do you do about it?

Are you one of those types who clings to the idea of youth, like an aging woman I saw still shopping in the junior department, who by rights should have been there only for her grandchildren. Or do you have a plan for how to enjoy those golden years when your hair turns silver? In *Enjoying Life After Sixty*, I explore those ideas and look at your approach to retirement. Even if you plan to keep working, there are things you want to do in the sunset of your life.

Being a grandparent is the joy of life in older age. In a way, it's your chance to be reborn, and to enjoy fun from the flip side of life. *Grandparenting* describes your ideal way of making the most of that special little person who has come along to remind you of life's pleasures.

ENJOYING LIFE AFTER SIXTY

I remember decades back listening to some much-older relatives talking about being senior citizens, and taking trips with their golden age club, and using special discounts. To me that seemed like something so far in the distance, it wasn't worth thinking about. But time flies, doesn't it, and now I do think about what it will be like to be old. Or should I say even older.

When my mother was 75, we had a party and a friend gave her a book titled, *When I Am Old, I Will Wear Purple*, or something like that. She laughed then because she was already old, although she didn't feel or act old, and she wasn't waiting to wear purple—or to do anything in particular. Whatever she wanted to do, she always did.

That's the thing about people. Some of us just do what we want as the mood strikes, some plan for the future and put off doing certain things until the time seems right. Can you imagine being old and finally having the time to crochet those afghans, build those bird houses, or become a champ at pinochle? Some people can. My dear elderly cousin told me that when you reach a certain age you must do two things: learn bridge and take up golf. I'm not much of a game player, so that didn't seem to be a philosophy suited to me, but for many people it's good advice. One keeps your mind active, the other provides exercise.

We all have different plans for our old age. I want to spend time being a gram. That doesn't seem like an unusual goal for the future, but it's the one I most care about. What about you? Does your Sun Sign have any insights about how you will handle those golden years? Read on!

ARIES: The idea of retirement appeals to you greatly because you'd love being able to do exactly what you want, every single day. Some Aries take an early retirement, then realize, gee, I'm only 40, what do I do now, like a guy I know who eventually decided to reenter his former field in a different capacity. That's very typical of your choices anyway—you tend to try things wholeheartedly and make sweeping changes without thinking about the long, long picture. It doesn't matter though, because in your life there are usually any number of new beginnings and you never mind going back to square one—in fact, you revel in doing so. What you can't envision is sitting in your rocker on a porch with an equally wrinkled mate, drinking lemonade and watching the world go by. Your view of life is that you want to be active, always involved in interesting things. So when you retire, you basically want more of the same. You want to travel, and maybe you can even envision owning one of those recreational vehicles that allows you to go anywhere you want. You love the outdoors and want to be able to spend more time outside, building that pond ecosystem you've been considering for your backyard, or joining a walking group of seniors who explore new mountain trails. You love the idea of having the freedom to try something new without the need to be back home at any given time. Wanderlust appeals to you, and when you're retired you won't have to punch a clock. Of course being able to retire requires money, and that means advance planning, something you seldom enjoy. So take some time now and consider your future. Are you saving for that day when you won't work any more, so that you can put all those exciting dreams into action? Otherwise you might find yourself working through your golden years because you have to, not because you want to.

TAURUS: You've been planning ahead almost from the moment of your conception. While you love to enjoy life as it happens, and there are many good times all through your life, you plan religiously for old age, and may have set up retirement income which kicks in quite early. You don't always plan to use that income and to stop working, but you feel it's nice to have it at the ready, no matter what. You have a strong personal attachment to the work ethic, so you can envision staying at your job quite late in life, and what you may opt to do is phase out working by moving into a part-time schedule for a few years. That way you enjoy a comforting sense of continuity that makes you feel safe, and find it easier to change your life by degrees, rather than all at once. There are many things you plan to enjoy when your life is less hectic. Perhaps you will catch up on your reading, or make scrapbooks of all those photos you've collected over the years. There are many enjoyable activities you plan that keep you close to home, because it feels so cozy to be chez you with few obligations and endless possibilities. You might duck into movies during the week, when the prices are cheaper, or try some of those early bird dinner specials seniors love so much. You can imagine spending endless hours in your garden, and even creating a new rose, if you're so inclined. If you have a big yard and a congenial climate, you might opt to grow lots of your own produce, if you're not doing so already. Having your family all around you is a nice thing, and you look forward to spending time with your grandchildren, doing all the things you remember as wonderful when your own kids were small, yet being able to send them home when you yearn for a few peaceful moments alone.

GEMINI: What, you get old? No way! Yours is the most youthful of all the signs and you love to play, no matter your age. You look young, think young, and want to stay young. New ideas and approaches to life appeal to you, and you'll never be the sort of person who grouses about the "young people," and what they're up to because you feel simpatico and want to be included in their fun and hijinks. You like reading, television, radio, conversation, and all other forms of intellectual stimulation, and you always will. You can imagine retiring and having the time to read all those books that you wish you could tackle right now. You might opt to become a tutor and help a child who needs a little push from a knowledgeable source. That would keep your mind sharp, while allowing you to share your knowledge and expertise. You love the idea of traveling and meeting new people, and you might decide to become one of those retirees who moves far away to a new place to take advantage of a special community or more hospitable climate. If so, you'll probably keep in touch with friends both old and new, sending out newsletters, cards, or even planning annual gatherings. You love the idea of having endless stretches of free time, the ability to start something without having to finish it, and the chance to be a little bit selfish so you can focus on only what appeals to you. It's nice to have more freedoms and fewer requirements, and if that's what retirement can be, you're all for it. The great thing about you is you're seldom lazy, and so you remain active all your life, enjoying life's pleasures as you go.

CANCER: You can easily imagine life as one endless weekend, with you surrounded by children and grandchildren. Life is hectic when you're raising a family, and you look forward to sharing quality moments with your grandchildren without having to race off to work. You might decide to baby-sit a grandchild or two while your kids concentrate on their careers. To you, that would be a joyous way to live. You take your responsibilities seriously, and focus on buying a home early so that it's paid for by the time you reach sixty. That way you know you have a secure base and a place where you can always live, no matter what. You also care about saving for the future, and focus early on putting money away for your kids' education and for your own old age. You want to be able to help your kids as they're starting their own families, and if you can give them a down payment for a home, you do so gladly. It's nice for you to have your whole family right nearby so whenever the urge to visit strikes, you can spend time together. If you do have loved ones at a distance, part of your retirement plan is to travel to spend time with them. Perhaps you even plan for a second residence so you can be near the people you love as often as possible. You have many hobbies you enjoy, and want to devote more time to them when you're older. Perhaps you'll perfect that cookie recipe, churn more batches of ice cream, fish more, or take up ping pong. You love to play, and being able to do so more often really appeals to you. It's easy for you to imagine writing a children's book, or at least reading some to a child you love.

LEO: The trouble with retirement is it's something generally considered suitable for people who are old. While you like the idea of having freedom and fun, you never want to admit you're getting older. Once you make peace with *that* idea, there are many things you'd love to do with your extra time. Of course you intend to remain busy and socially active, and being retired gives you more time to host parties of all sorts, and to share casual good fun with your pals. You adore the idea of traveling and can imagine yourself going on luxury cruises with a giant steamer trunk filled with elegant clothing. (Perhaps you picture Fred Astaire and Ginger Rogers, but really you mean yourself!) The hobbies you enjoy now can be developed further, and whether you want to become a master of something creative or simply a devotee of something fun, you enjoy the idea of immersing yourself more completely in your pleasures. You expect your golden years to be—well golden—and the elegance with which you live your current moments should be expanded upon when there's time to do it right. That could mean safaris, murder mystery weekends, tango lessons, jewelry making classes, or even a whole new career. Perhaps you want to become a fashion consultant, a mentor for children who need your wisdom and pizzazz, or a party planner. I know a senior who organizes cruises and gets to go on them for free; for her it's the best of both worlds because she is busy and active and has no shortage of good times. You might opt to spend more time at swap meets—perhaps as a dealer occasionally, selling some of your many collected treasures at a profit. That's the thing about retirement for you—you don't plan to lie about, doing nothing. You want your later years to be exciting and you intend to follow your fancies and make being over 60 as glamorous as possible.

VIRGO: Sometimes, on a very good day, when there are few crises nagging at you for immediate attention, you allow yourself the luxury of a bubble bath, or a nap on the couch, and in those blissfully peaceful moments, you imagine more time, just like this, a sort of temporal oasis, in which you have freedom and peace of mind. That to you is retirement. You almost never have a moment to yourself, because there's always that inner voice nagging at you to get up and do the dishes or the laundry, to organize your desk, to clean out the closets, in short to tackle every little chore that must be done to your satisfaction in order to engineer your perfect world. But in your fantasy life, retirement has none of these issues, because all the chores have been done! Does this make any sense at all? You tell me! When you do retire, you'll probably be just as busy as you were at work, although there will be different things to which you must attend. Your penchant for complicated hobbies must be answered, and you're likely to spend many hours hard at work at your computer, sewing machine, or work shop. Perhaps you'll make all your own bread (if you don't already), or start a day care center, even if only for your own grandkids. Maybe you'll learn to knit, or become a golf champ. Whatever you do, it won't be in a laissez-faire sort of way, because you're just not built for that. Instead you intend to immerse yourself in your many interests, and now you'll be able to do them even more skillfully than you did when responsibilities were your priority. Maybe you'll try to simplify. You might move to a smaller residence, where there are plenty of closets and no open shelves to hold dust-catching bric-a-brac. You might choose to increase your limberness through daily Yoga or Pilates, and you might even master meditation. Once you've gone that far, you will have developed the inner peace needed to survive life as a no-longer-driven retiree!

LIBRA: You can easily imagine yourself as one of the superstars of a very elegant over-60 community. Wouldn't it be fun to have a long list of social activities available to you and a congenial group of compatible friends with whom you could share them? Of course you don't picture yourself as old, nor elderly. You're youthful, perhaps not quite as young as you used to be, but still attractive and charming, and that's just how everyone else will see you too. Because you're so romantic, you hope to retire with your true love at your side, and to keep the romance alive, you want to go dancing on Saturday nights. Perhaps you can envision dancing every night in your living room or taking tango lessons. Learning bridge appeals to you, because it's an excellent, stimulating, yet social couples-oriented activity. And if you have a group of gal pals or guy pals, it's just as much fun. Those long lunches in which you share conversation and photos of the grandkids are so much fun, particularly when you don't have to race back to a job. You want to enjoy your grandchildren, but don't see them as a central part of your retirement. You want a life of your own, time with people on your own level, and the continued social involvements that have always meant so much to you. As a big fan of the good life, you realize that retirement on a shoe string is not your preference, so it's important for you to plan early and well for your golden years. Your tendency is to spend your cash as you get it, but take some time now to consider the future and what you must do to secure it. That way you can have an elegant retirement, and a long, pleasant one.

SCORPIO: You have a real need to be in control of your own destiny and thus you're willing to start planning quite early for your retirement. Although you love the idea of being close to your kids, you don't want to be a burden to them, nor the kids a burden to you! Independence is your preference, and then you know the time you spend with family members is by choice rather than need. You enjoy working and like spending time at something that gives you personal satisfaction. Continuity and routine often appeal quite a bit to you, so you may not be in any real hurry to retire. Eventually, though, you'd like some time to yourself, to pursue your favorite pastimes. Some Scorpios like to travel more than others—usually the ones with planets in neighboring Sagittarius enjoy a touch of wanderlust—and if that's you, it's fun to plan a trip now and then to an exotic location, even if it's just the distant city inhabited by one of your kids. Whether or not you love travel, all Scorpios love to come home. Puttering around your house is lots of fun, and you're quite content to spend time with your favorite television show, book, or music, while you sit in a cozy spot at home. The people you love are so important to you, and you look forward to additional time with them. You don't need a whole crowd of friends, just a few special people who've been in your life for a long time. This could be your chance to read more of those exciting whodunnit novels, to learn a foreign language, to play the stock market, even if only via a make-believe computer program. The point is to create a routine that feels perfect for you, so that every day is not just an adventure, but a source of fun and relaxation.

SAGITTARIUS: What you never get is why people wait to begin living until they retire. You live in the moment, and want to enjoy the here and now. If something interests you, it's not your modus operandi to wait forty years to give it a shot. You're always willing to try new things and to keep exploring old favorites. That to you is the right way to live. It's not just that you believe the old adage about all work and no play making you dull, you feel it hastens an early demise. You have to live, right now, today. But you do realize that some day you will be older, and you won't want to work forever. Often you feel you don't want to work at all. But you're not usually terribly frugal (unless you have planets in neighboring Scorpio or Capricorn) and thus it may be hard to amass the resources you need to stop working altogether. You might work as an elderly person, and it could be fun for you because by the time you're old, at last you feel a bit more stable. It could be fun to be one of those discount store meet and greet persons, or to work at a fast food place because by then all the pressure is off, and you can do what comes naturally—being friendly and enjoying life all around you. If you do have plenty of money, you love the idea of traveling—a lot. You might go around the world with a best pal, even taking up residence in a foreign place. You love to read and to learn, and might return to college or take up a foreign language. Perhaps you will raise more dogs, or work as their groomer. The idea for you is the same when you're old as when you were young—to live each day to the fullest and not sweat the small stuff along the way.

CAPRICORN: We've said it time and time again—you're all about working and building success. So does that mean you have no interest in retirement? Not exactly. One of the clichés about Capricorn is that you grow younger as you grow older. In other words, age becomes you, and once you've achieved the success you desperately crave, and the financial security you can't live without, you're somewhat willing to play. Do you envision yourself lying about at home, doing nothing? Of course not! To you that would be pure sloth. Instead you look forward to the time when you can pursue some of the hobbies you had to put off while you were so busy carving your path to success. You love the idea of spending more time with your family and getting to know your grandkids. You have many skills and talents, and it gives you great pleasure to share these things with those you love. You might take the grandkids miniature golfing, and might become a golf nut yourself. Walking those greens is relaxing and stimulating at the same time, and your mind comes up with interesting and useful ideas. Who says you have to retire completely? If you have a business, you might decide to keep a hand in and dabble here and there, or to act as a consultant in your field. You love tackling those do-it-yourself projects, and might decide to add a room onto your home, perhaps with your own two hands. Being a pillar of your community is meaningful to you, so why not consider running for office in your golden years. You could be the mayor of your town, or who knows—President Capricorn! The busier you stay, the happier you remain, and a vigorous retirement with many fascinating activities suits you perfectly.

AQUARIUS: The great thing about being retired is the time it gives you to make the world a better place. You love being involved in group activities and community projects, and as a retiree you can make a real difference in your world. Senior Citizens are a powerful force, and you love the idea of being a leader within that group. Because you have so many friends, it makes lots of sense for you to become active in one of those golden age groups. You could go on theater outings, trips to exciting locations, or just enjoy the day to day interaction with interesting people who have experiences and ideas to share. You also intend to maintain the interests that appeal to you now. Your high tech nature draws you to the computer and other modern gadgets, so perhaps you'll be part of an active online senior community. You like the idea of senior residences and retirement communities, and might plan to be part of something like that quite early in your life. It just makes sense to you to have a world designed for the activities and people you want to enjoy. Being retired gives you time for new and exciting intellectual pursuits. Perhaps you'll start a new charity, learn something about a subject you've always wanted to explore, or even return to college for an advanced degree. You're naturally intellectual, and you see getting older as an opportunity for personal growth, rather than personal decline. You might decide to work part-time or occasionally, if something interesting comes along. You could volunteer to register voters, help take the census, or be a counselor of some sort. Your wisdom is deep and valuable, and you want to take all possible opportunities to share what you know. Of course, you might not spend every moment trying to accomplish something. Some days you might opt just to sit in a coffee house with your friends and enjoy the moment. That, after all, is what makes the golden years golden!

PISCES: There are so many things that interest you in life that you see retirement as a way to pursue new dreams and old ones. Pisces Joanne Woodward went back to college in her later years, although this busy actress never really retired, but her Aquarian husband Paul Newman groused that he was the one who had to haul her out of bed in the morning for those early classes. If you have an equally accommodating partner, you might opt to lean on your mate for help of just this sort. You have a penchant for the theater, and retirement could be a great time for you to become involved (or increasingly involved) in community theater. You might not win an Oscar but it would be lots of fun. You enjoy the idea of sharing time with your grandchildren and look forward to doing fun little projects with them. You could go to school and help the kids learn to bake cookies or tie a fishing lure, work together on finger painting or pumpkin carving, and all the zillion other activities kids love that you continue to enjoy. The best thing about you is that zingy inner child who never seems to grow old. Your years may increase, but inside you have the soul of a tot, and that gives you the enthusiasm and passion to continue to enjoy life and its many fascinating activities. You might want to travel, even if it's only to explore a neighboring town, but chances are distant ports really appeal to you. You adore your friends, and look forward to quality time spent with them. You love the idea of becoming a member of a golden age group, so that you can go on theater tours, bus trips, and cruises. It's important to remember that retirement seldom pays for itself, so be willing to take a hard look at your finances today in order to see what needs to be done to ensure that active and interesting retirement that you were meant to have. Then when the time arrives, you can concentrate on the fun stuff—which is definitely your forte anyway!

GRANDPARENTING

Soon I will be an old, white-haired lady, into whose lap someone places a baby, saying, "Smile, Grandma!" - I, who myself so recently was photographed on my grandmother's lap. ~Liv Ullmann

Little kids are so much fun, particularly in short, grandparent-sized doses. When my little great niece, now grown, was a tot, she spent nearly every weekend with me, and we had the best times ever. I taught her to ride a bike. We had tea parties (but I always drank pretend lemonade in my pretend cups). Once after a tiring day, I was limp on the couch, and Kristen, still filled with energy, was bringing me fantasy cups of tea. Maybe that's why I always pictured having a granddaughter. They'll bring you tea. Little boys run around destroying things so you can't really recline while they visit. Little girls will talk with you. Boys will talk too, but then they run away urgently and hurriedly—off to their next search and destroy mission.

I did play with my nephew a lot when he was small and he often visited us when he lived in our area. A couple years back, he and his wife came for a visit and for the first time I got to meet my great nephew, who loves super heroes, and was enthused to meet and play with me—and to wear the shimmery super hero cape I had designed and sewn for him. "Logan," I shouted, demonstrating the meaning of the silver emblem on the back of the cape, "Speed of lightning, fists of thunder." It's as much fun being a great aunt as being a grandmother!

In fact, on one of my best days ever, the mother of my great niece confided that her own persnickety aunt asked Kristen who was her favorite aunt. Being the only aunt in the room, she felt assured of the upcoming response but was totally chagrinned when Kristen piped up and said, "Nancy!" I reminded Kristen of this recently and my heart went pitta-pat when she said I'm still her favorite aunt.

Although there are no neighbor kids around now, there have been in the past and what a pleasure it was to watch them grow up. Kids do and say such adorably amusing things and they're just wonderful. When a neighbor's visiting daughter recently gave me a hug after our first meeting, it really touched me. That's what being a gram is all about.

The history of our grandparents is remembered not with rose petals but in the laughter and tears of their children and their children's children. It is into us that the lives of grandparents have gone. It is in us that their history becomes a future. ~Charles and Ann Morse

When I picture my father's mother, it's always in the kitchen in an apron. Why this is I don't know. We never lived with her and in truth I recall no family meals she prepared. Although once I had some stewed fruits she'd made and that seemed a very exotic treat. But in the apron I see her, maybe because my daughter's first sewing project was an apron, one she gave to me, kind of an old fashioned atrocity really, and in it I feel myself transformed into my grandmother. She died when I was young, so she wasn't in my life as much as she was in my older cousins', who treasure her memory. My father's father did live with us a bit, off and on, and of him I remember some tales of a childhood in Russia, and the acrid smell of cigars, something that would make me flee the house when he was around. He worked in the garment industry, and had some giant scissors I still remember. Maybe it was from him that I inherited my ability to sew.

My mother's mother did live with us some of the time, and she was funny and could cook and sew. She grew up in a big family on a farm—and I remember her father too, called Grandpap, and the Maryland farm where he lived which had an actual outhouse. It was not the sort of thing a Virgo would remember fondly, but now at least I'm laughing. And there were the chickens that chased me about as a tot. That was more than half a century ago and now all these people are gone.

My family is spread out all over the place, and those who are left I don't often see. It's not the vision of everyone in the same small town with giant family gatherings and grandkids coming over all the time. But that is a wonderful vision, one I'd enjoy experiencing. That's what life is like for my Florida cousins, most of whom have spent their entire lives in one small beachside town.

Everyone says how much they love being a grandparent, and then usually they say it's all of the pleasure of having kids with none of the pain. It makes sense. To me, kids are easy to love, even when they're not your own. And being around them just makes life sweeter.

Nobody can do for little children what grandparents do. Grandparents sort of sprinkle stardust over the lives of little children. ~Alex Haley

Have you considered yourself as a grandparent? A friend recently confided he is to become one for the first time this year, although he claims to be neither old nor mature enough for such a momentous change in his life. The things is, though, if you believe what those in the role have said, grandparents are about fun more than responsibility. So maybe maturity isn't the main idea. Let's see what your sign might reveal about you in the role of a lifetime.

Our grandchildren accept us for ourselves, without rebuke or effort to change us, as no one in our entire lives has ever done, not our parents, siblings, spouses, friends - and hardly ever our own grown children. ~Ruth Goode

For **Aries**, this is so very true. Nothing is more important to you than being yourself and as a parent, often this trait can cause you problems, because you don't always want to buckle down and shoulder the heavy responsibility that comes with having control over someone else's life and destiny. Even when you do, sometimes you get into squabbles with your children because they see life differently than you do, and that to you echoes your own battles with your parents. Instead of it making you more tolerant, which admittedly is possible, it also can make you more stern, another posture that seems ill-fitting. With grandchildren, you can just have fun, and without a doubt, nobody exceeds your ability to do that. You are content to spend time with this tyke, particularly if you see yourself in him or her. Despite being colossally impatient in your normal daily life, as a grandparent you can relax and not click your heels, because at last you find someone as interesting to you as you are to yourself. And it doesn't matter at all if you have other plans, for this is someone for whom you don't mind changing those plans. Now you have a genuine excuse to haunt toy stores and buy tons of the coolest stuff. You have someone to show your own cool stuff as well, even if they're too young to drive/fly/whiz along on it. And now they have even newer cool stuff that you never had as a kid, whether you were poor or rich, and so this is your chance to play with even better toys than you had. If it sounds like I'm describing a second childhood, well I am. That's what being a grandparent is about—enjoying childhood from another perspective but with no limitations.

What a bargain grandchildren are! I give them my loose change, and they give me a million dollars' worth of pleasure. ~Gene Perret

As a **Taurus,** you discover something about yourself once you become a grandparent—you're willing to spend some of that money you've socked away. For years you've been eating early bird dinners at a discount, and now you'll think nothing of springing for designer ice cream cones or will shove spare cash in a grandchild's pocket, just because you don't want to think of this beloved person as going without. There's a lot to be said for frugality, and yes you're the one who said it, and now at last you know why—because someone has come along who is both so delightful and so downright worthy that you know why you saved all that cash, to lavish it like love or strawberry sauce on someone you adore. It's such a pleasure to take this child anywhere and to shop together. Your bargain hunting skills need to be passed down, and who better to absorb all your ways of wisdom. You're the one who taught your child how to calculate percentages by going to sales with deep discounts, and now this can be passed down to someone else. And then there are the family treats, the special dishes you've made or someone else has prepared to serve at holiday events. You must be the one to share the recipe, teach the technique, or just to regale this beloved child with the tangible—and tasty—evidence of your family history. It's as if you're the president of a club and you get to create the rules of order, and the pleasures as well, all to share with this brand new, perfect, indoctrinaire.

My grandmother started walking five miles a day when she was sixty. She's ninety-seven now, and we don't know where the hell she is. ~Ellen DeGeneres

There's no question that the **Gemini** grandparent remains youthful—and speedy. You're the one who takes the kid on bike rides and picnics, and whose lap is the perfect place to stop and read a book. Books are a big part of any Gemini's life, and to you this is such an important experience that the moment you learn you're expecting, you probably rush out and buy some books for the nursery. You don't worry initially about the crib or the layette, for to you those things mean far less than amassing a library that will provide so many hours of intellectual stimulation. You want a smart grandkid, after all, and books are the keys to—well—pretty much everything. You also like the noisy, wind up, and mechanical types of toys which drive a parent insane. Whistling, beeping, clicking, moving in circles and dumping upside down, well what can be better than that. You never fail to get a kick out of such nonsense, and may even buy that stuff for yourself just because it's so cute. Puzzles also appeal to you, and you'll happily spend hours with a grandchild assembling any sort of puzzle. Long after the tot has grown bored, you're still there, attaching part A to part Z. The thing you like most about little kids is the conversation, and in truth that's what you like best about pretty much everyone. Talking with your grandchild yields many laughs and even some amazingly interesting information. Never one to lag behind, you're enthused and interested in learning about the newest gadgets and toys, even when the parent—your child—is baffled or uninterested, you'll stand there and play video games, learn the iPad, or join in the rock band. Why not, you're a grandparent, not a corpse.

I loved their home. Everything smelled older, worn but

safe; the food aroma had baked itself into the furniture.
~Susan Strasberg

Can there be anyone more sweet and sentimental than the **Cancer** grandparent? Your heart is huge, you love to nurture, and a grandchild to you is the greatest blessing you could ever have. There's no question that you love your children and will go the extra mile for them, providing all they need and more, even if they're still asking you for things as they reach middle age. But a grandchild is someone who is there once again to provide you with a center to your world, a purpose, and more than that, the pleasure of seeing life grow and develop, all within the cozy embrace of your arms. Tradition is what matters to you, and those family dinners are the foundation of your life. Nothing feels happier than being surrounded by extended family members, and if it means you must stand for hours and cook and clean on painful and unsteady limbs, so what? Food speaks to you, and you love sharing the treats so much, just as a friend of mine said the moment he found his first grandchild was coming, he had visions of taking him for bagels on a Sunday. This is what it means to you, sharing the treasured moments of pleasure that really do define your life. There will be another person there, someone you love much more than yourself, and to this child you'll pass down all the good feelings and joys that have meant so much to you, and in so doing, the pleasure will multiply and so will the joy. You know all this instinctively and look forward to being a grandparent as early as you anticipate being a parent. Even as a child you played house willingly, and probably populated that doll house with a whole cast of characters, the family in your vision, the family you wanted to create and would always cherish.

One of life's greatest mysteries is how the boy who wasn't good enough to marry your daughter can be the father of the smartest grandchild in the world. ~Author Unknown.

Nobody can deny that being a **Leo** means clinging to your vanity. Yes, you're willing to be a grandparent, although you might opt never to be called by anything other than your first name, and you plan to remain a youthful, attractive, sexy grandparent of the sort who is confused by strangers as the child's parent, or better yet babysitter. One gram I know insists on being distinguished from the other grandmothers in her child's family by being called Gramma Pretty. You just don't see how having grandchildren should diminish you as yourself. Being a grandparent is a social opportunity to you, and you do enjoy sharing fun times and treats with your special guy or gal. You do together the indulgent things that you like to do, such as shopping, going for haircuts or mani-pedis, and it's a great thrill to you to introduce this (hopefully) well-mannered child to the army of caretakers who help you stay in such fine fiddle. Throwing parties to mark special events in your grandchild's life seems like your chance to have fun, and you do it with enthusiasm. Going to the park and wiping sand off this baby's face—well that's far less entertaining. The point is more to share the elegance of your world, not the poopiness of the baby's. Once the child is born, the race is on, and the biggest of all the big deals is determining whom the child resembles, hopefully you. The thought of him or her coming out looking like *their* side of the family, well why dwell on absurdities. The child will of course have taste, good judgment, and in general be the most perfect of all the earth's perfect creatures. That's not to say you won't take a stern tone if you spy bad behavior. You feel obliged to make sure your grandchild will live up to your standards, because otherwise you'll never be able to allow him or her to meet your friends. Humor is a great thing and you do enjoy the endless hours of fun you get from the antics of a grandchild. It's what gives you bragging rights among your buddies, because of course your peewee will say the first word, do the smartest things, and be the absolutely most gorgeous of all the children since the beginning of time.

My granddaughter came to spend a few weeks with me, and I decided to teach her to sew. After I had gone through a lengthy explanation of how to thread the machine, she stepped back, put her hands on her hips, and said in disbelief, "You mean you can do all that, but you can't play my Game Boy?" ~ Author Unknown

That's the great pleasure of being a **Virgo** grandparent—the opportunity to teach some of the things you know to a new audience, a child who is interested and open, and who can benefit from your knowledge and wisdom. It's so much fun for you to nurture in that way, because not only does it feel good, it truly makes you useful. You realize that a parent's job is to take care of the child, and of course you want to participate in that, and will make sure your child hears a word or two if you think something that should be done isn't being done. But you have other responsibilities, to enrich the life of your grandchild, to go beyond the call of a parent, to add to the life of this amazing little person everything that can be included that seems worthwhile to you. Whether you're buying clothes, or making them, choosing educational games that allow the child to grow intellectually and creatively—rather than that crap that you wind up and stand back while it does its own thing—you are thinking every moment about what your grandchild could use, need, or want. You're good with the details, that's for sure! Of course you did all that for your own child too, but now you realize that there's something else you can indulge in—fun. You're a worker bee and your to-do list is long and never ending, but once your grandchild comes, you finally have a reason to say the vacuuming can wait, the garage can be reorganized another day, and your life is richer for that. In fact, you may find that you learn some things as a result of this new focus on happiness that might have been useful as an attitude way earlier in your life. That doesn't mean you become lazy, far from it, and often you will let the grandchild help you with little chores, and to you that is a gift, for it teaches the child responsibility and gives him or her a sense of accomplishment. You like seeing this little person grow, and whatever you can do to make him or her feel good as it's happening, you will do.

If becoming a grandmother was only a matter of choice, I should advise every one of you straight away to become one. There is no fun for old people like it! ~Hannah Whithall Smith

As a **Libra**, fun is certainly important to you, and you

cherish the times you spend with your little tot. Tea parties are absolutely made for Libras, because they allow you to show your grandchild the niceties of social intercourse. And you happily reproduce such things in real life, when you bring your beaming and dressed up little guy or gal to your favorite luncheon spot for a grown up meal. It's as if by having a grandchild you have a new, favorite companion, one who sees you as beautiful/handsome and the most interesting person in the world, something you always endeavor to be. Bouncing the child on your toes while you whirl around the room to music, or even dancing side by side to any ditty is so much fun, it brings back memories of your own childhood. You love plopping Mr. or Miss Adorable down in your lap while you share stories of your own social triumphs. That tale of the prom may have grown dull to your children, but a grandchild really wants to know all about what happened that magical night, and not only are you passing down great stories, but you're equipping him or her for a future that will be as rich as your past was, filled with the luster of a life of charm, well lived. You love shopping for this child and dressing him or her up in nice clothes, clothes a parent might not buy, but which nevertheless must be acquired. No, a little boy won't get much use out of a suit, and most girls can't wear organdy all the time, but in having those things they know that life can be beautiful, and to you that is the best lesson of all to impart. Hector Elizondo wouldn't have had to instruct Julia Roberts in the art of fine dining in *Pretty Woman* had she had a grandparent who had taught her what fork to use. This is your job now and you take it seriously—and with the greatest of pleasure.

A grandmother pretends she doesn't know who you are on Halloween. ~ Erma Bombeck

The thing about being a **Scorpio** grandparent is you can see right through everyone—including your beloved grandchild, but in his or her case, you don't mind what you see. This child can always come to you as a confidant, and you will listen and keep all those secrets, or if something needs to be done in the way of a rescue, you will willingly do it, because nothing matters more to you than that this wonderful child be safe, secure, and happy. Your loyalty runs deep and is unstoppable, to the extent that if you feel a teacher is unfair, a friend is untrustworthy, or a future mate is unworthy, you will step in and do what's necessary. That might make you sound a little scary, and in fact you are. That doesn't mean you're not also fun, because you know how to enjoy life better than almost anyone. You have a true passion for living, and you transfer this zest to your grandchildren. Nothing is more fun than dragging the tyke up to your attic and opening all those trunks filled with the treasures of a lifetime. You can share the tales of life when you were young, and how your buddies tossed you into the river so you'd learn how to swim, or how you had to elope with Gramps because your dad wouldn't say yes to his request for your hand. No stranger to drama, you know how to make life seem like an adventure, and to you sharing all that with a grandchild brings home those memories once more, so you can relive them and feel the thrills and chills again and again. You can walk down the street, little hand in your big hand, and know that side by side you are history in the making, life in its grandest fulfillment, and the best part of DNA—having someone who is just like you, right there in your life to nurture and support.

The best baby-sitters, of course, are the baby's grandparents. You feel completely comfortable entrusting your baby to them for long periods, which is why most grandparents flee to Florida. ~Dave Barry

One of the most youthful of all the signs, **Sagittarius** knows how to have fun. It doesn't matter how old you get, you're still active, busy, and out there in life, doing the things you enjoy. There are always horses to ride, dogs to pet, and camping trips to take, and even if you've been going to the same desert rock to camp for thirty years, you still want to go again. And that to you is what being a grandparent is all about—making room in your life for a new friend, a companion in your adventures, and someone with whom you can share all the most special of special good times. You don't expect to be the one who inflicts discipline on a grandchild—or even on a pooch—you believe in live and let live, and because you have such a jaunty sense of humor, you're only too happy to make light and make merry of any behavior that someone else would describe as bad. Your grandchild isn't being bad, he or she is being an individual. Although parents are busy, you may not be so busy at the time of your life when a grandchild comes along, and that's a good thing, for who else will willingly push him or her along in a carriage or a stroller to enjoy the fresh air and see what adventures await. Who else will tirelessly hold a hand while a child totters along a riverbank, or push the same swing, high, high, higer up into the sky, amid peals of laughter and merriment. Those things are your specialty, and if you had to work too hard when your own children were young (though chances are you took plenty of time off, for there's not a Sag alive who gives up fun for work all the time) now you have your chance to enjoy those moments without any nagging at the back of your mind. To you a grandchild is a reward, a person who comes along at the right moment to share the best you have to offer.

It's one of nature's ways that we often feel closer to distant generations than to the generation immediately preceding us. ~Igor Stravinsky

Being a **Capricorn** can seem hard early in life because of your built in sense of responsibility. Nobody is more determined than you are to make a big success of your life, and of the task of building your family. There's always the sense of rules to be followed and standards to be upheld. Obviously, if you produce a child like yourself, it's an easy match, but if your child is of the wild and wooly type, much of your parenting years may have been filled with terror—on both sides—and strong words. You shook your head wryly at one point and recognized that you have turned into your father—or your mother. Was this a good thing? Maybe. As a grandparent, you have a new lease on life. You've learned a few things in the last forty or sixty years, and one of them is not to take everything so seriously. You have—dare we say it—lightened up. This is only to the good where a grandchild is concerned, because now at last you're able to concentrate on fun. You can enjoy flying that kite or dressing that doll, and it doesn't matter if the clock is ticking away, because you have all the time in the world to devote to this spectacular child—this little kid who—yes it's true—reminds you of yourself so long ago, before you focused all your energy on climbing that mountain. Of course that doesn't mean you won't have expectations. You might look forward to take your child to work day, and will press your arm around the tot's shoulders and confide with pride, "This will all be yours some day." Yes the child may meet that comment with a cringe and say, "Oh please give it to Daddy instead," but those things are to be expected. Even if your own child didn't want the future you envisioned, you can't expect that your grandchild will—except he or she just might. They say everything skips a generation, and to you that could be the best news ever.

Being grandparents sufficiently removes us from the responsibilities so that we can be friends. ~Allan Frome

Despite your happy-go-lucky reputation as the rebel of the universe, **Aquarius,** in fact you have a strong sensibility and the idea of precisely how things should be. You know what should be done in the best of all possible worlds, and often share these opinions with other people, who let's face it, are idiots when they don't concur. This point of view can be difficult during your parenting years because children often want to forge their own vision of what life should be, something one would think you'd understand, but which often you do not. With a grandchild, you get another chance to mold someone into the person you'd want him or her to be, but amazingly something happens, you let go a little, slow down a little, stop, look, listen, and basically fall deep into the anti-intellectual abyss that is love. Your heart begins to rule your head and you stop trying to rule the world. You consider what's before your eyes and say wow this little kid has some good ideas. Thus a grandchild is your chance to be reborn, to come to new conclusions, or simply to come to no conclusions at all. For some reason, although you know you're there to be the older person, the protective person, and yes, you're willing to do all that, somehow you feel that you and this little child are on equal footing, and that he or she has come along to be your best friend ever. You can spend hours talking about things with your grandchild, things that a normal kid that age might have no clue about, and in truth you realize that he or she is relatively clueless as well, but that's what makes it all so appealing. You get to watch a mind develop and to expose this already brilliant person to all the things in life that really appeal to you. You can bring him along to your barbershop to gab with your cronies, or take her to your bridge game. It doesn't matter. It just feels right to have this little person by your side, sharing in your world and opening up many new worlds right before your eyes.

Being pretty on the inside means you don't hit your brother and you eat all your peas - that's what my grandma taught me. ~Lord Chesterfield

The greatest thing about being a **Pisces**, other than your unbounded imagination, is your people skills. Genuinely interested in pretty much everyone, you can meet a new person and instantly be the one whom they want for a best friend. If you can do that with a stranger, imagine how wonderful and popular you'll be with a grandchild. You have the ability to understand the feelings of any other person and thus can be right there to dry tears when feelings are hurt, and you'll know just the right thing to say to bring sunshine back to that beloved child's face. Being a grandparent just makes your world better, because you are so immersed in the love you feel for this little person and the way in which it fills your life. You want to be there for every moment, and will happily agree to babysit virtually every day of the week if such is needed. To you it's a gift to have the time to spend with your grandchild. Each moment you share brings you closer, and it feels as though you have forged a bond you never before experienced. It's just raw emotion in your world, and that's what makes it so amazing. You love doing creative projects and nurturing talent, even if little actual talent exists, for you can see the good in any small accomplishment, and do wonders for pee wee's ego when you lavish him or her with heartfelt praise for a drawing, a clay model, or a tower made of blocks. The spirit of childlike wonder never leaves your heart, and thus you can relate to any little person in a way few other people can. You offer praise and little doses of advice, bestowed in such a subtle way that it just seems natural for your grandchild to learn the kindness, manners, and downright sweetness that comes as part of your ingrained people skills. It doesn't seem like teaching because few facts are involved, but in reality you are showing the best way to be a nice person, and that is something every child can use and count on.

It really doesn't matter what your sign is. It doesn't matter whom you ask. Everyone says being a grandparent is the best thing ever. It's the opportunity of a lifetime, so when it comes your way, count your blessings for they multiply and multiply with each new grandchild.

If I had known how wonderful it would be to have grandchildren, I'd have had them first. ~Lois Wyse

7
YOUR SPIRITUAL SIDE

Do you meditate? Some people find it difficult to turn off the inner static and open up blankly to the celestial vibrations all around us. The purpose of meditation is to channel in some of that divine light. One way to do this is repetition of a mantra, a collection of words designed to keep one part of your brain busy so the rest can open up blankly.

In the following article, I created twelve meditations, each one inspired by the issues and energies of the sign for which it's named. They weren't meant only for their own sign, however. Any meditation whose purpose appeals to you can be a good choice for you to try.

The meditations feature guided imagery. I create scenes or images for you to envision, and by doing so powerful changes occur within your heart and mind. These exercises can change your life.

Give it a try! It's much easier than learning to meditate when your primary goal is blankness. Here the goal is to attract good things or to release negativity. That's something we all can benefit from doing.

A MEDITATION FOR YOU

I'm a big fan of guided imagery. So much can be accomplished by closing your eyes and immersing yourself in a scene designed to heal, open you up, or release old woes. That's a wonderful meditation tool. Meditation is quite popular around the world, but there are many approaches to it. In some disciplines, people enjoy using a mantra, a phrase repeated over and over again. It's sort of the same idea your grammar school teacher had in requiring you to write a phrase over and over on the blackboard.

I thought it would be interesting to create a meditation for each sign, incorporating a mantra and some imagery. Normally with guided imagery, you need to close your eyes and have someone else read it to you. That approach will work here as well, but with these meditations you can simply read them, aloud or to yourself, perhaps daily for a couple of weeks, at bedtime, or also when awakening. They will help you gain clarity and focus.

Don't feel you must confine yourself only to the meditation written for your own sign. I list next to each sign the purpose of that particular meditation, so if you feel that any of the meditations would help you, give them a try. And then once you've done a few, see which provide the greatest sense of well being, healing, and ongoing growth and change. Those are the ones best suited to your needs now.

Before beginning, take a moment to breathe deeply. Relax in your favorite chair or on the couch. I always feel it's better to do this sort of thing sitting upright, because the light flows in more easily, and you're less inclined to fall asleep. But if you're more comfortable lying down, do what works for you. Take a few deep breaths, see a ball of white, luminous light all around you. Envision a sort of French doors on the front of you, and open them, out to the world. That provides a visual image in your mind to show that you've opened up to the meditation. Continue the deep and relaxed breathing, and read your meditation.

When finished, don't race right back into your daily life. Give yourself a few moments to rest in the afterglow. Enjoy the peace of the moment. Then resume your day a little more centered and better able to accomplish your goals.

And remember that although the meditations were designed with each of the specific signs in mind, there's no reason why you can't try another sign's meditation, particularly if you feel it could help you.

Aries—To get in touch with your destiny and find the right path today:

I walk into the fire of creation and emerge cleaner, leaner, purified. The distractions of my life melt away, along with any static surrounding me. There is light around me, the sound of a calming, peaceful hum, and I merge with the light and the sound. All confusion is gone; I am receptive and one with the universe. I take a breath, and into my lungs flows pure energy, which inside my body is transformed into a river of inspiration. I flow along those waters and feel myself alive, secure, assured, and guided toward my truest inner truths. Whatever bewildered me before flows out of me, into that river, and flows away forever. It doesn't matter what happened before, or what I never understood. Today I understand and can see clearly. I walk into the fire of creation and emerge cleaner, leaner, purified. My breath is clean and I can feel tomorrow pulling at me; I know what I must do. I breathe, once, twice, three times. A vision begins to form in the back of my mind. The more peacefully I breathe, the more clearly the vision appears. This is my true desire. This is the path of happiness and fulfillment. Momentary concerns fade away. Nothing is now frivolous or casual. I see the truth. I see the things I have chosen which I no longer want. I see what I might have had, what will be right for me now and for tomorrow, and I see how easy it will be to make those choices. I walk into the fire of creation and emerge cleaner, leaner, purified. A stronger sense of self radiates through me. I know who I am. I can just be, whether I do something or not, because in being, I express who I am, and I share those inner lights with the world. I send out love to those around me and open up to their love and approval. I am alive in this world, attuned to my own vibration and in harmony with all that is.

Taurus—To create security and the courage to take risks.

I climb into the hands of God, and am held there, safe in a cocoon of luminous light. My breath flows peacefully, filling my lungs with love, joy and happiness. My heart beats calmly, the blood in my body flowing perfectly through my veins. I am alive in my body, and am held in harmony, safely cosseted by the universe. I feel my worries flow through me and out, falling away, gone forever. The fears that held me back rise up and flow down, dribbling out and disappearing. I breathe and feel new energy flow in. I am alive. I climb into the hands of God, and am held there, safe in a cocoon of luminous light. My past flows before my eyes briefly, and I see the chances I missed, the things I grasped for too long, the choices that brought me genuine joy. As my breath flows, I float into those things I wished I'd done, and feel the unlived possibilities tugging at me, then I release them. I choose not to worry any more. What's done is done and I will hold no regrets. They flow down and away. I breathe in the happiness of the moment. I am alive. I am safe. I can do with my life what I choose. I climb into the hands of God, and am held there, safe in a cocoon of luminous light. My future is as clear to me as a movie on a screen. I know what I want, and see how easy it will be to create. I can feel the anticipation building in my heart. My tomorrow is right there, almost ready, moving toward me, and I fearlessly move toward it. Joy is there, and love, and harmony, and I must only reach out my hand, say yes, and grasp it. My breath flows in and my lungs expand, not just with light, but with happiness. I am alive and I am safe. I can have everything I want and more, much more.

Gemini—To release static and increase mental acuity.

I walk into an apple orchard and hear nothing but the gentle green breeze, the rustling of the branches, and I sit calmly on the ground. My breath is smooth and clean, the fragrance of apple blossoms in the air. I breathe in that smell, and relax into the scent. The day is warm, and I am comfortable. Above me is the blue sky, and it is wide and free of clouds. I look up at the sky, and follow it all the way to the horizon. I breathe and am in my breath, peacefully alive. As my eyes flow down to the horizon, my thoughts flow down, into the ground, where they stay, seeds that one day might be planted, but for now, all inside me is silence. I walk into an apple orchard and hear nothing but the gentle green breeze, the rustling of the branches, and I sit calmly on the ground. I feel the breeze blow through me, all around me, inside me. I am one with the breeze. I am, I exist, I breathe. Time flows away from me, and all responsibilities and demands flow with it. I am in this one and only moment, detached from yesterday, unaware of tomorrow. Five minutes from now is irrelevant. I am here, breathing, right now. My senses open up, and I am aware of the randomness all around me. A blossom detaches and falls to the ground. A bird's wings ruffle the air and create a breeze. I feel it all, yet none of it. I walk into an apple orchard and hear nothing but the gentle green breeze, the rustling of the branches, and I sit calmly on the ground. There is one sound, off in the distance, a feeling, a thought, an idea. Nothing is more important than that. I focus on that and all around me falls away. I am in that one thing and nothing else. My mind takes hold of that one thing, and it is like a feast. Everything I need to know about it is clear. Everything I would want to know or to say is clear. I am alive and my mind is clear, my thoughts clean and at peace.

Cancer—To nurture and be nurtured.

I walk through a tunnel of luminous pink light, and the years I've lived fall away, revealing the child inside me. There by the mossy bank of a stream, I sit, and I dangle my feet in the water. The stream bubbles along, and it flows between my toes, tickling me. I laugh in the light, I splash the water, I am filled with pleasure and joy. The cares of the past flow out of me, right through the tips of my toes, and everything I thought I missed flows away, far down the stream and out of sight. Sadness and regret flow away. Hurt and anguish flow away. My child's heart is at peace. I walk through a tunnel of luminous pink light, and the years I've lived fall away, revealing the child inside me. I walk into the shallow waters and feel them bubbling all around me. The water is clean and cool, and I am safe. The sky above is reflected in the stream, and I don't know which is which, ground, water, sky. All is one, and I am part of it all. I breathe in the light of the sky, the peace of the ground, the love of the water. I am safe and happy, and nourished by the water. I sit down in the stream and feel the water flow all through me, filling my heart with happiness. I walk through a tunnel of luminous pink light, and the years I've lived fall away, revealing the child inside me. I am alive, safe, and surrounded by love. The child I am merges with the adult I am, peacefully. I feel the world around me, remember the people I love, and feel them alive in my heart. I reach out my hands, and the ones I love best take them, and we embrace. I lead us all into the stream, arm in arm. The water flows comfortingly all around us. I hold the ones I love tightly, knowing nothing will ever separate us, that we will always be fine, always together, always we will love.

Leo—To release insecurity and stimulate the creative process:

I walk into an empty, white room, the walls glowing and clean, and in the distance I hear a drum, beating in the rhythm of my heart. I stand in the middle of the room and breathe in the sound, and my heart matches the beats until the drum and my heartbeat are one comforting sound. I flow into and out of the sound of my heart beating. I am alive, and my heartbeat comforts me. I breathe, and let all thoughts slip away. Nothing is there but the sound of the drum and the matching sound of my heart. I walk into an empty, white room, the walls glowing and clean, and in the distance I hear a drum, beating in the rhythm of my heart. Images flash briefly on the wall, then fade away. Things I tried but failed to complete, things I regret, things I could not do, are there on the wall, briefly, and then they're gone. I breathe in the emotions connected to these things, and take from them all I was supposed to learn, then they fade away, leaving the walls blank and clean. I breathe in the light in the room, feeling it fill and balance my heart, my lungs, my mind. I flow out of myself into the light of the room, and I breathe it in. I am alive, and my heart is open to the light all around me. My heart beats calmly, in perfect rhythm. I walk into an empty, white room, the walls glowing and clean, and in the distance I hear a drum, beating in the rhythm of my heart. I watch serenely as the walls are flooded with splashes of color. Each color washes over me, leaving behind an image, an idea, a feeling, and then is gone. I radiate with the color, breathing it in, letting it fade peacefully away. I breathe calmly, my heart in perfect rhythm. The colors fade, but inside me is the rainbow left behind. I feel it expanding and ebbing along with my breath. My thoughts are clear. I can see my future and what I will do next. I am calm. There is no harm in trying. I trust I will get it right and it will be beautiful. I am alive with light and color. I am alive.

Virgo—To release stress and find acceptance:

I step into the hurricane that is fate, the winds buffeting me all around, blowing all thoughts from my mind, and pushing me into the calming eye of the storm. I am in an empty, serene place. I look around me and the winds are blowing, but nothing touches me. My thoughts and feelings fly out into the winds and away. The obligations that plague me daily fly out of my mind and into the winds and away. My worries fly out into the winds and away. I breathe and feel the serenity of the eye of the storm. I am surrounded by electricity, but I am calm. I step into the hurricane that is fate, the winds buffeting me all around, blowing all thoughts from my mind, and pushing me into the calming eye of the storm. The possibilities that make up my future swirl around me, and I can choose any or none, but I do nothing. I breathe and let life be, let myself be. I feel nothing compelling me. Time stretches before me like an endless, elastic ribbon. I am part of the fabric of life, but it doesn't bind me. I breathe in the blue light of the hurricane, feeling my blood flow calmly through my veins. I step into the hurricane that is fate, the winds buffeting me all around, blowing all thoughts from my mind, and pushing me into the calming eye of the storm. I reach out my arm into the winds and feel life pulling at me. I can fall into the hurricane and let it blow me in any direction it will, knowing I will always be safe and the best choice will be made. My mind is calm. I am in the hands of fate, and I trust that fate knows what is best for me, whether I do anything or not. I am safe. Fate is my teacher, leading me in the journey of my life. The winds subside and at my feet is a stream with a little boat. I step into the boat and flow down the stream of life, letting the boat take me into tomorrow. It knows the way. I am safe.

Libra—To release fear and attract true love:

I dive into a pool of clear green water, and swim deeper and deeper toward a tunnel of light. My breath is strong and secure, and I see the bubbles float out of my mouth and nose as I swim. My arms are strong and the water gives way as I go down, down, down into the tunnel. I am all alone in the pool of water, completely safe, and buoyed by the bubbles all around me. I feel my skin and the water flowing by as I swim strongly. I am alive under the pool of water, like a sea creature with no thought but moving through the sea. I dive into a pool of clear green water, and swim deeper and deeper toward a tunnel of light. Floating above me are the people in my life, some I love, some I hate, some to whom I'm indifferent. Some reach out to me. Some float by. I allow all the feelings connected to them to flow through me, and out into the water. I send a ball of love up through the bubbles to float above me, where all can see. I am a force of light and love, and receive all I need from the water. I dive into a pool of clear green water, and swim deeper and deeper toward a tunnel of light. I swim through the tunnel and float upward toward the shore. The bank is grassy, planted with pink flowers. I sit alone on the bank, knowing I am safe and content. Nothing must happen today, but whatever comes I will embrace. My heart beats calmly, a cloud of pink joy rising up from inside me and floating out to the sky. I am alive. I am here. I live in a world of love. I breathe in the pink cloud and sigh. Life is beautiful.

Scorpio—To release negativity and promote healing and transformation:

I blaze across an endless river of ice on a toboggan of light, through a wall of fire, and out again, purified and serene. I fly into the light, white along the icy river, and I float from inside myself out into the light. The light floats into me, opening me up and filling me with white, luminous energy. I am a balloon, floating along a river of ice. I breathe in, filling my lungs and my heart with light. My thoughts fall asleep, my mind falls asleep, my worries become a tight little sneeze, and they fly out my nose. I blaze across an endless river of ice on a toboggan of light, through a wall of fire, and out again, purified and serene. Before me is the wall of fire, but I am not afraid. I walk slowly into the fire and feel the warmth. What does not belong inside me melts away in the fire and puddles at my feet. I release bad habits and mean thoughts, and watch them melt away. Any illness in my body bubbles and melts out through my toes. I stand in the fire, comforted by its heat, knowing that I am molten and raw, being reborn in the flames. I blaze across an endless river of ice on a toboggan of light, through a wall of fire, and out again, purified and serene. In the distance is a geyser, and I walk toward it. Up in and through me goes the yellow water of the geyser, and I bubble on top of it, a buoy. I breathe in the yellow light. I breathe in the yellow water, feeling it flow into and through my skin. I become the light, newborn and ready to begin again. I am myself. I am alive. I am renewed. I breathe in the light and fill my cheeks with the fat yellow light. I blow and blow and blow, sending a giant cloud of yellow light into the universe, to illuminate and recreate the world.

Sagittarius—To bring peace and harmony:
I walk past a screaming crowd into a garden planted with beautiful flowers. My feet are bare and the grass tickles me. I breathe in the scent of grass and the flowers. I sink down onto a bank and lean against a calm old tree. My thoughts and worries sift down through me, into the ground below, and are transformed into mulch for the grass. I breathe in the smell of green, I breathe in the smell of life, I relax in the garden. Above me, the blossoms open on the tree limbs and birds fly over, singing a sweet song. I breathe in the smell of the blossoms and the sound of the bird's song. I am alive, and I am one with life. I walk past a screaming crowd into a garden planted with beautiful flowers. A wind blows from the ground, gathering force, swelling to a giant green bubble, filled with the scent of the trees, and it swells all around the crowd of screaming people. Gray light flows out of the people all around me, and up into the green gust of wind, where it is purified. I reach out my hands and am embraced by all who see me. We walk together through the light, and we hear the birds singing. I walk past a screaming crowd into a garden planted with beautiful flowers. The people walk with me into the garden and their screams turn into song, the music of the birds, the scent of the flowers, the color of light. All around me are people playing, singing, lying on the grass holding hands. I breathe in the light of the day, the love in the air, the songs of joy. I am alive. The world is a beautiful place, filled with happiness and love. I am at the center of the world. I am a force for love. I share my heart with all around me, and I embrace them, one and all.

CAPRICORN: To increase self-esteem and promote success:
I dive into an icy river and swim against the current, my arms pumping fiercely, my lungs pulling clean air into my body. The water twists and bubbles, and it pulls at me. The cold is bracing, and the chill invigorates me. I breathe and breathe and breathe, my face dipping into the icy depths, my

legs kicking, the water giving way to the strength of my stroke. Rocks piled on the bank jut out into the water, and I know I can grab one and climb out if I choose. The banks are gray and unplanted, and I could get out and fill the dirt with flowers. My arms and legs will not stop. The current and I are one as I swim upstream. I dive into an icy river and swim against the current, my arms pumping fiercely, my lungs pulling clean air into my body. I dive beneath the waters, seeing life below, fish swimming, green plants billowing, bubbles rising from the sea bed. There is life under me, around me, above me, and I swim through the stream, gaining momentum, floating on a cushion of air and determination. My heart beats firmly. I could swim forever. I dive into an icy river and swim against the current, my arms pumping fiercely, my lungs pulling clean air into my body. Upstream I swim, going onward, gaining energy with every stroke. I am calm. The waters are choppy, and I glide through them like a power boat, the bubbles falling away from my hand as I swim. Before me is a grassy knoll, and I rise onto the bank, watching the water flow away. I breathe in the light of day, the water dripping off my skin. The air is warm and I sit in the sun and embrace the yellow light. My mind is clear. My thoughts are focused. I know what I will do next.

Aquarius—to promote friendship and empathy:

I walk through a choir, and my heart is filled with its song. All around me there is music, sounds I know, sounds I've never heard, sounds I remember from long ago and had forgotten, and I open up to the song all around me. In my mind is the hum of music, the hum of life, life all around me. And my heart sings along. I smile, and my heart beats. This is life, and I am alive, and there is song all around me. I breathe, knowing that no matter where I am, I can hear the music. I breathe in the rhythms I hear, I sing along, the words clear in my mind. I walk through a choir, and my heart is filled with its song. I reach out my hand, and instantly another hand is in mine. I squeeze that hand, smile and walk on. I reach out my hand again. A hand reaches out to me, and I take it, smiling. I offer a hug to someone next to me, singing. I laugh and sing along. A voice pipes up, solitary and alone, and another joins it, filling in the harmony. I listen, and then my voice pipes up. The room is filled with song, different voices singing in harmony. I walk through a choir, and my heart is filled with its song. Each voice fills the room, each voice sends a billow of color, filling the room, each voice is a peal of light, a rainbow, and I am alive in the rainbow. I walk in the light, singing. I sing and am surrounded by light and harmony. My hands are touched. My shoulders are patted. In my arms, people come and go, leaving a hug and a moment of tenderness. My heart vibrates with music. I am alive. The world is a song. I walk into the choir and am part of it. I join the choir, and am part of the song. I am alive, and the song is part of me. I give my song to the choir, and let its song fill my heart.

Pisces—to absorb universal love and oneness.

I float on a beam of sunlight up into the sky, where a cloud becomes my hammock. I fly higher into the sky and beyond the blue, into a field of lavender. I breathe in the lilac light, breathing, breathing, breathing, a feeling of peace and calm floating over me like a quilt. I am alive in the lavender sky. I stretch out my arms and they float away from me, off into the infinite. I stretch out my legs and they expand beyond the edge of time. I stretch into the universe, elastic, and filled with light, my breathing calm and perfect. I float on a beam of sunlight up into the sky, where a cloud becomes my hammock. I feel my lungs expand with my breath, and I feel myself expand with my breath. I have stretched to fill the universe. The universe fills me and I fill it. I breathe in the light of the universe, and allow it to radiate through me. I feel myself whirl around in the light, feel all the energy that is me disperse and come together again. I am alive in the world, and the world is alive in me. I float on a beam of sunlight up into the sky, where a cloud becomes my hammock. I breathe in silence, safe in the sky. A ball of white light envelops me and I am surrounded by purity. My hands open and reach out. All that I am opens and reaches out. The light flows into me, merging with all that I am. I am part of the light and it radiates through me. I lie peacefully in the clouds, a part of the light, vibrating with love and peace and harmony.

Nancy Frederick is an internationally acclaimed astrologer who has been consistently in print for over twenty years. If you read astrology magazines, you've read Nancy! She has published thousands of articles in all the national astrology magazines. Nancy contributes frequently to *Dell Horoscope Magazine*, with a bi-monthly column, many articles, features like the Yearbook, Purse Books, and Love Sign Guides. As the founding editor of *ASTRO SIGNS*, she conceptualized the popular mini-magazine, designed its format, and wrote much of its contents for many years. She also wrote most of the contents of *Astrology Your Daily Horoscope* for fifteen years.

She is the author of six books combining various aspects of metaphysics with romance. They are: *Love and Sex Under the Stars*, Dell, 1989 and a new version for 2014; *Tarot: Love is in the Cards*; *The Lover's Dream*; *Palmistry: All Lines Lead to Love*; *Love Games: Psychic Paths to Love*, Lynx Books, 1988. She's also the author of a comprehensive astrology text, *The Astro Tutor,* a book that teaches beginners astrology or helps more advanced students gain greater expertise.

Nancy is certified by many astrology

organizations, and has taught astrology privately in New York and Los Angeles, has lectured in New York and taught through the Learning Annex in Los Angeles as well as at conferences sponsored by the AFA.

In addition to being an astrologer, she is a master of the Tarot and uses the cards in her counseling work. Nancy has done much research over many years into other aspects of metaphysics. A spiritualist, she worked for some years with a trance medium, talking directly to spirit and getting information about Karma, reincarnation, and technical astrological details.

Ms. Frederick spends much of her time counseling a large international clientele. She's also the author of six popular novels. Visit www.nancyfrederick.com to learn about the readings she offers and to contact her.

www.ingramcontent.com/pod-product-compliance
Lightning Source LLC
Chambersburg PA
CBHW030921090426
42737CB00007B/278